Translating Baudelaire

This book is the record of an apprenticeship in translating Baudelaire, and in translating poetry more generally. Re-assessing the translator's task and art, Clive Scott explores various theoretical approaches as he goes in search of his own style of translation. But, equally, he undertakes detailed analyses of the seventeen poems of which he offers renderings, so that the book is as much an evaluation of Baudelaire's writing as it is of the available ways of re-imagining that writing in another language.

As the apprenticeship unfolds, Scott also addresses two other questions which translation studies have left relatively neglected: What form should the criticism of translation take, if the critic is to do justice to the translator's project? How can a translator persuade readers to respond to a translation as a text with its own creative dynamic and expressive ambitions? These two questions motivate the answer that the book itself provides: the presentation of translations not as isolated products, but as texts embedded in a discourse which traces their emergence.

Translating Baudelaire is thus an experiment in 'contextualised' translation, where the translator's visibility is radically increased, where translation is seen as a kind of spiritual autobiography, where the relationships between translation and criticism, translation and reading, are acted out. The book ends with a magnificent translation of Baudelaire's 'Le Voyage', which is accompanied by a justification of free verse as a translational medium and as the goal of Scott's stylistic search.

Clive Scott is Professor of European Literature, University of East Anglia and Fellow of the British Academy. His most recent books include *The Poetics of French Verse: Studies in Reading* (Clarendon Press, 1998) and *The Spoken Image: Photography and Language* (Reaktion Books, 1999).

Translating Baudelaire

Clive Scott

UNIVERSITY
of
EXETER
PRESS

First published in 2000 by
University of Exeter Press
Reed Hall, Streatham Drive
Exeter EX4 4QR
UK
www.ex.ac.uk/uep/

British Library Cataloguing in Publication Data
A catalogue record for this book is available
from the British Library.

Paperback ISBN 0 85989 658 7
Hardback ISBN 0 85989 657 9

Typeset in 10.5/13pt Plantin Light
by XL Publishing Services, Tiverton

Printed in Great Britain by Short Run Press Ltd, Exeter

Contents

Acknowledgements

An earlier version of Chapter 2, 'Translating Rhythm', first appeared in *Translation and Literature* (Edinburgh University Press), Volume 6, 1997. I would particularly like to thank students and faculty involved in workshops for the MA in Literary Translation at the University of East Anglia for their invaluable comments on the first drafts of chapters, and parts of chapters, of this book. I would also like to thank Sam Scott for helping me to think through some of the arguments in Chapter 3, and Marie-Noëlle Guillot for keeping me focused and for lending me her expertise in the solution of textual problems. Last, but not least, the team at the University of Exeter Press (Simon Baker, Anna Henderson, Genevieve Davey) gave much in the way of creative advice and ready help, and I am very grateful to them, too.

Introduction

This book is about an apprenticeship, my own, in the translation of Baudelaire. I did not set out to teach myself how to translate Baudelaire, so much as to learn what approaches might be brought to the translation of Baudelaire. This latter task has two aspects: on the one hand, the reading of theory and my own theorizing; and, on the other, exploring selected Baudelairean poems specifically from the point of view of the translator. But in the end, of course, I did want to translate Baudelaire, to discover what my own translational persuasion was, and to try it out. I wanted, too, to discover, through translation, what my response to certain Baudelairean texts was. And this last concern, in turn, raised another issue: how does the translator reconcile in his work the often conflicting demands of a pedagogic/promotional role (product champion of Baudelaire) and a self-expressive impulse (what Baudelaire sounds like in my voice, what my voice sounds like in Baudelaire)? And there were still other reasons for turning to this topic, reasons relating to my perception of the present state of translation studies.

Translation had always left me feeling uneasy. The more the difficulties in a particular source text (ST) persisted, the less fruitful, for the target text (TT), seemed to be the possible solutions. Or rather, the more the difficulties persisted, the more they seemed to de-textualize themselves, to become problems 'for their own sake', demanding specific mental dexterities, or options, or strategies, which 'technicalized' the problems and made them exemplary of certain categories of difficulty. The difficulty, in short, became more interesting than the text.

Some confirmation of this tendency seemed to be provided by the appetite for linguistically difficult texts—Lewis Carroll, Apollinaire, e.e. cummings, Jacques Roubaud—and for the puns, idioms, and other word-play associated with them. And the concern with such texts inevitably led to what struck me, paradoxically, as a carelessness about text, because such translations—not all, by any means, I hasten to add—inevitably let linguistic difficulty supplant properly textual difficulty. When it came, therefore, to my own pursuit of translation, I found myself gravitating towards the view that the TT and TL (target language) should not be confused with each other, that the TL should certainly not mask the TT, and that the 'health' of the TT might well depend on its setting itself against the TL, while necessarily the translator operated within it. Correspondingly, the translator should imagine a similar tension between the ST and SL (source language), without which the ST might be assumed to exemplify the SL rather than constructing its own linguistic being.

Much continues to be said, and with justification, about the translator's lack of literary credibility, about the translator's invisibility, about the impossibility of any translation worth the name. All these symptoms of a condemned condition can, however, be turned round, if we are prepared to change our expectations and our prejudices. The translator must be allowed to take possession of his/her work, even if this involves textual intrusions—why has translation been for so long blighted with 'La note en bas de page est la honte du traducteur' [The footnote is the translator's humiliation] (Aury in Mounin 1963: xi)?—and creating new settings for translations (translations as part of a diary of reading, translation as an inbuilt supplement to literary criticism, translation as the destination of a creative meditation). And translations themselves must be treated more integrally, as whole texts, as part of the translator's ongoing or completed *œuvre*, as an irrepressible phenomenon which must for ever be undertaken afresh, so that every translation is felt to be supersedable though it is never superseded.

Translation asks: 'Given the language you have, how would you want to express this foreign-language poem?' To say that the task of translation is impossible is already disqualified. This question has the advantage of interesting itself in motive, in personal vision, in the way in which the translator possesses his own language (not simply in how much of it he knows, but in which parts of it he feels most at home, most a self-speaker). Commentators on translation too often either assume that some individuals have a richer grasp of their own language than others (poets should translate poems) and this gives them greater rights to freedoms; or they assume that everyone has at least the same *access*, because everywhere language is the same, equal to itself, and there are dictionaries and thesauruses—this is most frequently the heresy of a linguistics-based approach.

The question also assumes that translation needs ever to be started afresh, not because available translations are wrong, have avoidable infelicities, misunderstand, but because all ages, as all individuals, want to say things differently, have different ways of projecting a self into a response. What does Baudelaire sound like when passed through my mentality?

Translation asks not 'What does this ST mean?' but rather 'What does this ST mean to you in your retextualization of it?' As we have already argued, poetic translation is about the conversion not of an SL into a TL, but of an ST into a TT, a fact which has two important consequences.

First, the translation of verse reaches into the peculiar nature of the reading of verse, that reading which is both a reading and a listening to the self read, a communication more between the reader and himself than between a poet and a reader. In Maulnier's rather heady words:

> Pureté pleine de possibles, cristal où chaque homme vient comme Narcisse se pencher pour aimer une figure inconnue de soi-même, diamant nocturne où chacun vient allumer ses propres étoiles, le poème naît ainsi en chaque âme à une vie différente, et chaque âme naît en lui à sa propre vie.
>
> (1939: 12).
>
> [Purity full of possibilities, crystal which each person comes to gaze into, to fall in love with a figure unknown to him/her, nocturnal diamond at which each person comes to light his/her own stars, the poem is thus born, in each soul, to a new life, and each soul is born to its own life in the poem.]

In fact translation's great benefit to literary criticism is the contribution of a dimension of textual experience which literary criticism cannot itself properly provide—the experience of reading itself (i.e. not just a hermeneutic or interpretative activity, but an involvement in the making of meaning, in the making of a meaning peculiarly significant to the maker). It is for this reason that the undoubted contribution which linguistics has made and continues to make (particularly in stylistics) is less reliable when it comes to the translation of poetry.

Secondly, the contribution of linguistics needs to be qualified by a further warning in relation to verse translation: while a central tenet of any modern poetics remains the auto-reflexivity of the work, despite much justifiably precautionary debate, then we must also suppose that the poem is a linguistic system within the linguistic system, but that this inner system creates its own principles of operation, principles which are by no means

3

consistent across the totality of verse products. Besides, we still know very little about the modes of signification of verse structures, partly because semantics is absorbed into psycho-physiological eventfulness, partly because questions about the meaning and function of rhyme, metre, acousticity, etc. have been relatively little asked and less answered. If we add to these observations the propositions of the so-called neo-Humboldtians, as expressed by, for example, Jost Trier:

> Chaque langue est un système qui opère une sélection au travers et aux dépens de la réalité objective. En fait, chaque langue crée une image de la réalité complète, et qui se suffit à elle-même.
>
> (quoted in Mounin, 1963: 44)
>
> [Each language is a system which makes a selection from, and at the expense of, objective reality. In fact, each language creates a complete image of reality, which is self-sufficient.]

then we would have to assert that each poem has the potentiality to create a new (image of) reality, by implication complete, and held in a state of tension with the native language system.

That the neo-Humboldtians, too, are persuaded of the impossibility of translation—

> On ne peut pas traduire parce qu'on ne parle jamais tout à fait de la même chose, même quand on parle du même objet, dans deux langues différentes.
>
> (Mounin 1963: 53)
>
> [Translation is impossible because no two people are ever quite talking about the same thing, even when they *are* talking about the same thing, in two different languages.]

—should act as no deterrent, even if one adds that what is here said of speakers of different languages might also be said of individual users within a single language; what makes literature necessary to us all is the opportunity to discover our own world through the challenge of someone else's, and vice versa. It is the impossibility of translation which founds the desirability of translation. But we should ensure that translation defines its true objectives by reference to an acceptance of its impossibility; to try to achieve a perfect translation is quite simply a misuse of translation, and were such a perfect version achievable, it would make translation a *process* of absolutely no interest to any audience other than machine translators; this is not of course to say that translations as *products* would not continue to be fully enjoyed. Perfect translations in a world in which translation was justified only by the pursuit of the perfect would be the only versions, the definitive ones, and translations would be a series of termini, as if removing works, one by one, from consciousness.

The impossibility of translation makes translation possible, gives it its worth. It is an integral part of the survival and multiplication of the ST; it is a valuable source of interactive writing; it is, as we have said, an embodiment of the experience of reading, a record of an encounter with an other which is negotiated into a self (either persona or 'real' identity); it is a way of transforming one world view into another (*text* into *text*) rather than merely transferring a single world view from one language to another. *Understanding* a translation in relation to an original is a profoundly more valuable activity than assessing a translation's proximity to an ST, which is, as previously mentioned, to misunderstand what translation is.

Languages do not exist in impermeable compartments, but rather in dialectical relationships with each other; the more translation that is done, the more translatable languages become. Verse-translation, we are often told, is the least possible of all translations, because of the complexity of the interplay between language and formal structure. But in the communication stakes, verse-translation has the huge compensatory advantage that, in order to be effective, it must be built, like all verse-communication, on a version of that bilateral solipsism which we look upon, in other communicative contexts, as undermining, if not disqualifying. The factor of bilateral solipsism is what makes verse-communication so rich, so rewarding an experience.

But this means that, in verse-translation, the stakes are very high, for verse-translation is tantamount to *resisting* communication, or at least paying little heed to it. If communication can only be guaranteed at the level of an average of its various linguistic uses, or of a lowest common communicator, or of an invariant core, then verse will want nothing to do with the kind of public, consensus language that communication is inevitably tied to, since it is verse's business to increase access to (one's own) privacy by correspondingly increasing language's capacity for variability. I prefer this account of verse-communication to the multilevel one, i.e. verse, being the most sophisticated form of linguistic expression, maximizes the number of levels on which communication can take place. In the multi-level account, a really sensitive, well-trained reader will be able to capture, for example, a text's intertextual allusions, and rhythmic and acoustic nuances, in a way denied to a less informed or responsive reader; but this latter will still derive benefit from the text, albeit at a different (lower) level of apprehension. This approach is a patronizing one, but, more dangerously, it is a mechanistic one: it assumes that all readers at a certain level have access to, and enjoy, the same experience.

It does not seem likely that any radically new method of translation will be discovered; even multi-media versions will still leave the translator with the same kinds of problem, the same range of solutions. F.W. Leakey's Introduction to his *Selected Poems from 'Les Fleurs du Mal'* (1994) presents a typical sequence of moves to highlight the translator's predicament. First, an analysis of the practical challenges facing a translator, which involves breaking the poem down into its component parts, so that each class of difficulty can be identified and measured, but which immediately raises concerns about the preservation of the text's integrity; Leakey rather slides away from these concerns:

> these various elements [meaning, sound (including metre, rhythm and rhyme), imagery, vocabulary, syntax, dramatic quality and tempo, tone] no doubt on occasion overlap, but the challenges they severally present to the creator of the poem remain distinct and measurable.
>
> (1994: 1)

Secondly, these component parts are passed in review, and many of them, that is the most specific and technical, are declared untranslatable (equivalence, rightly perhaps, is considered a delusion); thirdly, given the intractability of these particular components, one should concentrate on the others (meaning, imagery, vocabulary, dramatic quality and tempo, tone), combining them in a version that gives priority to essentials rather than to details (what are 'essentials', and do they not derive from, or find expression in, details?); fourthly, but of paramount importance, is the production of a translation that is itself 'aesthetically pleasing':

> [...] the translator, far from being a mere intermediary, must strive to achieve somehow a happy compromise between, on the one hand, the proper transmission of the essential content of his chosen poem ('essential', in the sense that mere word-for-word equivalence is not here the primary goal) and, on the other, the creation of an aesthetically pleasing parallel poem of his or her own.
>
> (1994: 2–3).

Unfortunately, 'essential', now with 'proper' as a companion, continues suspended in the realm of unelaborated credo and question-begging; unfortunately, the translator's own writerly input is left unexplored and unexplained. Lastly, a reason for this latter is that what is given with one hand is taken back with the other: the translator is not really invited to be himself/herself, but rather his/her idea of an English Baudelaire:

> Better still, in the present case, he or she should seek (if only ideally)
> to compose the kind of poem Baudelaire might himself have written,
> if English had been his native tongue.
>
> (1994: 3)

The same idea is to be found in Lowell,[1] and though it often operates as a useful excuse for certain choices, the very notion of a (contemporary?) English Baudelaire is clearly absurd, since the implicit argument about his untranslatability is that Baudelaire's inimitable selfhood as a writer lies in his nineteenth-century Frenchness. The trouble with this last strategy, and with other parts of the plan, is that it absolves the translator from having to say anything about himself/herself as a writer, and indeed, as a reader of Baudelaire (as opposed to an interpretative critic). And this shying away from confrontation with the task of *writing* translations, which may be no more than modesty, is no more apparent than in Leakey's final introductory words:

> I would add, finally, remembering Baudelaire's own constant
> concern for the proper declamation of his poems, that I have been
> careful to test, in actual spoken performance, the rhythms and
> metres I have adopted in each case.
>
> (1994: 4)

'To test'? Against what criteria? In what *special* sense does this mean 'I think most of my versions are acceptably iambic'? Once again the art of the translator is being stowed away somewhere out of sight, and the reader is asked to take Leakey's 'testing' on trust. I have no quarrel of principle with Leakey's translations, but his Introduction troubles me (a) because it does the visibility of the translator no favours (does the translator really need any more than a rudimentary knowledge of verse, a thesaurus and a good dictionary to do a competent job?), and (b) because it does nothing to develop the relationship between the translator and his/her reader. What this book attempts to do is follow the thought processes which a translator might have, and at the same time find ways of crediting readers of translation with more creative intelligence than is usually the case. It is easy for 'knowledgeable' readers of translations to act as back-seat translators. They also need to find ways of sympathizing with the driver, of adopting his/her point of view. Don't shoot the pianist. An important task of this book is to discover an appropriate approach to the criticism of translations (see Chapter 8).

The mystifications to be found in Leakey's Introduction are, unfortunately, all too frequent in translator's prefaces. Walter Martin's laudable versions (1997) do not need the support of impenetrable statements like:

> By forcing you to 'play it by ear', to rely on your ear to capture the poet's varying pace and tone, syllabics tend to circumvent metrical solutions. Numbers—it seems to this practitioner—are essential to the probity of verse.
>
> (1997: 441)

Syllabics, one might argue, are linguistic, while pace and tone are partly, if not wholly, paralinguistic, and belong as much to the reader as to the text. Why 'tend to'? What does 'circumvent' mean here? Are syllabics non-metrical? In what sense is metre a provider of solutions? What is the 'probity' of verse and is it the moral criterion it sounds like?

Moral criteria, overt or covert, drive more of translation practice than they should perhaps. Martin, like some others, is an apologist of the inherent virtues of strict form, of the bracing self-denials of rhyme and regularity; these disciplines are seen as a necessary defence against a free verse which is endemically sloppy:

> Floppiness has made great strides in the intervening seventy-five years, and *vers libre* has been watered down to an extent that Eliot and Pound (much less Gautier and Baudelaire) would have found hard to imagine. Until some new and improved remedy has been discovered, rhymes and regular strophes will have to do.
>
> (1997: 441)

'Much less' here probably means 'much more'. But the general view is echoed by Norman Shapiro, in his comments on available translations:

> some, elegant exercises in idiosyncratic paraphrase; others, intentional attempts to turn Baudelaire into a formless twentieth-century free-versifier; some, hewing closely to his formal constraints, but often tortured and contrived in the process; others, endeavouring to echo the richness of his music, but forced to resort to wan assonances, almost-rhymes, and graceless, limping meters.
>
> (1998: xxx)

8

as pedagogic mediator has always been important; (c) it raises questions about what parameters of tolerance the translational contract might establish. The chapter's destination is a foreignizing translation of 'Parfum exotique'. This same poem is the subject of a free-verse rendering in Chapter 2, which opposes itself to the first chapter in two ways: it abandons the pedagogic to embrace the self-expressive, and it turns abruptly away from the ST in its rhythmic and formal choices. Some of the implications of free verse as a translational medium are investigated through the writing of Yves Bonnefoy and the translation of Shakespeare. If Bonnefoy presides over Chapter 2, Henri Meschonnic, as already mentioned, is an important critical witness in Chapter 3, which returns to translation's relationship with pedagogy as its point of departure. This chapter focuses on the dangers of that relationship—the transformation of the ST into a 'dead language'—and suggests that the way round such a danger, the way to revivify the ST, and animate its interaction with the TT, lies in a better understanding of textuality and intertextual exchange. Baudelaire's 'Sed non satiata' is the text around which the discussion revolves, and a translation in the spirit of the chapter is presented. While this translation is irregular, it is not free in the way that the translation of 'La Cloche fêlée' in the following chapter is. This fourth chapter is about the way in which the translation process itself can be theorized, to ensure that the translator finds his own territory for translation, and that his version can intimately complement the ST, in a partnership tantamount to co-authorship. The pace of translation accelerates in Chapter 5: two versions of 'A une passante', one of 'Le Goût du néant', one of 'Le Balcon', one of 'Bien loin d'ici' and one of 'Harmonie du soir' are offered. These serve an investigation into translation as formal transposition, as a means of exploring the expressive range of various fixed forms, called upon to deal with material which puts their flexibility to the test. The self-conscious nature of fixed forms also makes more acute the conflicts between persona and self in translation, between the critical and the existential in the 'position traductive [translational position]' (Berman 1995: 74–5). Chapter 6, which includes translations of 'Quand le ciel bas et lourd pèse comme un couvercle', 'Obsession', 'A une dame créole' and 'Les Aveugles', examines the possibilities of 're-authoring' the ST by shifting the position of the presiding consciousness from outside to inside the text, and from poet ('shot') to subject ('reversed shot'). Consciousness can also be multiplied, either with the help of paratextual resources (title, epigraph), or by installing multivocality within the text, or across variant versions. Chapter 7 looks into 'plain prose' translations and suggests that these, unwittingly, have impeded the development of prose translations of verse.

As a way of enquiring into the relatively little known art of prose, analyses of prose translations of two Baudelaire poems—'Correspondances' and 'Le Mort joyeux'—are undertaken. The prose poem and the prose translation are intimate bedfellows; indeed, prose poets have been in the habit of imagining their work as the translation of lost verse originals. Chapter 7 ends with the search for a verse original: I attempt a verse translation of Baudelaire's 'Assommons les pauvres!' Before a final chapter devoted to a single, but relatively large-scale, translation, Chapter 8 takes stock, in the light of the previous approaches, of the criticism of translation, and suggests how greater account might be taken of the translator as practising writer, and of the particularity of translation projects. Different versions of 'Recueillement' constitute the chapter's primary material, and are the source of an argument about the differences between reading and interpretation. Concordancing is briefly assessed as a possible route to a better understanding of the principles of choice which govern a translator's posture towards the ST. Chapter 9 occupies itself with a translation of 'Le Voyage'. This, too, is a free-verse rendering, with the difference that it includes, montaged into it, quotations from other writers and some verse insertions of my own. The purpose of this chapter is twofold: to show how a TT can expand the ST, to take account of not only of the translator, in person as it were, but also of the time and space, with all their added voices, which have 'elapsed' between the ST and the TT; and to further argue the case for free verse as a translational medium.

This book certainly does not claim to provide a comprehensive review of available translation theory; its agenda is rather too partisan for that. Nor does it look to arm the reader with a history of 'Baudelaire in English'—this has already been admirably done by Clark and Sykes (1997)—nor to undertake a thorough comparative assessment of the work of different translators—although there is some comparative analysis, particularly in Chapter 8—nor to trace Baudelaire's assimilation into the English tradition (see Clements 1985). Rather I have tried to move through those theoretical issues which relate particularly to verse translation, in order to make clearer to myself my own 'position traductive'—I say 'make clearer' rather than 'define', because each new translating situation tends to require some adjustment of one's position, some re-configuration of strategies. I can only hope that the translations which do emerge from this series of ruminations seem to make the ruminations worthwhile.

Note on the text: I have provided translations of all foreign-language critical extracts and of all material in Latin. Poems, and extracts from poems, in French (and German) are not translated.

1

In Defence of Foreignizing Translation

Much of what I write in the coming chapters will be preoccupied with the ways in which the translator moves away from the source text (ST), or rather draws away from the ST while pulling it along with him. But this chapter describes a move in the other direction, towards the source text. It considers the efforts of the translator to foreignize the target text (TT) sufficiently for a reader to be able, or wish, to reach through the TT to the poem which has survived within it as a shadowy, but still imperious, presence. I want to start in that dimension of translation which is more concerned with acting as the mediator of another culture, the pedagogic dimension, than with expressing a translating self, the psycho-existential dimension. I am less interested in translations as achievements, as finished texts, and more interested in them as activators of a special kind of reading. Translation theory takes little account of the reader, in the sense that the answer to the question 'How should one read a translation?' (apart from assessing its distance from the ST) still remains to be formulated. The foreignizing translation provokes the reader, makes demands on the reader's patience, requires the reader to fill out the TT with all manner of imaginative supplements—at the risk of alienating the reader. Foreignizing translation is, in short, a calculated gamble, always likely to fall flat on its face when put alongside the unassuming sanity of a domesticating translation. Translation can often seem to be a test of cultural allegiances, and the translator may often feel wary of consorting with the enemy. At all events, I take as my 'text', as a formulation of what translation is about, a passage from Bonnefoy's Introduction to the French translation of poems by George Seferis: 'Je salue avec grande affection et respect Georges Séféris, en cet heureux moment où sa poésie, tout atténuée qu'elle soit par la disparité de nos langues, est offerte en volume au lecteur

13

français. Puisse-t-il, ce lecteur trop sollicité, impatient, entendre au loin cette voix: il n'en est pas de plus pure' [I salute, with much affection and respect, George Seferis, at this happy moment when his poetry, attenuated though it is by the disparity between our languages, is offered as a volume to the French reader. May he, the impatient reader, with too many demands on his attention, make out, in the distance, this voice: there is none purer] (1989: 16). The foreignizer is the translator who wants his translation to minimize linguistic disparity, who wants the easily distracted reader to strain to hear the voice of the original.

I would like to begin with a set of indictments. When translations tend towards the domesticated, as has been only too often observed, the result is all too often a bland consensus translation, the version that causes the least linguistic offence to the largest number of people. This, for me, is why the reading of translations produces one of the least—when it should be one of the most—imaginative and challenging kinds of reading there is. Translation should be at the forefront of experimental writing, but it is only when the source text is itself experimental, playful, punning, that the translator feels licensed to break out of the strait-jacket of 'the way we say it in English', or 'what sounds natural to the English ear'. Peculiarly, the language of translation performs in a permanent crisis of credibility, is an extremely fragile confection, and very rarely are readers prepared to suspend their disbelief; correspondingly, translators lose their nerve. And yet the very idea of translation—trying to get a foreign language into your own, trying to wear a dress that was made for someone else—requires creative self-disfigurement. This dress parallel might be usefully taken further: in borrowing someone else's dress, and given that no alterations are possible—you cannot alter the source text—would you pretend that it *does* fit, by a bit of surreptitious tucking here, a bit of drawing in of the stomach there, even though it patently does not? Or would you get round the difficulty by proclaiming its ill-fittingness a new fashion which others might profitably follow? If our aim is the glorification of the dress—the celebration of the source text—then it is clear that the latter option makes best sense. Translation is emphatically *not* the equivalent of the judicious use of a bilingual dictionary. It is the exploration of cultural and linguistic spaces not known to the native language.

Part of the reason for this threat of normativization is the failure to think of translation functionally. What are translations for, what kinds of translation do different genres demand, what particular objectives does a particular translation have in mind, what kind of context or performance is a particular translation intended for, what kind of audience or ambience or voice has the translator, or indeed an alternative performer of the translation, in view? The relationship between text and performance has always been difficult to measure, and for that reason has been unjustifiably neglected. Is there any translation theory which really concerns itself with variable appropriacy, not just the appropriacy of the translation to the source text, but the appropriacy of the translation to its own many possible roles in the world. One might argue that, for much of the time, translation has remained an irresponsible, or excessively self-regarding, activity.

The principal victim of this vagueness about function is, as already intimated, the audience, the reader. To my knowledge, there is no developed theory about the reading of translations, about what kind of reading experience it is, about where the reader should place himself in relation to the text, about the implicit understandings and the perceptual adaptations with which a translation should be read, about the compensation mechanisms necessary for a fruitful reading of what is, in many respects, an inadequate text. The standard attitude of the translator writing for an *ignorant* reader (i.e. ignorant of the language and culture of the source text) would seem to be that his reader reads the translation but cannot decode it. All the reader can do is read the translator's own decoding of the source text, but without any instruments to judge it by. Consequently, the translator, for the ignorant reader, becomes an unjustified authority on the text he has translated, an indispensable mediator. Riffaterre's imagined translation-reading process, wherein he posits the direct transmission of the decoding processes of the translator, via the translation, to the reader —'The signals guiding readers in such a decoding in the original must be reproduced in the translation' (Schulte and Biguenet 1992: 205)—is pie in the sky, since it is quite clear that no one can really know what the signals guiding the translator in his decoding of the original are, nor how much they are interfered with by purely practical constraints. We must, therefore, read *through* the translator, or round the translator, make a spectre of him, prevent him from becoming the target of our reading. It is just as absurd to suppose that a translator is in full possession of his own native language, or of the language of his translation, as it is to suppose that the original writer is in full possession of his. So, ironically and tragically, translation has the effect of closing the source text down for the reader, not opening it up, and the reader is consequently, if implicitly, disempowered, treated as a passive consumer, without rights of appeal.

We know that translation is inadequate. 'Necessary and impossible' is the catch-22 which Derrida describes in his allegorization of Babel (Schulte and Biguenet 1992: 226). But it is not for translation meekly to undergo these inadequacies, nor to try to conceal them. Inadequacy is the factor which must be built upon, exploited, developed, made *expressively* visible. I emphasize this word 'expressively', because it is expressiveness which provokes and engages a readerly response, and, as I have already mentioned, we need a theory of translation in relation to the way a reader might most profitably engage with a translation.

Translation is a peculiarly interactive undertaking. The translation interacts with the original, both interpretatively and linguistically. This interaction involves the intertexts within the source text and the whole intertextualization generated by the mere presence of an historical and cultural distance between the source text and the translator. On top of this, is the interaction between the translator and his reader, by which the reader is invited, by a process of linguistic and *presentational* interaction, to take a journey through the intervening layers of intertext to the source, that is to say, to make contact with the source text as a twentieth-century reader. So expressivity involves three dimensions of the text, its expressivity as an interpreted and therefore *interpretable* text, its linguistic expressivity and its presentational expressivity.

What one can imagine is the development of a particular kind of translationese. By this I evidently do not mean that translationese which is a lame and lumpy version of the target language, a set of linguistic compromises deriving from a peculiarly half-hearted or untheorized faithfulness. I mean a translationese which tries to arrive at a more uncompromising faithfulness, which does not seem to be constantly apologizing for itself, but one which calls for the reader to comprehend, to compensate for, and complete it; a translationese which is prepared to use a whole range of diacritical and graphic signs, and a range of language structures, which the target language can only just bear. When I translate Baudelaire, I am not trying to produce an English or Englished Baudelaire, though I shall do that to some degree without trying. What I want to do is produce a text which invites the reader to pass back through something half-familiar, half-recognized, palimpsestic, to something which is in many respects alien and culturally unassimilated. My translation must be designed as a journey back, a journey back to the decipherment of a text which is alien. So I am translating in order to mobilize the reader, to provide an acclimatization, or the first step of a cultural reorientation, which will at least put the original within reach. Above all, even for the reader who has little or no knowledge of the source language, the translation must be a *terminus a quo* and not a *terminus ad quem*.

If translation does not require a linguistic/cultural reorientation of the reader, then it has perhaps failed in its objective *as a translation*. To take the crassest of examples: we 'translate' French's 'encre de Chine' by

'Indian ink'. If we look these two things up in their respective monolingual dictionaries, we discover:

> **encre de Chine**: composition solide ou liquide de noir de fumée, pour le dessin au lavis [encre de Chine: solid or liquid preparation of lampblack, for wash drawing] (*Petit Larousse*, Paris 1960, p. 372); employée pour les dessins au pinceau, à la plume [used for brush or pen drawings] (*Le Nouveau Petit Robert*, Paris 1993, p. 756).
>
> **Indian ink**: very black ink, used for writing, drawing etc. (*Penguin English Student's Dictionary*, London 1991, p. 474); **1.** a black pigment made from a mixture of lampblack and a binding agent such as gelatin or glue: usually formed into solid cakes and sticks. **2.** a black liquid ink made from this pigment (*Collins English Dictionary*, London 1979, p. 744).

We might think these definitions have much in common; but we equally might think that while, for the French, images of Oriental scrolls, delicate calligraphy, spontaneous gestures of the hand, are made available, for the English some product springs to mind whose colour and unpleasant constituents relate it to a colonized people and the attendant administrative responsibilities. There is still much work to be done on dictionary definitions as sources of differential acculturation. But the factors which make this translation especially dispiriting are twofold: first, there is a tendency to associate the triumphant correctness of the translation with the very difference it affirms; the guarantee of the target language's idiomaticness is its very distance from the source language. Secondly, in choosing 'Indian ink' as a translation, we willy-nilly suppose that the average English reader is incapable of thinking his/her way into 'Chinese or China ink', of re-imagining the context of this ink.

French characteristically postposes its adjectives; postposition in English usage connotes the poetic and the archaic. Do we then conclude that the English reader cannot, even temporarily, be persuaded out of his/her culturally stereotyped thinking? Do we believe that, forewarned, the English reader cannot be persuaded to think of the postposition of adjectives as determined by other considerations? Normative translations are to be deprecated as an insult to the reader's intelligence.

Let us imagine we have a source text whose stanzas are rhymed *abba*. This rhyme-scheme will (a) make rhyme-partners of particular words; (b) generate a certain intonational pattern for the reading of the stanza; (c) set up certain possibilities and expectations of syntactic segmentation. Are we then to suppose that a reader, faced with a rhymeless TT, but informed, directly or indirectly, that the ST rhymes *abba*, cannot imaginatively re-enact the line-terminal combinations, albeit now between unrhyming words, and the intonational patterns, and indeed expect certain syntactic divisions?

I have suggested that the assumption most dangerous to our proper understanding of translation is its assimilation to the use of the bilingual dictionary. By that I mean that the translator, in his/her unguarded moments, may ask 'What does X [a source word] mean?' His answer may be 'Y' (a target word), as if Y were the *signified* of X. Of course it is not. Y is an alternative of X as *signifier*, more synonym than definition. It is the acceptance of this latter 'truth' which justifies Benjamin's view (Schulte and Biguenet 1992: 71–82) that, together, source language and target language might point to a universal, pre-Babel language, Mallarmé's 'supreme' language: one signifier (source) is supplemented, complemented, forms new linguistic coordinates with, another signifier (target), and out of this relationship a third signifier is projected, the ghost of a pre-lapsarian language. However, this view is not adequate either. Source text and target text are not two equivalent or alternative texts. As I have argued, the latter should lead back to the former; in other words, even if we were using an invalid bilingual-dictionary model, we would have to say that the target language does not translate the source language, but vice versa. In *some* senses, a process of signification, of Y *means* X does obtain. But how?

The distinction we are making here is the well-known one, between two processes of translation: the process of systemic equivalence and the process of signification (translating a signifying text into a signified text). This distinction is particularly useful in translation studies, and more so in the translation of poetry, in three ways:

1. The distinction can be used the better to understand mistranslation. In Baudelaire's 'Parfum exotique', for example, the translator has to negotiate the shift from 'chaud' to 'chaleureux', which occupy different locations on the systemic map of French. Scarfe (1964: 56) supposes that 'chaleureux' is to 'chaud' as 'sultry' is to 'warm' in English. Well, he has judged the distance correctly perhaps, but not the direction: 'sultry' has negative associations of oppressiveness and humidity unknown to 'chaleureux'. Similarly, Wagner (1971: 31) sees 'heated' to 'close' as the equivalent of 'chaleureux' to 'chaud'. But what might be forgivable as a systemic miscalculation is cruelly punished in the mind of the 'knowing' reader by being read as a miscalculation of signification, a lack of familiarity with the meanings of the target language: 'heated' means either 'animated in the direction of anger' ('a heated discussion') or 'having its temperature raised,

usually by electrical means'. Laughs at the expense of translations come cheap and reveal a lack of appreciation of (a) the systemic imperatives and (b) the need to think about the target language differently, as though it were no longer quite so predicted and so constrained by cultural givens and automatic associations. Readers must be encouraged to think back through signification to system, back to a space of meaning occupied by a word in relation to others. It is probable, here, that 'chaleureux' is to 'chaud' as 'warm' is to 'warm'; the question is how to indicate 'warm's' shift from questions of temperature to questions of spiritual attitude or being. Sometimes this problem is automatically solved, by what 'warm' is collocated with—'a warm welcome'—but there is no reason, as far as I am concerned, why this shift should not be indicated diacritically.

2. The distinction can be used to unpack the remark 'I cannot say what it means', which might mean either 'I understand what it means, but cannot say it' (systemic failure), or 'I cannot say what it means because I cannot understand it' (refusal of signification in the source language). In 'Parfum exotique' a problem of signification is posed, for example, by the closing phrase 'le chant des mariniers'. 'Chant' is not only the act, or art, of singing, but also song in noble, elevated style, or canto, and one thinks, too, inevitably, of the 'chant des sirènes'; but 'chanter' is also the source of 'shanty' ('chanson des marins'); 'marinier' is a deep-sea sailor, or seaman, but as an archaism; more recently it means a sailor who works on rivers, canals, inland or inshore waters, and, more particularly, a bargeman. In these circumstances it is nonsensical to say that one translation is preferable to another—'boatman's chant', 'song of the sailor-sirens', 'the shiphands' song', 'the shanties of the deep-sea men', 'the singing of the inshoremen'. But then let us multiply the meanings to show that we are in the throes of unsteady signification and use, say, round brackets as our code, to gather in the various possibilities. There is no necessary virtue in a choice made; there is more virtue in choices offered, in disseminated meaning.

Before moving on to the third way in which the distinction between the systemic and the significatory may be useful, we must make a further distinction: between the systemic as transferred system and the systemic as equivalent system; between, in other words, a foreign system transferred bodily from source language to target language, and a foreign system translated into the native system. In my contention, it is the former of these which is desirable.

3. The distinction between the systemic and significatory, and between the transferred systemic and the equivalent systemic, helps to define the

Foreignizing	**Naturalizing**

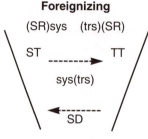

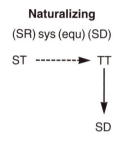

i.e. systemic *is* signifying	i.e. the systemic is superseded by the signifying
interactive at level of translation itself	interactive prior to translation
because interactive at level of translation, it also *involves* the reader	because interactivity precedes, its results *are reported to* the reader
danger: systemic activity interrupted and undermined by signifying process	danger: the TT is emptied of its own activity, by both being a signified (of ST) and having a (normative) signified

Figure 1.1

difference between the foreignizing and the domesticating translation, which I represent graphically in Figure 1.1 (where SR = signifier, SD = signified, trs = transferred, equ = equivalent, ST = source text, TT = target text).

Clearly, if prejudicially, this schema suggests that foreignization not only serves the ST better, but that its strategy harmonizes better with that of poetry generally, in that it seeks to suspend or postpone, in order to more richly synthesize, the process of signification.

It will be clear from the foregoing that I would relate foreignization to Barthes's notion of the *scriptible*, the writerly, and domestication to the *lisible*, the readerly (1970: 9–18). In other words, the domesticated text aims at a certain assimilability, unselfconsciousness, comprehensibility, and thus produces a certain passivity, receptivity, in the reader. Foreignization, on the other hand, is Brechtian in its self-interruptions, in those refusals of cohesion, which make it impossible for the reader to know how to read it. The *scriptible* text constantly opens itself up, projects multiplicity of structure and meaning, invites the reader to re-write it, declines wholeness.

So far we have made a distinction between processes of systemic transference/equivalence and processes of signification, and suggested critical and theoretical ways in which this might be used. But as we return to the foreignizing text, we shall need to sharpen our terms. The model outlined above suggests an equality of position between ST and TT. But however much we might wish to theorize on such an equality, as the ultimate desideratum of translation, we know empirically that it is not so, particularly in literary translation: ST has a priority, both in status and authorship, over TT. In fact, our wish to see ST and TT as paired SRs conspiring to produce an SD, where ST, let us remember, is, for the ignorant reader, an aided projection out of TT (TT is, as it were, both text and palimpsest, both itself and another text) is out of true, simply because ST is not only a free-standing SR but also a REFERENT and SD of TT. What I mean, more specifically, by the latter is this: for the ignorant reader,

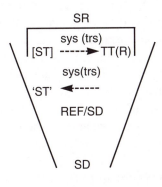

Figure 1.2

the ST is a text, something which can be, and is, referred to by the TT— 'warm', in a translation of Baudelaire's 'Parfum exotique', means both 'of a certain temperature' and 'the word "chaud" in Baudelaire's "Parfum exotique"'. Without a bilingual translation, this meaning circuit is impossible to verify and acknowledge, and should disqualify non-bilingual translations by definition. But the ignorant reader may look at 'chaud' in the ST, may think that 'warm' = 'chaud' (Baudelaire), but will be little the wiser; unless, unless of course, the translation also produces 'Parfum exotique' as a signified, that is as an image, a representation, a set of concepts, a pattern of feeling. ST constitutes TT, so that it can itself be reconstituted. ST only becomes an SR, for the ignorant reader, because TT has been able to regenerate it, not only as an SR, by referring the reader to it, but as an SR likely to signify adequately within the parameters that TT has managed to indicate. Our model, then, more accurately, should appear as that shown in Figure 1.2 where [ST] is a pre-text by definition inaccessible to the reader, and 'ST' a semi-accessible version of [ST], produced by the mediation of TT. I have changed TT to TT(R) to emphasize that TT's role as mediator can only be activated by readerly participation. And since the TT is *scriptible* rather than *lisible*, the reader does not simply bring the TT into existence by registering it, but does so by using it as a scenario for his own writing of it.

The projection of [ST] by the TT as a text (REF) with a potential signified (SD) begins to imply, as we have already adumbrated, that ST is in fact a translation of TT, or at least a translation *back* from TT. This plunges us deep in deconstructionist territory and will bring us shortly face to face with the perennial issue of authorship. But before confronting that issue, let us briefly bemoan the relative absence of postmodernist thinking in translational practice. So far, translation's use *to* postmodernism has resided largely in translation's aptness, because of its necessarily inadequate relation to an original, as an allegory or exemplum of disseminated or deferred or constantly self-relocating meaning. So far, translation's use *of* postmodernist thinking has been connected with feminist accounts of translation (see, e.g., Simon 1996; Flotow 1997), and, more generally, with the debunking of 'essentialist' translation theories (see, e.g., Arrojo 1998). There are at least three ways, all closely related, in which postmodernism can immediately help us to re-present translation:

1. It can loosen our commitment to the unprovable aesthetic prejudices of organic wholeness, textual integrity, systemic completeness. Deconstruction tells us, convincingly enough, that texts are in fact incomplete, incoherent, undermined by uncontrollable variables and shifting priorities. The recent history of translation has been as old-fashioned, as anachronistic, as that of photography. Where photography has perpetuated Renaissance perspective, the window-aesthetic of rectangular visual constructs, and the collapsing of three-dimensional stereoscopy into two-dimensional monocularity, so translation has continued to pursue the chimaera of textual autonomy, the transfixing of textual being, the notion that the text is self-justifying and self-completing, and the notion that the text is temporally coincident with itself. In order to break photography's unregenerate imprisonment in window-aesthetics, David Hockney's SLR (as opposed to polaroid) photocollages (1982–6) introduced a wandering frame, the self-improvising frame, or framelessness (depending on your point of view) and the reversed perspective of Oriental art. This, it seems to me, is the solution which translation, in its turn, must pursue. Translation is a provisional, self-improvising, ragged writing, and thus, formally, it is a ruin of its original even while being a younger version of it. Translation is a second-hand,

citational, delapidated form of the ST at the same time as it re-originates, re-engenders that same text. This complex, dialectical relationship between the ST and the TT depends for its existence on the reader's ability to reverse perspective: the point of infinity, the vanishing point, is no longer solely in a text which reaches out, in a process of increasing legibility, towards the reader, who, in his turn, is increasingly fixed, or positioned, by the lines radiating out from the text's vanishing point; no, concomitantly, the translation locates the point of infinity in the reader, so that the TT, and the ST buried in it, or concealed behind it, or visible alongside it, radiates out of the process of reading, a process able constantly to relocate itself, since it carries its point of infinity within it. In conventional perspective, our seeing is organized by the conventions of the picture; in reversed perspective, our perceptual experience organizes, composes, the 'being seen'.

2. Postmodern thinking can suggest to us that, since translation makes explicit the sense of layered, and possibly self-contradictory, strata of perception, translation is not locked into a purely linguistic dialogue with the ST. It is perfectly easy to produce *performances* of translated texts, or indeed of any text, in which the performance bypasses the text, to appeal to an origin prior to the translation, prior to the ST even, to arrive at which the intervening texts must be abused, distorted or disregarded. In 1987, the Heavy Metal group Celtic Frost produced an album entitled *Into the Pandemonium*, which contained performances both of Baudelaire's 'Tristesses de la lune', and of its translation by Joanna Richardson (1975). The French text, to a melody by the group's bass-player Martin Ain, is sung by Manü Moan (Man You Moan)—the female singer's name as comment on the poet—while the Richardson translation is sung by the group's lead singer, Tom Warrior. The poem's theme of transferred masturbation—the Moon is figured as an auto-erotic muse who stimulates the poet to an onanistic response, by which creativity is self-directed and life-resistant—is here transposed into a feminine ST answered by a masculine TT; conversely, however, the feminine ST is to a melody by a male composer, while the masculine TT is a translation by a female writer. The performance of the TT quite clearly answers the provocations of the ST. But two further features should be commented upon. First, on the album itself, the ST and the TT are separated by four other tracks, so that the TT does require a real effort if the ST is to be recovered; the listener must traverse a set of intervening intertexts, so that the album foreshortens the historical processes at work in any reception of a translation. The four intervening tracks include 'Babylon Fell':

Tears drift in the shadows sleep
Turn innocence into excess
Fragments of a dying world
And destiny lies beneath

'Caress into Oblivion', 'One in Their Pride' and 'I Won't Dance':

Journey into a wicked world
My body beneath the skies
Erotic wishes, my heart has failed
Incalculable is the surface's breath
Paralyzed form—the ring of death
Steps on the stairs to my silent ecstasy.

Secondly, whilst Tom Warrior's vocal delivery is like a violation of, or an ironic flirtation with, Joanna Richardson's archaizing, perhaps Pre-Raphaelite, syntax and lexicon ('some fair woman', 'lost in cushions deep', 'with gentle hand', 'avalanches soft', 'white visions aloft', etc.), the style of Richardson's translation is, ironically, peculiarly in tune with the style of Martin Ain's own original lyrics (see quotations above). Translation can now draw on the resources of multi-media and hyper-text and other electronic aids. The models of translation with which we formerly lived have, at a stroke, in theory if not in fact, become anachronistic. It is up to translation, still stuck in hard copy, to produce the kinds of hard copy which can anticipate translation's future.

3. Deconstruction can suggest that translation is not only an allegory or exemplum of the postmodernist signifying condition, but that it is the actual locus of postmodernism. Just as Linda Hutcheon (1989: 120) argues that 'photography may be the perfect postmodern vehicle in many ways, for it is based on a set of paradoxes inherent in its medium', so we might make the same proposal for translation: by introducing the notion of duplication or doubling, by opening up the spaces in textuality, by diversifying styles and registers, translation opens up both itself and its source text to the effects of difference, deferral, of one thing after, or within, another (Krauss 1985: 109). Corrosive succession is introduced into unanimous simultaneity.

But the deconstructive re-writing of the notion of authorship, as described by Gentzler (1993: 149) in his account of Foucault—

> The notion that the translator creates the original is one which is introduced by deconstructionists and serves to undermine the notion of authorship and with it the authority on which to base a comparison of subsequent translated versions of a text. Deconstructionists argue that original texts are constantly being rewritten in the present and each reading/translation reconstructs the source text.

—will be a harder task. Any translation which involves an act of interpretation as well as one of transference or equivalence inevitably ascribes an authority to a source. Any endeavour to resurrect a source ascribes a priority to that source. But this is not to say that the source enjoys an integrity which the translation does not; it merely indicates a will to assign a *greater* integrity to the ST than to the TT; it is, in other words, a question of degree rather than of kind. The ST has an authority, too, by belonging conspicuously to history (even if it is a contemporary text), and by virtue of its foreignness, its irreducible otherness. Perhaps it is a constitutive perception of the modern translator that he always stands at the end of history, at the terminus of geographical distance, that he is not in a position to make history, that he cannot author anything, that he has been written before he can write. Faced with this condition, he can only recirculate himself into history and into authorship by making his text palimpsestic, a ghostly trace underwritten by a source and its intervening manifestations. And even if the translator has confidence in the projective power of his work, it is likely that he will draw psychological sustenance from a nostalgia for a work deemed to have more integrity than his own. But these attitudes need to be revised, not merely in the name of postmodernism, but in the name of translation newly understood, and of a translation process more purposefully defined. These are the issues with which the chapters following busy themselves.

In the translation of Baudelaire's 'Parfum exotique' which follows, I make two broad assumptions: first, that verse, because of the suspensive nature of the line, sustains an unusual syntactic tolerance. Syntactic improbability is, as it were, masked, partly by satisfied metrical structure, partly by the line's ability to trap readerly attention within it, partly by the stanza's supplanting the sentence as the measure of sense-fulfilment (Grimaud 1992: 7–10; Scott 1998: 57–9). Secondly, the more obtrusive the imperatives of rhythmic structure, the more the reader is receptive to, and tolerant of, word-coinage and syntactic innovation—a supposition borne out by the poetry of, for example, Hopkins.

Parfum exotique

Quand, les deux yeux fermés, en un soir chaud d'automne,	4+2+4+2
Je respire l'odeur de ton sein chaleureux,	3+3+3+3
Je vois se dérouler des rivages heureux	2+4+3+3
Qu'éblouissent les feux d'un soleil monotone;	3+3+3+3
Une île paresseuse où la nature donne	2+4+4+2
Des arbres singuliers et des fruits savoureux;	2+4+3+3
Des hommes dont le corps est mince et vigoureux,	2+4+2+4
Et des femmes dont l'œil par sa franchise étonne.	3+3+4+2
Guidé par ton odeur vers de charmants climats,	2+4+4+2
Je vois un port rempli de voiles et de mâts	4+2+2+4
Encor tout fatigués par la vague marine,	2+4+3+3
Pendant que le parfum des verts tamariniers,	2+4+2+4
Qui circule dans l'air et m'enfle la narine,	3+3+2+4
Se mêle dans mon âme au chant des mariniers.	2+4+2+4

I have attempted, first and foremost, to convey to the English reader the rhythmic movement of the French line: the dodecasyllabic alexandrine, with its fixed medial caesura at the sixth syllable and, since metrical/rhythmic stresses (accents) are word-group-terminal in French, with fixed metrical accents on the sixth and twelfth syllables, and, usually, two further accents, one within each half-line, each with a variable position. I have followed the accentual pattern in Baudelaire's lines to the letter. French verse is also characterized, up to the 1860s, by the 'loi de l'alternance des rimes', by, that is to say, the alternation of masculine (oxytonic) and feminine (paroxytonic: word ending with a 'mute' syllable) rhymes; I have tried to embody this principle, indicating the 'feminine' syllable by square brackets; where the French line has a feminine ending, and my translation none, I have indicated the omission by '[...]'. I have, throughout, avoided padding to make up syllables, and instead resorted to the sign ^ , in the belief that the English metrical mind is accustomed to the provision of silent off-beats, and that, anyway, the reader can be relied upon mentally to 'fill' syllabic gaps when asked to by a diacritical sign. I have also indicated where the reading mind should collapse two syllables into one by the superscribed mark ⌢ . Where words with an apparently concrete, or physical, signified have shifted into a figurative register, either by virtue of their morphology or position in the ST, I have alerted the reader to the shift by a preposed ! . I have supplied the mark ′ not only to indicate where the accents fall in the equivalent French line, but also to warn the reader to demote to weak any preceding syllables in the particular measure, which might more naturally be felt to be strong in a 'native' English reading; thus, at line 10, we should read 'I see a port' rather than 'I see a port'. But it has not always been possible to engineer measure-terminal stresses/accents; in these instances, I have placed the stress-mark in its natural English position, but added the mark > to encourage the reader to 'float' the stress forward, if only in imagination, on to the final syllable of the measure. Finally, I have respected, wherever possible, that feature of French verse known as the *coupe enjambante*; this concerns hemistich-internal accents which fall on a syllable succeeded by a 'mute' ending; when not elided by a following vowel or mute h, these mute syllables are counted as syllables in French, and thus to a greater or lesser degree articulated; for scansional purposes, they become the first syllable of the rhythmic measure succeeding the word they terminate, and have the added effect of lengthening the syllable which precedes them, particularly if it is accentuated: thus, 'Je respire l'odeur' (line 2) would be phonetically represented as /ʒəRɛspi:/RələdœR/; in my diacritical language, this phenomenon is represented by a . following the stressed syllable.

I do not wish here to embark upon a detailed account of the reading which has guided some of my choices; such an account can be found elsewhere (Scott 1998: 138–44). Suffice it to say that I view the structure of the poem as an expansion of the initial pattern of progression 'les deux yeux fermés' > 'Je respire l'odeur' > 'Je vois', or , expressed acoustically, the pattern of progression from /ø/ ('deux yeux'), through /œ/ ('odeur') to /a/ ('vois'). Observation will confirm that /ø/ occurs only in the octave, that /œ/ occurs only once, in the repeated 'odeur' (line 9), in the sestet, and that the sestet as a whole is fairly saturated with /a/. This movement of progression and expansion is reinforced by other linguistic features: the poem's rhythm is increasingly informed by the expanding 2+4 hemistich; the paratactic nature of the syntax of the octave gives way the the hypotaxis of the sestet, with its embedding of phrases and clauses; the poet's 'I', absent from the second stanza, undergoes a transformation from agent ('Je vois') to patient ('m'enfle') to focal site ('dans mon âme') in the third and fourth stanzas; the essentially visual emphasis of the second stanza gives way to the amalgamation of sight, smell and sound in the course of the sestet; the predominantly adjectival mode of the octave, the mode of rhetorical embroidery and qualitative appreciation, gives way to a predominantly substantival mode in the sestet, the mode of confident being, of unmediated inhabitation; the adjectives which remain in the sestet

2

Translating Rhythm

My foreignizing translation of 'Parfum exotique' is designed, among other things, to suggest:

(a) that translation, by its very nature, is committed to sustaining, or creating, the openness, the unfinishedness in time and across national boundaries, of the ST;

(b) that, in a successful translation, the ST becomes a potential or intuited translation of the TT (i.e. a visible, but unspoken ST is, as it were, animated or inhabited by the voice of its translation);

(c) that a text can be accompanied by graphic and diacritical information, which guide reading without interfering with it, and that translations should make their premises clear in explanatory notes; and

(d) that the rhythmic ear can be re-attuned, that alternative rhythmic versions of a language can be explored, in comfort, while apparently disregarding that language's 'natural' prosody.[1]

It is the question raised by the last of these—the degree of a reader's rhythmic tolerance and adaptability—that I wish to address in this chapter, but I wish to approach it from the opposite direction: to ask not how much 'distortion' of native rhythms a reader will tolerate, but how great a deviation from the rhythms (and form) of the original. I want, in short, to investigate the plausibility of free-verse translation, and to essay a free-verse rendering of 'Parfum exotique'. This necessarily entails a shift from a pedagogic stance to a self-expressive one, since free verse is, to quote from Pound's 'Credo', 'an "absolute rhythm" [...] which corresponds exactly to the emotion or shade of emotion to be expressed. A man's rhythm must be interpretative, it will be, therefore, in the end, his own, uncounterfeiting, uncounterfeitable' (1954: 9). The enterprise also entails a somewhat circuitous route, through Yves Bonnefoy and the translation of Shakespeare, since Bonnefoy has been the steadiest champion of free verse as a universal translational medium for all poetry, however regular.

The difficulties which a reader might have with my gallicized version of English rhythm in 'A Perfume to Foreign Places' is no greater than the difficulties an English reader might encounter in reading Wyatt, or Coleridge, or Hopkins. These three poets are, in fact, the subject of Ted Hughes's 'Myths, Metres, Rhythms' (1995: 310–72), in which he challenges the reader to leap the gap between metrical expectations and the adaptation of those expectations required by particular verse-instances:

> Each line is like a dancer who, if you are going to read the line at all, forces you to be a partner and dance. [...] You can pronounce the line as silently as you like, but that launching of the inner self into full kinaesthetic participation is, so to speak, compulsory. Otherwise, you can't read the line. You have to back off, stay a wallflower, and call it 'unsayable'.
>
> (1995: 335)

This 'kinaesthetic participation' requires two related modifications in the reading mind: first, the substitution of a scansional mode for a metre-analytical one, reading for the unpredictable, the aleatory, rather than for the preordained, reading metre as expression rather than as knowledge, or convention aptly handled; secondly, reading rhythm with the paralinguistic (tempo, tone, pausing, stress-degree) in mind, that is to say, reading rhythm not only as expression but as self-expression. This latter proposition reminds us of the need for rhythmic parameters which include both the expressivity of the author (foreignizing translation) and the expressivity of the translator (idiolectal rather than domesticating). Indeed, one should put this more comprehensively: the need to develop a metrico-rhythmic medium which embraces the rhythmic nature of the ST, the rhythmic self-insertion of the translator, and the rhythmic input of the translation's readers. Over-normativized metricity has transformed metre into a code which merely over-determines verse as verse; far from releasing expressivity in verse, metre, and specifically metrical correctness, has come to mean, to adapt Hughes's telling phrase (1995: 356), the cultural maiming of sensibility. The need for broad rhythmic parameters, and for rhythms both responsive and adjustable, suggests, of itself, a recourse to free verse.

There are two reasons why, in translation, one should privilege rhythmic considerations over lexical ones, reasons which reveal a paradox at the heart of rhythm. First, rhythm is peculiarly independent of the historicity of lexicon; it is a strange but not surprising feature of translation that the consumer is more sensitive to the historicity of the TT (and specifically its lexicon) than to that of the ST. A translation may be taxed with being archaic or anachronistic, but not on rhythmic grounds. In this perspective, rhythm can be seen to constitute something transhistorical and perdurable, beyond the vulnerabilities of change. Secondly, what destabilizes the TT lexically is the fact that the place of the creative mind is taken by a dictionary or thesaurus (even if these exist within the translator's head). The translator asks 'What does this text mean?' and then 'What words will express that meaning?' The words, correspondingly, come from elsewhere, from a lexical repository which cannot itself guarantee family likeness or consistency of tone, temper, register. Of course, this particular argument can be overstated; of course, translators can create styles, construct consistencies. But the fact remains that the source of lexical solutions is not itself a whole, a work.[2] If lexical considerations, then, threaten the dispersal of the translator as a subjectivity, we may argue that the translator can re-ground his subjectivity in a free but adequate, diverse but inclusive, pattern of rhythmicity, that is to say, in that dimension of verse, rhythm, in which experiential response is uppermost.[3] And this recourse to rhythm is motivated by rhythm's capacity to inscribe in lexical sequences the here-and-now responsiveness, the continuously present expressivity, of the translating, and then of the reading, self.

But there are other historical justifications for adopting free verse as a universal translational medium:

1. Translations might be looked upon as one of the contributory factors in the emergence of free verse (see Scott 1982, 1990).

2. We have long been duped, as I have tried to suggest elsewhere (1993), by a misconceived view of the relationship between metre and rhythm. Because it is more abstract and absolute, metre, it is assumed, is more fundamental than rhythm, is the deep structure to rhythm's surface structure, the underlying competence to rhythm's performance. Generative metrists have only served to strengthen this misconception. Personally, I favour a Bergsonian reversal of this view, a reversal whereby rhythm, the acoustic dimension of *durée*, of inner time, is located in the *moi profond* [deep self] and thus predates or antecedes metre, that

rationalization of rhythm by a *moi superficiel* [surface self], operating in the quantitative rather than qualitative realm of chronometric time. In re-affirming the rhythmic, the non-metrical, against the metrical, free verse is merely restoring a priority which, masochistically, self-mutilatingly, we have been at pains to suppress.

3. There is evidence for the assertion above in verse itself. The diversification of metres in English—pure-stress, accentual-syllabic, syllabic—seems like an attempt to respond metrically to freedoms which will have their way. And as for French, we know of the anxiety which beset theorists, that French verse was too much like French prose in its principles of accentuation, that metricity had to be invested in syllabic number, caesura, rhyme, and that these safeguards of regularity had to be pursued with unusual punctiliousness (rules of pronunciation, rules of rhyme, degrees of rhyme, sensitivity of the sixth and seventh syllables of an alexandrine). And yet some commentators have argued that with the thirty-six rhythmic variations allowed by the classical alexandrine (that is, excluding the variations of the *trimètre*) the invention of free verse was hardly necessary (Champigny 1963: 61).

4. But regular verse is free in another dimension, too. The degree of metrical awareness even in the most regular verse is regulated by the voice, by the poise and insistence of the voice, and by other paralinguistic features (e.g. tempo, pausing). Immediately the recitation of verse is de-ritualized, shifts towards the spoken, towards extensive rather than intensive reading, then verse-structure loosens and diversifies itself. In the opening lines of Shakespeare's sonnet LXXI, for example, we can abandon a strict iambic pentameter to install, in its place, a 'slacker' rhythm, which fixes on 'nuclear' stresses, with some additional expressive support:

	No. of stresses
No longer mourn for me/ when I am dead	2(3)
Than you shall hear/ the surly sullen bell	4
Give warning to the world/ that I am fled	3
From this vile world,/ with vilest worms to dwell.	4

But the placing of the nuclear stress is itself open to dispute, and its characteristic terminal position may be challenged—as in the first unit 'No longer *mourn* for me' as against 'No longer mourn for *me*'. However, it is easy to see how the tendency for nuclear stress to occur phrase-terminally would make the verse in this form more amenable to French translation. The process of stress-demotion here does not, of course, affect the alternating syllabic segmentations created by the caesura, i.e. 6/4; 4/6; 6/4; 4/6; and the alternating rhyme-scheme is registered more emphatically— ironically—by a pattern of stressing which is denser in the *b* lines, or rather, denser in the second hemistichs of the *b* lines, as the quatrain's two *ab* pairs are each brought to a close.

Correspondingly, we should remember that the French Romantics' revolutionizing of the classical alexandrine, including the view that the caesura might become entirely mobile (see Wilhem Ténint's *Prosodie de l'école moderne*, 1844), coincided with the death of classical declamation and the arrival of the new 'spokenness' of French verse drama; Hugo praises Ténint for his understanding of this new situation: 'Le vers brisé est en particulier un besoin du drame; du moment où le naturel s'est fait jour dans le langage théâtral, il lui a fallu un vers qui pût se parler' [The broken line is particularly necessary for drama; from the moment that the natural emerged in theatrical language, it needed a verse which could be spoken] (Siegel 1986: 57–8).

In these circumstances, and whatever Bonnefoy might have said to the contrary,[4] the translation of verse into prose (other than the prose of the crib) is by no means an admission of defeat or a *pis-aller* (see Chapter 7); it is a translation of the verse-text re-cast at a lower level of metricity. In approaching Pierre Jean Jouve's prose translations of Shakespeare's sonnets, we should immediately remember the voice which Jouve himself ascribes to these poems:

> Ces Sonnets n'étaient point faits, du reste, pour être lus par le public; ils étaient conçus pour une récitation à voix basse, ou une confidence amoureuse, ou une sourde querelle. Cette suprême poésie n'a aucune ambition d'être une poésie. Elle est ambitieuse de *secret*.
>
> (1969: 9–10)
>
> [Besides, these Sonnets were not written to be read by the public; they were designed to be spoken in a low voice, or as amorous confidences, or as a muted quarrel. This supreme poetry has no ambition to be poetry; it is ambitious for *secrecy*.]

What policy has Jouve pursued in his translation? First, he has introduced certain archaisms into French (omission of articles and pronouns, use of inversion, archaic lexicon), not in quest of some historical literalism, but as a reminder of our distance from Shakespeare, as a 'supplément de contact' [contact support] (p. 19), as an act of sympathy. Secondly, he has set out to 'établir d'abord un poème français, avec tout l'appareil de ses correspondances, et ce poème doit être en outre constamment nourri de la substance du poème étranger' [create first and foremost a French poem, with all its apparatus of correspondences, and this poem must furthermore be constantly nourished with the substance of the foreign poem] (p. 17). Jouve further explains this latter point: 'Il faut faire le contraire de "franciser"; il faut porter la poésie français jusqu'aux modes poétiques d'une autre langue, et qu'elle rivalise avec l'étrangère' [One should do the opposite of 'gallicizing'; one should extend French poetry as far as the poetic conventions of another language, so that it can compete with that foreign tongue] (pp. 17–18). Jouve is not trying to make French syllabics, with their weaker accentuation, equivalent to English stress-timing, whose starkness is often reinforced by monosyllabicity; instead, taking his cue from Mallarmé's translations of Poe, he opts for a 'prose scandée' [cadenced prose], a 'prose subdivisée en mesures variables, en inventions variables et sensibles qui, sans avoir les appuis de la répétition, doivent s'imposer à l'esprit' [prose segmented into variable measures, into a variety of perceptible configurations, which, without the support of repetition, should impose themselves on the reading mind] (p. 18). Traditional verse-rules—e.g. those concerning the *e atone* (mute e)—are not always observed, of course, but connections between different rhythmic measures are often pointed up by assonance, and the English rhyme-scheme is echoed typographically, in the pattern of paragraphs.

The first four lines of Shakespeare's sonnet LXXI run, in Jouve's translation:

> Ne me pleurez pas plus longtémps,/ quand je serai mórt,//que
> vous n'entendrez/ la lénte lugubre clóche,// donnant avis
> au món/de que j'ai fui,// du monde víl/ pour habiter au vers
> encor plus víls [all 'metrical' markings are mine].

One notices immediately that Jouve's lines preserve, albeit more approximately, the alternating hemistichial balances singled out in Shakespeare's lines: 8/5 (6/4); 5/7 (4/6); 6/4 (6/4); 4/10 (4/6). There is also a close correspondence between the two texts in the number of accents/stresses per line—Jouve's 'lines' produce the sequence: 2(3); 4; 2(3); 3(4). Additionally, Jouve maintains the central alliterations—'mourn...me' ('pleurez pas plus'), 'surly sullen bell' ('la lente lugubre cloche')—and manages to echo Shakespeare's insistent /w/, /v/ and /ɜː/ in lines 3–4, in a variant string: 'avis...fui...vil...vers...vils'. My syllabic tabulation indicates that, in these lines, the maintenance of an articulated *e atone* is necessary, and/or desirable, to avoid consonantal congestion and/or to decelerate and elegize delivery. Jouve's version, then, is far from a counsel of despair; it is a TT which meets the ST at a more relaxed and elastic level, a level which allows the TT not only to intimate more formal and disciplined alternatives, alexandrine or iambic pentameter, but also to make rhythmic room for itself, to inhabit the ST and come away from it with a rhythm which is like a commentary, or meditation, on the ST's rhythm, a meditation in which the original rhythm, shadowy though it is, is not effaced.

In defending the use of free verse as a medium of translation (1979), Bonnefoy argues that the function of regularity has changed, that we no longer operate with the orthodoxies, the common set of beliefs, promoted by regularity, and that therefore we are unable to use regularity instinct-ively. We already notice two causally connected assumptions made by Bonnefoy: (a) that translation should be non-historicizing, because (b) the translator aspires to the condition of poet. The translator must therefore use the medium which most permits his own authenticity and the multi-dimensionality of the contemporary mind to express themselves.[5] Furthermore, Bonnefoy supposes that, in the process of translation, form and content must necessarily come apart from each other, unless the form itself is newly adapted. Why? Because where the ST poet could think his content into a form already chosen, for the TT poet the content is now the given, the pre-existent, which the form can no longer happily mould itself to: 'Consequently, were he to decide to adopt the alexandrine or the pentameter, this regular pattern would be for him nothing but a frame to which the meaning would have to adjust itself, obliging him to pure virtuosity' (1979: 377). I am not in accord with this line of thinking, for two reasons: first, for the foreignizing translator, the TL itself becomes the adaptable element, not the ST's form; secondly, regularity, even if we accept Bonnefoy's ideological interpretation of it, is relevant today as cultural memory, and memory is very different from either anachronism or nostalgia; memory is part of our present being.

But the arguments for free verse as a translational medium remain deeply persuasive, for the reasons already outlined, but most particularly because free verse's non-metricality operates as a plurality of metrical intimations, because free verse is an *inclusive* verse-form in which regularities of various kinds can survive, because, in free verse, metricity is restored to rhythmicity and the rhythmic fabric thus becomes available to an input from both translator and reader, or put with a different emphasis, the metrical ceases to be pre-determined, transcendent, abstractable, prescriptive, and becomes deduced, immanent, instantiated and optional.

In order to illustrate a little of what I mean by these last remarks, I offer, to begin with, a free-verse rendering of the quatrains of Baudelaire's 'Parfum exotique':

```
        /    x  x  /    x   x /   x
 1.  give me an evening, in autumn
        /
 2.  warm
        x  x   /    x /    x  /
 3.  and I'll close my eyes, just so
        x  /   x /   /  x  x     /
 4.  and take a lung full of the smell
                        x   x        /
 5.                    of your    breasts
                                /    x  x    /  x
 6.                           warm, yes, and warming
        x    x   / x  x    /   x   / x  /
 7.  and see faraway beaches, far away
        x   /    x    x   x   /  x
 8.  sun-drenched, sun-smitten, sun-haunted


        x  /  x   x  x   /    / x   x  x    /
 9.  An island if you like, moving at a stroll
        x      / x
10. Where Nature
        x x   /   x   /
11. Has invented trees
        /     x   x   /  x x  /    x    /
12. Straight out of fantasy hung with fruit
        x   /  x  /  x  /   x (/)
13. To whet a whetted appetite
        x    /    x   x  / x  x    /    x
14. And men with the bodies of beach-boys
        x    /   x   x   /  x /   x
15. And women whose look, unflinching
        /      x  x  x    /
16. Roots you to the spot
```

The iconic advantages that free verse has over poetic prose are immediately apparent: the two quatrains have become two eight-line stanzas, whose second lines have, as we shall see, certain structural similarities; the consistency of the left-hand margin in the second stanza is designed to suggest a certain undifferentiatedness in the experience of the island, a certain homologousness among things seen, a certain complacency of consciousness; this complacency, this rhetorical self-satisfaction, finds further confirmation in the line-initial capital letters. In the first stanza, on the other hand, we find not only line-initial lower case, suggesting perhaps more intimacy, less conventionality, but also a variable margin which makes available variations in 'depth' of consciousness and experience, and other imitative manoeuvres: the breasts are lexically separated, 'of your   breasts', so that 'smell' can seem to have risen from between them, and so that a doubling process can be initiated—'warm, yes, and warming'; 'faraway....far away'—in which the second term acts as the achievement of the desire of the first and which, in turn, leads into a tripling, both lexical and rhythmic, in the final line of the stanza.

This free version is designed, above all, to make possible the rhythmic shaping of my own perception of the subject. I start with a so-called 'falling' rhythm, trochees and dactyls, to imitate the contextual falling (evening, autumn). The monolexical second line then acts as a pivot, in two senses: it allows the rhythm to swing into 'rising' iambs and anapaests in the line following, and, bound into line 3 by a coordinating 'and', it reveals an underlying choriambic pattern (/xx/: 'warm and I'll close'), which has appeared in an imbricated form in the first line:

$$\text{give me an eve/ning}$$
$$\text{evening in au/tumn.}$$

This spectral, but still unconfirmed measure breaks out into the open in 'full of the smell', is echoed in the following line, where 'full' is absent but implied: '(full) of your breasts', and then re-affirmed in 'warm, yes, and warming', now with an added feminine syllable. The syntactic juncture after 'and see' allows the liberation of 'faraway beaches' as an independent unit, with the same /xx/x configuration (which might also be called an adonic foot). If, hitherto, the choriamb, with or without added weak syllable, has been embedded in a predominantly iambic/anapaestic economy, it is half glimpsed, in the final line of the stanza, in a swinging amphibrachic sequence:

$$\text{sun-drenched,/ sun-smitten,/ sun-haunted}$$
$$\text{sun-drenched, sun-/smitten, sun-haunted.}$$

In the second stanza, an expanded form of the choriamb—/xxx/— immediately makes itself felt:

$$\text{An] island if you like, moving at a stroll.}$$

Once again, the second line acts as a pivot, both echoing the amphibrachic pattern of the the previous stanza's final line—'Where Nature'—and at the same time leading us again into into the /xxx/ pattern: 'Nature/Has invented'. After revisiting the choriamb in line 12 ('Straight out of fan/tasy') and an iambic sequence in line 13, we find the inhabitants of the exotic island also bound together by the choriambic spell:

> And/men with the bo/dies...
> And/women whose look/...

And in this latter instance, the choriamb leads into an amphibrachic measure ('unflinching') which echoes the sun's patterns of line 8, and its mixed modality of seductive relentlessness. Finally, line 16 provides a closing instance of the pentasyllabic measure (/×××/) which has characterized the stanza as a whole.

I have described the principal rhythmic implants in this sequence of lines. Not only have I tried to install a sense of expansion, as choriamb moves to /×××/, but I have also tried to modulate experience by localized echoes (e.g. the amphibrachs of line 8 are picked up by the amphibrach of 'unflinching', line 15). The important thing, however, is that the rhythms I have identified are incorporated into a predominantly iambic, anapaestic and then also fourth paeonic (×××/) ground, which ultimately makes them indeterminate. If any English rhythmic family affiliates itself with French counterparts, it is the iambic/anapaestic/fourth paeonic one. In other words, I have tried to create a rhythmic texture which allows the reader to align the translation with a French performance, while providing sufficient variability and indeterminacy equally to allow the reader to make expressive room for himself. The only rhythmic distortions involved in this version are perhaps the stress-demotions on 'see' (line 7) and on the first 'sun' of line 8.

Yves Bonnefoy's arguments for free-verse translation relate to his own versions of Donne, Yeats and especially of Shakespeare. In his article 'On the Translation of Form in Poetry' (1979), Bonnefoy begins by explaining why the alexandrine is not an option as a translator's medium for Shakespeare:

> And the very decision to render the English pentameter with the French alexandrine is in my view a mistake, because this French verse, which normally has two equal and symmetric parts, works spontaneously as a closed system, existing in itself and by itself, that is quite apart from the realities of existence, from the throes of time and labor and death through which Shakespeare's pentameters are walking, sometimes even faltering.
>
> (p. 378)

This assertion will come to many as a surprise, for two reasons. First, Bonnefoy, in other contexts, affirms the contrary, namely that the classical alexandrine, like other long lines, is sufficiently self-investigative, and complex, to encompass the *vécu*, the existentially volatile; in particular, Bonnefoy points to the *e atone*, and to *coupes*, and to the 'rythmes de vides et de pleins sonores' [rhythms of acoustic vacuums and plenums], as the sources of 'failles' [fissures] and uncertainty, and adds to these features the alexandrine's 'relativisation dans la strophe, qui est tout de même la vraie vérité' [relativization in the stanza, which is, nonetheless, real truth] (Thélot 1983: 255). Secondly, and building on Bonnefoy's observation that one effect of the *group* of lines is the relativization of each of its members, one might propose that the modern alexandrine bears little resemblance to its classical forebear: alongside the regular *tétramètre* with medial caesura, we find a range of quasi-metrical trimetric alternatives, and non-metrical dodecasyllables. To read a sequence of 'modern' alexandrines is to shift back and forth along the continuum between the controlled and the improvised, the metrically grounded and the roughly approximate. The opening lines of Pierre Leyris's translation of Shakespeare's *Twelfth Night* (*La Nuit des rois*) (1994) give some indication:

1. Si la musique est la pâture de l'amour,   4+4+4
2. Jouez encore, donnez-m'en jusqu'à l'excès   5'+3+4
3. En sorte que ma faim gavée languisse et meure.
                              6+2+2+2/2+6+2+2 (8//4)
4. Ce passage à nouveau! pour son rythme mourant;   3+3+3+3
5. Oh! il m'a flatté l'oreille comme un zéphyr   5+2+5
6. Dont l'haleine, en frôlant un lit de violettes   3+3+2+4
7. Dérobe et donne du parfum...Suffit! Assez! 4+4+2+2 (8//4)
8. Sa douceur de tout à l'heure s'en est allée.   3+4+5

[where the apostrophe in the notation of line 2—5'+3+4—denotes a *coupe lyrique*, i.e. the final e of 'encore' is not counted in the following rhythmic measure (*coupe enjambante*), to give 4+4+4, but is the final, unaccentuated syllable of the first measure.]

In these first eight lines, we find a combination of standard tetrameter (ll. 3, 4, 6), regular trimeter (l. 1), irregular trimeter (ll. 2, 5, 8), and asymmetrical tetrameter with a major juncture after syllable 8, in which dissyllabic measures are juxtaposed (ll. 3(?), 7). This fluid combination which relativizes the 'regular' lines and transforms them into nonce reformulations of other, very different configurations, produces a sense of a dodecasyllabic outline whose appropriate metrical constitution has yet to be discovered. But what is important is that any necessary relation between syllabic number and accentual pattern has been erased, so that accent is unconstrained by number and can respond to its own (the voice's) demands. This brings the French line remarkably close to the English:

	No. of stresses
˟ ⁄ ˟ ˟ ˟ ⁄ ˟ ⁄ ˟ ⁄ If music be the food of love, play on,	4
⁄ ˟ ˟ ⁄ ˟ ˟ ˟ ⁄ ˟ ˟ Give me excess of it; that, surfeiting,	3
˟ ⁄ ˟ ˟ ˟ ⁄ ˟ ˟ ⁄ ⁄ The appetite may sicken, and so die...	4
˟ ⁄ ˟ ˟ ˟ ⁄ ˟ ⁄ ˟ ⁄ That strain again! it had a dying fall:	4
˟ ˟ ⁄ ˟ ˟ ⁄ ˟ ˟ ⁄ ⁄ O, it came o'er my ear like the sweet sound	4
˟ ⁄ ˟ ˟ ˟ ⁄ ˟ ⁄ ˟ ˟ That breathes upon a bank of violets;	3
⁄ ˟ ˟ ⁄ ˟ ⁄ ˟ ˟ ⁄ ˟ ⁄ Stealing and giving odour...Enough, no more!	5
˟ ⁄ ˟ ˟ ⁄ ˟ ˟ ⁄ ˟ ⁄ 'Tis not so sweet now as it was before.	4

None of these lines adds up to a regular iambic pentameter, and in all but one line, the seventh, natural voice rhythms, focusing on nuclear stresses and using pause to multiply weak syllables—it is through-reading which tends to sustain metrical continuity—reduce the stresses per line to 4, and sometimes 3. The French lines equally vary between 3 and 4 accents. Those phrasal rhythms of the theatre, which bring English rhythms towards French ones, not only intensify variations in pacing, but make iambic a frequently inaudible, shadowy ground, as shadowy as any regularity in the French dodecasyllable.

Be that as it may, however, Bonnefoy goes on to describe how, in his alternative solution, that is a free verse form in which the majority of lines vary between 9 and 15 syllables, a recurrent hendecasyllable began to make itself felt, a line sufficiently insistent to appear to be reinventing 'the repetitive pattern of the original poetry', but not sufficiently so 'to dissipate the atmosphere of free verse' (1979: 379). This hendecasyllable begins 'like an alexandrine—that is, with these six syllables which lead in the alexandrine to their symmetrical image in the second hemistich', but it then 'ends with only five syllables and thus breaks the arrogant symmetry of the great verse of Racine or Mallarmé, with its refusal of time, of everyday life, of death' (p. 379). How is the obsessive presence of the hendecasyllable to be accounted for? Because it combines within it 'the spiritual quality of Shakespeare's verses', that form which is 'a reference to the absolute' (6 syll.), and also the direct encounter with life (5 syll.). Thus 'free verse was able to find an image of the pentameter more faithful to it than any traditional renderings could be' (p. 379). And yet, to have written the entire translation in hendecasyllables would have amounted to an attempt to re-metrify the line, and would have denied Bonnefoy options on other verse-lines which might prove, in certain contexts, to be more appropriate: 'While continuing to write with no prosodic restraint, I can from time to time come across some words which spontaneously organize themselves in a twelve-syllable pattern, adding then to my translation this *indication of plenitude* which the alexandrine alone is able to give in French, despite all its ambiguities or defects' (p. 379). Not surprisingly, Bonnefoy went on to use the hendecasyllable more frequently in his own verse: from a percentage of 3.68 in *Du mouvement et de l'immobilité de Douve* (1953), it rises to 13.24 per cent in *Dans le leurre du seuil* (1975).

It is not difficult to find instances of this 6//5 hendecasyllable in Bonnefoy's 1978[6] *Hamlet* translation:

HAMLET	Oui, oui que Dieu vous garde…Me voici seul.	2+4+5
	Oh, quel valet je suis, quel ignoble esclave!	4+2+3+2
		(2.2.552–3)

Nor is it difficult to see how the hendecasyllable's existential stumbling and groping can resolve itself into the alexandrine's lapidary and assured abstraction:

LE ROI	Mes mots prennent leur vol, ma pensée se traîne.	2+4+3+2
	Et des mots sans pensée n'atteignent pas le ciel.	3+3+4+2
		(3.3.97–8)

But we should equally remember: (a) that the hendecasyllable's disruptive force, its capacity to flirt with existential panic, is directly proportional to its scarcity; (b) that the hendecasyllable is a much more complicated machine than the 6//5 rationalization implies; (c) that the free verse of Bonnefoy's *Hamlet* adds up to much more than a context for the hendecasyllable. In Act 3, Scene 4, after the short visitation of the Ghost, Hamlet answers his mother's charge with these words:

Le délire!	3
Mon pouls est régulier autant que le vôtre	2+4+2+3
Il fait le bruit de la santé—ce n'est pas la folie	4+4+3+3

41

Qui hantait ma parole, la preuve en est	3+3+3+2 (7'//4)
Que je puis tout redire, quand la folie	4+2+5 (7'//4)
Ne sait que divaguer.	2+4
	(3.4.139–44)

There is much to enjoy in the ironic 'défaillance' [moment of weakness] in the rhythm when Hamlet mentions his mother's pulse (2+4+2+*3*), much to enjoy in Hamlet's iron-willed, but fragile recovery of control in line 141, with its overall syllabic parity, but pairing of imparisyllabic measures with parisyllabic ones. But lines 142–3 are a rhythmic quicksands, where no footing is to be had. In a manner similar to those Shakespearean lines in which a line-internal pause produces a phrase-terminal weak syllable, which leads on to another weak syllable as the iambic pattern is resumed, e.g.:

$$\acute{\text{S}}\text{t}\overset{/}{\text{e}}\text{aling}\overset{\times}{\text{ a}}\text{nd}\overset{\times}{\text{ giving}}\overset{/}{\text{ }}\overset{\times}{\text{o}}\text{dour}\ldots\text{Enough, no more!}$$

Stealing and giving odour…Enough, no more!

or

And make as healthful music—it is not madness

Bonnefoy introduces an articulated *e atone* at syllable 7; the connection with the Shakespearean pattern is clearer in a line already quoted (2.2.552):

Oui, oui que Dieu vous garde…Me voici seul
[Ay, so, God bye to you! now I am alone]

To Shakespeare's syntactic 'faille' corresponds Bonnefoy's prosodic 'faille', the *e atone*, and in a syllabic position, the seventh, which intensifies its powers of rupture and disorientation. My original 2+4+5 reading, with its *césure enjambante* ('Oui, oui/que Dieu vous gar//de…Me voici seul'), attempts to use a prosodic plaster to dress a syntactic wound. If I had allowed the *e* to reinforce the syntactic break, then my reading would, and probably should, have been 2+5'+4 ('Oui, oui/que Dieu vous garde//…Me voici seul'), i.e. the really haunting hendecasyllable is not 6//5 but 7'//4. Alternatively, I might have opted to read the *e atone*, at the seventh syllable, as a so-called *césure épique*, i.e. as an extra-metrical syllable, producing a 6//4 decasyllable ('Oui, oui/que Dieu vous gard(e)//…Me voici seul', 2+4//4) (Thélot tells us (1983: 68) how much Bonnefoy prefers the 6//4 decasyllable to the classical 4//6 variety). These comments apply equally to lines 142–3 of Act 3, Scene 4. And we come to understand, perhaps, that Bonnefoy's hendecasyllable is not a line of verse, in the sense that it has no structural or metrical credentials, although it does have certain expressive potentialities and corrosive ways of relating to its consecrated neighbours, the decasyllable and the alexandrine. It is a free-verse line, a number of syllables constantly exploring their combinational possibilities, influenced by, and influencing, contextual lines, with nothing given or predicted, a space free for the translator and the translator's reader to exercise their variable responses. At the same time, as we have seen, it is a rhythmic space which does recall, by number of accents, by rhythmic instability, by nuances of medial articulation, the Shakespearean pentameter; indeed, a free-verse TT does not stand off from its ST, but seems to draw the ST into itself, to encompass it, both by enacting the ST's futurity/survival and by potentiating the multifarious inputs of its consumers (translators and readers of translation); this is a cumulative process which leaves the ST half-buried in rhythmic accretions, covered with the rhythmic barnacles of its continuing multi-cultural existence.

Finally and briefly, I would like to look more closely at the way in which lines are relativized by those around them, particularly in the sense that they relate to each other as distributors of specific measures. Bonnefoy's account of Laertes's words to Hamlet in Act 5, Scene 2 (lines 311–18) runs:

O Hamlet, le voici. Hamlet, on t'a tué,	3+3+2+4
Aucun remède au monde ne te sauvera,	4+2+6
Il n'y a plus en toi une demi-heure de vie.	4+2+5+3
Et l'arme de la trahison est dans ta main,	2+6+4
Démouchetée et empoisonnée. La hideuse ruse	4+5+3+2
S'est retournée contre moi; vois, je m'écroule	4+3+1+4
Pour ne me relever jamais…Ta mère est empoisonnée…	6+2+2+5
Je n'en peux plus…Le roi, le roi est coupable.	4+2+2+3

As one reads this sequence of lines, one may begin to feel that certain measures are the voice of destiny, or of cruel chance, that a rhythmic web of fate is being woven, however 'free' the lines, *across* the lines in a transverse design: the hexasyllables are negativity, with a short-term future orientation (how apt that two of them have the 'faille' of an *e atone* as their first syllables); the pentasyllabic measures bind son and mother together in the short term of their poisoning; and the dissyllabic measures are the wavering, self-contradictory thread of Hamlet himself: 'Hamlet', 'au monde', 'en toi', 'Et l'arme', '—e ruse', 'jamais', 'Ta mère', 'Le roi'. The speech ends with our familiar 6//5 hendecasyllable, about which two things should be added: we first hear the pentasyllabic second hemistich three lines earlier in 'La hideuse ruse' (that which belongs to both Hamlet and to Claudius); and in the final line, the 6//5 hendecasyllable overrides the syntax: 'Je n'en peux plus…Le roi,// le roi est coupable', so that the king exists both in the hexasyllable of order and essence and form, and in the pentasyllable of disorder, contingency, finitude. Two kings, two orders, Hamlet and Claudius. And yet for the first king, Hamlet's father, 'Je n'en peux plus'; and the syntax tries to pull together two kings, whom verse-structure struggles to keep apart.

Bonnefoy himself, of course, reveals the secret kinship between Claudius and Hamlet *fils*, in the preface to his translation of *Hamlet* and *King Lear* (1978: 11):

> son [Hamlet's] proche dans l'oeuvre, hélas, ce n'est ni Laërte ni Fortinbras, […] mais celui qui dit une chose et en pense une autre, et feint de respecter, de célébrer des valeurs auxquelles il ne doit pas beaucoup croire: Claudius, le destructeur, l'ennemi….
> [his (Hamlet's) soulmate in the play, alas, is neither Laertes nor Fortinbras, (…) but the one who says one thing and thinks another, and pretends to respect, to celebrate, values in which he can have hardly any belief: Claudius, the destroyer, the enemy….]

These are two figures who tend towards the *impair*, the incomplete, matter without form. But Hamlet maintains, too, his nostalgia for the other king, the other, 'archaic' order, the order of essence and transcendence, of which the hexasyllable is part. This dividedness, this tension, this dialectic, is the being of the hendecasyllable, which is both Hamlet and Bonnefoy. But the 'readiness', the 'disponibilité', which, for Bonnefoy, is the mark of Hamlet's self, is at the heart of translation, too, not just in the act of Bonnefoy's translation of *Hamlet*, as described by Heylen (1992: 339):

> By constantly recasting his translations, Bonnefoy's French will ultimately disentangle itself from the limitations of its idiom, and with each new version will hint at the presence of a pure, pre-Babelian 'language of truth'.

but in all translation, inasmuch as it resembles the hendecasyllable, with the hexasyllabic hemistich as the ST, past, 'archaic', whole, transcendent, and the pentasyllabic hemistich as the TT, partial, provisional, fragile. But within the translation of poetry, we might look upon free verse itself as a version of the hendecasyllable, as a verse which looks at the hexasyllable from the perspective of the pentasyllable.

Armed with these findings, I can now again take up, after long interruption, my free-verse translation of 'Parfum exotique', and complete it with the sestet:

17. Drawn by your skin's smell
18. to enravishing places
19.   a harbour's
20.   my landfall
21. bristling with sails and masts
22. still catching breath
23. after the heaving swell
24.   the long haul

25. while the lush-green
26.   tamarinds
27. steep the air in scent
28. set billowing
29.   my nostrils
30. with an aromatic wind
31.   and mingle
32. in the heart's core
33. with the shanties
34.   of sailors
35. putting out to sea

I have taken up some of the music of the octave, in particular the choriamb (/××/), as a line-initiating measure in the first 'tercet' (lines 17, 21, 22, 23), and the amphibrach (×/×) across the 'tercets' (lines 19, 20, 29, 31, 34). It is the amphibrach which sustains the second-margin trisyllabic measures, although there are two variations (bacchic (×//): 'the long haul'; dactyl (/××): 'tamarinds') occurring consecutively and confronting each other across the stanzaic division; it is as if the bacchic of 'the long haul' needs the dactyl of 'tamarinds' to recover the amphibrach, which is then to be seen as a 'mingling' of sails on the open sea and a tropical evergreen in the shelter of port. The 'developed' form of the bacchic, the ionic (××//), is to be found in line 32, 'in the heart's core', and the distant rhyme-echo on /ɔ:/ is intended not only to suggest a coming home to self, to an expanded and free-associating interiority, but also to recall those other members of the acoustic family : 'Drawn' > 'landfall' > 'haul' > 'core'. And this ionic might also echo line 25, which many might wish to read with a stress on both 'green' and 'lush'. A moment of much sharper acoustic focus occurs at lines 28–33, on the sound /I/; here the sheer frequency of the sound knits experience together into an undifferentiated state, an experience which, in my hearing of the text, has its sources in 'skin' (line 17) and 'tamarinds' (line 26). This moment of sensory and spiritual unanimity is supported rhythmically by the emergence of an anapaestic (××/) line-initial configuration (lines 30, 32, 33), which is really the signature of the tercet as a whole (see line 25). The final line of the translation takes up the rhythmic configuration of line 27, and these two lines act as the frame of the intensfied interactivity we have just described. Finally, I have maintained the eight-line stanza of the 'quatrains' for the first 'tercet', but have allowed it to stretch to eleven lines in the second tercet, not only to enact the expansion of consciousness which occurs there, but also to allow for a freer circulation of the breeze-filled tropic air.

3

The Dead Language of Translation

This chapter turns back to translation's relationship with pedagogy, initially at least. It explores some of the dangers of that relationship and suggests ways in which they might be circumvented by a better understanding of textuality and intertextual exchange. The 'product' of this chapter is a translation of Baudelaire's 'Sed non satiata', and before embarking on the argument, I give both texts, the ST and my account of it:

Sed non satiata

1. Bizarre déité, brune comme les nuits,
2. Au parfum mélangé de musc et de havane,
3. Œuvre de quelque obi, le Faust de la savane,
4. Sorcière au flanc d'ébène, enfant des noirs minuits,

5. Je préfère au constance, à l'opium, au nuits,
6. L'élixir de ta bouche où l'amour se pavane;
7. Quand vers toi mes désirs partent en caravane,
8. Tes yeux sont la citerne où boivent mes ennuis.

9. Par ces deux grands yeux noirs, soupiraux de ton âme,
10. O démon sans pitié! verse-moi moins de flamme;
11. Je ne suis pas le Styx pour t'embrasser neuf fois,

12. Hélas! et je ne puis, Mégère libertine,
13. Pour briser ton courage et te mettre aux abois,
14. Dans l'enfer de ton lit devenir Proserpine!

... but not satisfied

1.   Bizarre deity,
                        duskier than dusky dark,
2.   Wrapped in a mix of musk,
                        and Havanese cigar,
3.   Fashioned by some obi,
                        the savannah's Dr Faust,
4.   Ebony bewitcher,
                        child of the black midnight.

5.   Which? Opium? A glass of Nuits?
                        Perhaps wine from the Cape?
6.   No, the elixir of your tongue
                        and its amorous pavanes;
7.   When the caravan of my desires
                        sets out across the sands,
8.   Your eyes are the water-holes
                        for my nagging ennuis.

9.   Oh staunch the flow of flame,
                        relentless tormentor!
10. From those large, coal-black eyes,
                        the sigh-grates of your soul;
11. I'm no encircling Styx
                        to take your body nine times,

12. More's the pity! nor can I,
                        pleasure-hungry Megaera,
13. So as to break your will
                        and force you down on your back,
14. In the Hades of your bed,
                        play the part of Proserpine!

Teaching methodology in modern languages shifted, during the 1960s, from a discredited grammar/translation foundation to a communicative one. This shift coincided, broadly speaking, with the supplanting, in school curricula, of the so-called dead languages by living ones, and a diminution of the credit of the written in favour of that of the spoken. The pedagogy of the dead languages is peculiar in several respects. First, dead languages are, relatively speaking, without a pragmatics, without those recuperable speech environments and conventions of exchange which allow us to reconstitute underlying linguistic assumptions. It is not surprising, therefore, that in our contact with these languages, the mediation of a living one, usually our own, is seen as unavoidable, indeed desirable—we cannot establish a direct contact with a dead language, we cannot correct or verify our understandings with the help of a native speaker.

Secondly, our contact with a dead language is not only mediated by a living one, but by specialists in the dead language. We can learn a living language with the help of any native speaker, whether that speaker has a metacognitive awareness of his/her language or not; the mediator of a dead language, on the other hand, must have this metacognitive awareness as an essential part of the teaching capacity.

A third factor in this pedagogy is the necessary presence of decipherment. The verse of a dead language is for ever out of reach, and the authority of the mediator is based on a knowledge which identifies ignorance without removing it. The fact is, that in this kind of situation, ignorance itself is an integral part of authority. The trouble is that, in the process of translation, ignorance becomes elided or transformed *into* authority. If we turn to my scansion of those lines from Juvenal's Sixth Satire (129–32) which lie behind Baudelaire's title 'Sed non satiata', we can see a little of what we might mean:

clausit, ad/huc ar/dens//rigi/dae ten/tigine/ volvae,

et las/sata vi/ris//nec/dum sati/ata re/cessit,

obscu/risque ge/nis//tur/pis fu/moque lu/cernae

foeda/ lupana/ris//tu/lit ad pul/vinar o/dorem.

[// = caesura; / = foot boundary; ᵕ = short vowel; ⁄ = ictus (metrical accent); o = word-accent; φ = coincidence of ictus and word-accent; – = long vowel]

Nussbaum, in his *Vergil's Metre: A Practical Guide for Reading Latin Hexameters* (1986), states:

> Ever since the 'reformed' pronunciation of Latin was pioneered in this country a century or so ago, we have aspired more and more to an 'authentic' experience of Latin literature—to read it more nearly as if we were Romans living in the great age of Cicero and Catullus, Vergil and Horace. [...] And of course the aspiration is unattainable.

> [...] we cannot know when and how far we are sharing the authentic
> quality of their experience, for there is no feedback to tell us so.
>
> (p. 56)

And yet Nussbaum has earlier (p. v) referred to the 'counterpoint' of ictus
and word-accent as the key to 'authentic' reading, just as, further on, he
adds: 'to read Vergil authentically is to read him aloud' (p. 1). Authenticity,
it seems, is both non-achievable and a requirement for the self-respecting
scholar. As we look at these lines, we might wonder whether we can even
discover, reliably, how to pronounce the words, yet alone read them
rhythmically. Nussbaum tells us (p. 12) that the standard guide to the
pronunciation of Classical Latin is W.S. Allen's *Vox Latina* (2nd ed., CUP,
1978), but does not tell us how 'standard' was established.

What we can deduce, from the coincidence of metrical accent and
word-accent in the last two feet of each line, is that the terminus of the line,
as in so many other versifications, is the location of metrical authority (see
Gasparov 1996: 49). We note a similar but less marked incidence of
accentual coincidence at the beginnings of the lines. Oddly, the area of
greatest divergence occurs around an important structural boundary, the
caesura. Why? And what function does the caesura have? Nussbaum
suggests that it divides the line intonationally, but what do we know about
patterns of intonation in Latin, an aspect of speech about which we are
likely to have false ideas anyway, because texts like this are provided by
their editors with punctuation marks which are culturally alien to them?

Furthermore, we still know nothing about the relationship, in recitation,
between metrical accent and word-accent (although we know that German
philologists of the eighteenth century introduced a mode of declamation
which consistently privileged the metrical accent over the word-accent)
(see Gasparov 1996: 86–7); and although we speak of Latin verse as
quantitative, we may suspect that this Greek importation never really
smothered a rhythmicity in the Latin language which was based on word-
accent. Yet there are those like Beare (1957: 50–5) who argue that Latin
word-accent was an accent of pitch, not of stress, and would not therefore
affect the versification.

Just as we cannot know the features of the voice that Latin verse
activated, so we cannot know what mental processes and meanings the
words produced. The phrase 'adhuc ardens rigidae tentigine volvae' calls
forth the following translations:

> and with passion still raging hot within her
>
> (G.G. Ramsay 1961: 93)

50

Still burning from the strain of her stiff womb
>   (Steven Robinson 1983: 116)

still with a burning hard on
>   (Peter Green 1974: 131)

and still with fire in her womb/Erect like a man in her heat
>   (Hubert Creekmore 1963: 89)

The lust, though, still raged hotly in her bosom
>   (Jerome Mazzaro 1965: 67)

The point I would make about these versions is simply this: their diversity seems to derive not from a process of informed choice, but from reasonable guesses about the anatomical range of 'volva' in Roman usage and the sexual state to be perceived in 'rigidus' and 'tentigo'. Such guesses are complicated by the inevitable modesties of Victorian dictionaries. The 1968 *Oxford Latin Dictionary* is forthright enough, without being anatomically specific: 'tentigo' = 'immoderate sexual tumescence' (p. 1921); 'uulua' ('volva') = '1. The womb.[...] 2. The female sexual organ' (p. 2123). But if we turn back to those dictionaries based on Wilhelm Freund's four-volume dictionary (Leipzig, 1834–45), we find more evasive answers, answers likely to take refuge in the abstract. E.A. Andrews's edition of Freund (*A Copious and Critical Latin–English Lexicon*, London, 1861 [1850] defines 'tentigo' as 'A tension of the privy member, lecherousness, lust' (p. 1530), and 'volva', in its (secondary) sexual sense as 'womb, matrix' (p. 1646) (its primary sense is given as 'wrapping, covering, integument'). The same account of 'volva' is to be found in both Lewis and Short's *A Latin Dictionary* (London, 1962 [1879], p. 2013) and William Smith's *Smaller Latin–English Dictionary* (revised J.F. Lockwood; London, 1968 [1933, 1855], p. 815). 'Tentigo', on the other hand, loses its attachment to the 'privy member' and in Lewis and Short becomes 'A tension; lecherousness, lust' (p. 1855), and in Smith/Lockwood just 'lust' (p. 748). About 'rigidus' one might also ask whether, in this context, it makes available the ironic overtones of moral severity, and whether the reader should see in it the bitterness of an assimilation to 'rigor mortis' (given that 'rigor' is used, too, for sexual erection). Adams (1982: vii) additionally warns us that 'the terminology in which that [sexual] behaviour is described can vary revealingly from genre to genre, and also within a genre', and his work alerts us to the displacement of body parts, thanks to metaphor and metonymy. What does at least seem certain, and important for the presence of Juvenal in 'Sed non satiata', is that Juvenal has changed Messalina's sex: given that 'tentigo' and 'rigidus' are typically used of male erection—although such language might be used of the clitoris ('landica') (see Adams 1982: 103–4)—Juvenal imagines a phallic Messalina, guilty of sexual usurpation. This perhaps helps us to understand Baudelaire's final line, not so much as a reference to lesbianism as a sexual role reversal.

My underlying insinuation will have long become clear: that, in translation, the ST is too often treated as a dead language, or is transformed into a dead language. It is in the interests of the translator to imply to the reader that the mediation necessary to reach the ST cannot be obtained from *any* source, but that the translator himself is the indispensable authority. But this policy has two pernicious consequences. The authority of the translation as authentic, as a reliable *corrigé*, entails the disappearance of the teacher into his own authority, into an aura of objectivity and sound judgement. Secondly, translators, like teachers, have a peculiar tendency to hide the sources and methodology of their authority; translation's lack of status and prestige derives from its inability to wed a globalizing theory to an empirical practice, and, more particularly, from its inability to theorize that empirical practice (Meschonnic 1973: 318–19). And part of the reason for the latter is that translation is much better at theorizing linguistic difference than it is at theorizing textual difference, a characteristic of the teaching of translation in the classroom. Furthermore, by transforming the ST into a dead language, even if the ST was written only yesterday, the translator sacralizes the ST as literature, although, again, it be at translation's expense, and, at the same time, locates himself in the too narrow space of 'translator'.

But if the language of the ST is, or becomes, a dead language, the language of the TT is a metalanguage, both metatextual and meta-linguistic. The metatextual is a re-presentation of an ST, *in its textuality*, in another language; the metalinguistic is the presentation of the meaning of an ST, an interpretation of an ST, in a companion text in another language. About this classification, we should immediately say two things. First, it is in verse specifically that the metatextual and the metalinguistic dimensions of translation are peculiarly prominent: the poem has such marked textual definition and renders such textual autonomy to its signifying devices, that not only does the text demand to survive as a self-conscious text, but the interpretative problems posed by it are proportionately greater. Secondly, this fact brings with it two real dangers: (i) the metalinguistic activity takes precedence over, indeed threatens to exclude, the metatextual one, because it is assumed that the reader will be impatient to know what the ST means rather than how it constructs its meanings; thus the ST's structure is superseded by its meaning even before, reconstituted in the TT, it has had the chance to re-activate the

ST's interpretive problems; (ii) the translator is thereby put in a false position, since he finds that he cannot opt out of the responsibility of interpretation, that the reader will not allow him not to know. And we can see that the meta-status of the TT derives in part from this separation of the metatextual and the metalinguistic, which is all but unavoidable. Why? Because the separation of text from language which takes place in the process of translation leaves the language of the TT uninstantiated in, unintegrated into, the text's own expressive/semantic system. Word/phrase in ST *means* word/phrase in TT, rather than *being* word/phrase in TT. In other words, the TT might claim equivalence at the semantic level but cannot do so at the ontological level.

One might argue, of course, that the deadness of the ST and the meta-status of the TT are mutually dependent, and that by promoting its meta-status, the TT has it within it to intensify the deadness of the ST and thus to supersede it. This process seems to occur in advertising. 'Beanz means Heinz' leads us to believe that 'beanz' is a dead lexical and alimentary item, that the name 'Heinz' is a *presence* on the supermarket shelf, an updated form of beanz, a modern gustatory experience. The trouble with literature is that it has a more visible and valorized debt to origins. If consumerism thrives on desirable supersedability, on novelty ever renewed, literature observes the order of mimesis, the order of truth, whereby an originating presence (truth) begets imitation which comes to supplement it (add to it, provisionally supplant it), but does not efface it (see Derrida 1972: 219–20). What are we to do to improve this situation?

First, we must remember that there are certain *innate* ways in which verse is both dead—in the sense of 'non-communicative'—and metalinguistic. Although some analysts have applied pragmatics approaches to verse, there are reasons for arguing that verse is antipathetic to pragmatics, among which I cite the following: a verse text, indeed any literary text, feeds itself into so many situations across time and space that no reliable interactive context can be established; in Sperber and Wilson's argument (1986: 236), poetic effects, and metaphoric ones in particular, are so weak in implicature that implicature is multiplied beyond any possible contextual specificity; verse is not a communication addressed by a psychologically circumscribable speaker to a separate addressee, but a text governed by shifters, in which the reader listens predominantly to himself, that is, is both speaker and listener in a complex and varying pattern of explored selfhood and acknowledged otherness, itself imaginable only as a possibility of the self. In these senses, the verse text is dead, necessitates a process of decipherment.

The verse text necessitates decipherment, too, in the sense in which

Baudelaire says of Hugo's verse 'tout est hiéroglyphique' [everything is hieroglyphic] (*Œuvres complètes*, II, 133), or in which, in an essay on Gautier, he maintains: 'Il y a dans le mot, dans le *verbe*, quelque chose de *sacré* qui nous défend d'en faire un jeu de hasard. Manier savamment une langue, c'est pratiquer une espèce de sorcellerie évocatoire' [There is in the word, in the Word, something *sacred* which forbids us to make it a game of chance. The skilful manipulation of language is the practice of a kind of evocative sorcery] (*OC*, II, 118). It is the task of poetic writing generally to transform 'mot' into 'verbe', and the process of transformation is aided by the 'deadness' inherent in any versification, a deadness deriving from our inability ever completely to rationalize it. Again we might turn to Baudelaire: 'Que la poésie française possède une prosodie mystérieuse et méconnue, comme les langues latine et anglaise' [That French poetry possesses a mysterious and unrecognized prosody, like the Latin and English languages] (*OC*, I, 183). But in affirming this inaccessibility, Baudelaire also reminds us that versification's mystery, its complex music, is what enables it to reach into the inner duration of the reader, is what allows it to transform meaning into experience, language into psycho-physiological perception: 'comment la poésie touche à la musique par une prosodie dont les racines plongent plus avant dans l'âme humaine que ne l'indique aucune théorie classique' [how poetry is affiliated to music through its prosody, whose roots plunge further into the human soul than any classical theory indicates] (*OC*, I, 197183).

Finally, if the language of verse is already a metalanguage, it is because its various exploitations of the principle of repetition make it auto-reflexive, a message poetic by virtue of its self-regardingness. This familiar Jakobsonian position is reformulated by Claudette Oriol-Boyer in the following terms:

> Il faut dès maintenant noter que ce retour *susceptible d'attirer l'attention* qui fonde le poétique fait de la fonction poétique une variété de la fonction métalinguistique.
>
> (1992: 59)
>
> [One should immediately note that this principle of recurrence, *likely to attract attention,* on which poetics is based, makes the poetic function a variety of the metalinguistic function.]

However, this should be treated with care. We usually suppose that the shift from language to metalanguage involves us in a loss of linguistic substance, that metalanguage, being about the meaning of meaning, is abstract, philosophical, language in the second degree of contact. This is certainly what we have primarily meant to date, in our description of the TT as metalingual. When Francis Scarfe translates the opening 'Bizarre' of 'Sed non satiata' as 'Outlandish', we understand 'Outlandish' not in and for itself, as a value in a whole text, but as a version of 'Bizarre', owing its value to this word-to-word relationship. 'Outlandish', we might say, while it has the welcome colour of the barbarous, suggests something too eccentric, and is not provocative, not perceptually teasing, in the way that 'Bizarre' is. Besides, '-ish' is a pejorative suffix in English which expresses either the indeterminate and wishy-washy ('greenish', 'fairish') or an attitude of condescending superiority ('childish', 'foolish', 'modish'). These overtones are not in 'Bizarre'. But when we use 'metalinguistic' of verse, we mean a state of metacognitive awareness which sharpens our sense of language's materiality, of its phonemic, graphemic, morphemic presence, so that far from producing a process of abstraction, it does the opposite, it concretizes language and dramatizes the relationship between meaning and being, the semantic and the physical. Curiously enough, it is the 'informed' reader who is more likely to read translation as an entropic metalinguistics; but the 'ignorant' reader is not likely to opt for the converse, the metalinguistics of heightened physicality. At all events, the translator must concentrate on installing the latter at the expense of the former. The question is: how is he to prevent the devaluation of his own utterance?

One way forward, as already indicated in the first chapter, is to multiply the TT, to set up competitive texts and thus erode both the translator's authority and the authority by which the language of the TT can justify its meta-status. But this strategy is likely to perpetuate the view that the quality of a translation depends on, is to be judged by, the quality of its choices. The existence of variants might lead us to suppose that the quality of creative writing has also to do with choice, but, as we have mentioned before, the process of creative writing is a process during the course of which the choice factor is increasingly masked, to the point of invisibility. As Valéry would have it, creative writing is the art of giving the arbitrary the force of necessity (*Œuvres*, I, 1308, 1314). Translation, on the other hand, displays choice, makes it public, and, crucially, invites the participation of the reader. And the judgement of writing on a choice basis undermines the creative, self-expressive function in favour of linguistic competence and stylistic skills. The true concern of the reader of translations should be not how to judge them, but in what spirit to read them.

How, then, is this danger to be minimized? First, even if our appreciation of translation gravitates towards choice, at least we must shift our conception of choice from the lexical level to the textual level, so that assessing choice becomes a way of developing a sensitivity to the designs of the whole text. Secondly, we should exercise awareness of choice among the variants of the translator himself rather than immediately importing other versions, so that the reader has the sense of a unified voice in search of its own satisfaction. A further strategy is the Benjaminian one: to translate the ST with the intention not of translating it, but of complementing it, supplementing it, with another text, so that from the convergence of the ST and the TT, or in the gap between them, might grow up a 'third text', a 'text-idea' which neither the ST nor the TT could realize on its own. We shall have more to say about the Benjaminian proposal in the next chapter. For the moment, we should note that it is in the assumption of this 'third text' that we might begin to imagine the TT as an improvement on the ST, as being nearer the 'text-idea'. That would create a reversal of the order of mimesis and of truth; we would have arrived at that achronicity which operates in the psyche as it shifts unpredictably between anticipation and recuperation, fantasy and memory. Derrida draws our attention (1972: 216–17) to that quotation from Diderot's 'Pensées détachées sur la peinture', in which the desire of the posterior to become the anterior, or of the metalinguistic to become the referential (in the Jakobsonian sense), by virtue of the vivid immediacy of its expression, is encapsulated:

> Antoine Coypel était certainement un homme d'esprit, lorsqu'il a dit aux artistes: 'Faisons, s'il se peut, que les figures de nos tableaux soient plutôt les modèles vivants des statues antiques, que ces statues les originaux des figures que nous peignons'. On peut donner le même conseil aux littérateurs.
>
> (1959: 816)
>
> [Antoine Coypel was certainly witty when he told his fellow-artists: 'Let us, if possible, ensure that the figures in our pictures are the living models of ancient statues, rather than those statues being the originals of the figures we paint'. One might give the same advice to writers.]

Were such a strategy to be realizable, both the deadness of the ST and the meta-status of the TT would be abolished. How adequate is Baudelaire's 'sorcière aux flancs d'ébène' (2+4) as a translation of my 'Ebony bewitcher' (/×××/×)?

A final strategy is, in fact, a cluster of strategies, designed to establish (a) the continuity of literary history so that the dead continues to have a voice, and (b) the status of the translation *as text*, able to affirm its own system of language against or within the system of the TL. Translation is more concerned with the transformation of the ST into the TT, than with the transformation of the SL into the TL, or as Meschonnic puts it:

> On peut construire un *rapport prosodique* entre les structures du signifiant, d'un texte de départ à sa traduction-texte, là où l'opinion, opposant deux phonologies sur le plan de la langue, et terme à terme, concluait à l'intraduisible. En effet, on ne traduit pas une phonologie. Mais on ne traduit pas de la langue non plus, dans un texte. On construit et on théorise un rapport de texte à texte, non de langue à langue. Le rapport interlinguistique vient par le rapport intertextuel, et non le rapport intertextuel par le rapport interlinguistique.
>
> (1973: 314)
>
> [One can construct a *prosodic relationship* between the structures of the signifier, from the ST to its TT, where critical opinion, setting two phonological systems against each other, on the linguistic level, and term for term, concluded that translation was impossible. In fact, it is not a phonology that one translates. But nor is it language either, in a text. One constructs and theorizes a text-to-text, not a language-to-language, relationship. The interlinguistic relationship derives from the intertextual one, and not the other way round.]

To activate a sense of continuity as part of a creative readerly attitude is an integral part of the translator's task and has to do with his own apprenticeship as a reader of the ST, and with the apprenticeship of the TT in the reading of the ST. Of the former of these apprenticeships I do not wish to speak here; it will receive a fuller treatment in due course (see Chapter 8). Of the latter more should be said, since it directly concerns the textuality of the TT. The image of the dead-language ST as a photograph (the Barthesian tragedy of the rupture between the 'still-there' and the 'that-has-been'), or as the interrogation of an uncommunicative suspect, presents history as voluntary memory, as a series of temporal gaps between known incidents which have to be bridged by efforts of investigation. But history is the vehicle of involuntary memory, a cumulative accretion in which all is always potentially present to itself, continuously carried forward; no voice stops speaking. Intertextuality is the name of this unremitting survival, this persistent and growing congregation of voices, mixing together in complex and changing choruses.

What kind of voice has Juvenal, then, and how does this voice survive in the voice of Baudelaire? How does it blend with other voices in Baudelaire, with the voices of Ovid, Vergil, Nerval, and the other voices of Baudelaire himself? And more especially how do all these voices interact with those in the translator's head, and how are they textually patterned in the TT? This last question already indicates a sense in which the TT *must* be an enlargement of the ST. If 'transparent' translations were at all possible, they would be a betrayal not only of the translating subject, but also of all the accretions of writing and reading which intervene between the ST and the TT.

We know very little about Juvenal. He was probably born in Aquinum in about AD 55. He probably died in about AD 138, but was he at that time still in exile in Egypt, or had he returned to Italy after Domitian's death in AD 96, to farm at Tivoli (Tibur) under Hadrian? What was the cause of this exile? Was it because of lines against the actor Paris in the Seventh Satire (86–92), a favourite of Domitian's, but executed by him in AD 87? It is likely that the five books of Juvenal's sixteen satires were published between AD 105 and AD 135, but no exact date for any of the books can be reliably established. And if the first was published when Juvenal had already reached fifty, how early do passages within it date back to? Or are they indeed principally the product of an embittered man past his prime?

We know more about the voice than the man, more about the writerly methods than the times. Baudelaire lived with Juvenal's voice for a long time. It was in 1833, at the age of twelve, in Lyon (where his stepfather, Lieutenant Colonel Aupick, had been stationed), that Baudelaire received an edition of Juvenal as a gift from his brother Alphonse. If we may roughly distinguish between left-wing satire and right-wing satire, as between a satire which attempts to undo a stagnant or complacent or repressive status quo, and a satire which bitterly regrets a decline in the quality of life, a gradual erosion of earlier virtues, then Juvenal, like Baudelaire, is a satirist of the latter persuasion: 'nunc patimur longae pacis mala' [now we are suffering the ills of a long peace] (VI, 292) is the way Juvenal puts it. Republican Baudelaire may have been, but Progress is the worst of abominations. The trouble is that the past is not believed in either. Virtue is no virtue in a woman: 'quis feret uxorem cui constant omnia?' [who can put up with a wife in whom all virtues are found?] (VI, 166). And the golden age that Baudelaire celebrates in the opening lines of 'J'aime le souvenir…':

> L'homme, élégant, robuste et fort, avait le droit
> D'être fier des beautés qui le nommaient leur roi;

Fruits purs de tout outrage et vierge de gerçures,
Dont la chair lisse et ferme appelait les morsures!

(ll. 11–14)

strikes me as an ironic, derisorily idealized gloss on the opening lines of Juvenal's Sixth Satire in which the hill-bred wife is an earth-mother 'whose breasts gave suck to lusty babes, often more unkempt herself than her acorn-belching husband' (VI, 9–10, trans. G.G. Ramsay 1961: 85).[1] Caught in this limbo of intolerable alternatives, both poets frequently use the diction of epic as a *repoussoir* for modern bathos and petty-mindedness. Satire (satura) is the genre of mixture, miscellany, medley, and both Juvenal and Baudelaire mix registers, temporal perspectives, fact and fiction, the grave crime and the petty vice. Mock-epic as much mocks the epic as it does the trivial. In the new pantheon in which 'Ennui' has usurped Zeus's throne, we connive in our own delusions: Juvenal lets contemporary Roman figures rub shoulders with heroes from the Trojan War, just as Baudelaire can liken his relationship with Jeanne Duval to a Hadean adventure. Who was Baudelaire kidding when he insisted on the heroism of modern life?

How many implicit reminiscences of Juvenal there are in Baudelaire's work is impossible to say; but there can be no doubt that there are many waiting still to be suggested. We have mentioned the parallels between the openings of the Sixth Satire and of 'J'aime le souvenir…'. And from the same satire, we might want to draw out one of the images of Messalina— 'tenditque tuum generose Britannice ventrem' [and flaunted the womb whence you, O noble Britannicus, came] (VI, 124, trans. H. Creekmore, 1963: 89)—and put it alongside Baudelaire's 'Une charogne', 'Les jambes en l'air, comme une femme lubrique,/Brûlante et suant les poisons,/Ouvrait d'une façon nonchalante et cynique/Son ventre plein d'exhalaisons.' As one reads through the Third Satire, on life in Rome, one cannot but think that the lines:

> quod spatium tectis sublimibus unde cerebrum
> testa ferit, quotiens rimosa et curta fenestris
> vasa cadant, quanto percussum pondere signent
> et laedant silicem…

(269–72)

[See what height it is to that towering roof from which a potsherd comes crack upon my head every time that some broken or leaky vessel is pitched out of the window!]

trans. G.G. Ramsay 1961: 53]

59

lie at the root of 'Le Mauvais Vitrier', just as the description of the street brawl, which follows almost immediately at lines 286–301, takes us forward to 'Assommons les pauvres':

> ... libertas pauperis haec est:
> pulsatus rogat et pugnis concisus adorat
> ut licet paucis cum dentibus inde reverti
>
> (299–301)
>
> [Such is the liberty of the poor man: having been pounded and cuffed into a jelly, he begs and prays to be allowed to return home with a few teeth in his head!]
>
> trans. G.G. Ramsay 1961: 55]

What is noticeable in these borrowings, however, if borrowings they are, is that Baudelaire has reversed the roles: leaving Juvenal to be the pitiable victim, he assumes the role of instigator of pain, of streetwise sadist.

Baudelaire's explicit allusions to Juvenal are fewer and less wide-ranging than one might expect. One such allusion appears in his article on Auguste Barbier, whose *Iambes* (1831) directed their satirical verve at the July monarchy. In Baudelaire's view, Barbier's verse is *over*-adapted to his target, is too occasional in spirit, and too often betrays Barbier's 'grimace dantesque'[Dantean grimace]. But Baudelaire admires his Latinity ('sa langue, vigoureux et pittoresque, a presque le charme du latin' [his energetic and picturesque language has almost the charm of Latin], *OC*, II, 142), and goes on to quote Satires I, 79—'Facit indignatio versum' [indignation writes the line of verse]—while pointing out that it was in Juvenal's interests to say so. In his 'Lettre de Jules Janin', Baudelaire refers to Juvenal's 'éclats de rire pleins de fureur' [bursts of laughter filled with fury], and goes on to call him 'le vilain sale' [the dirty scoundrel] because 'il se fâche toujours au profit du pauvre et de l'opprimé' [he always loses his temper to the advantage of the poor and the oppressed] (*OC*, II, 236), a typically dialectical touch of irony. Finally, in what is Baudelaire's equivalent of the Sixth Satire, namely the twelfth section of *Le Peintre de la vie moderne* (1863) (*OC*, II, 718–22), entitled 'Les Femmes et les filles', he makes use of Juvenal's phrase 'femina simplex' [one-trick woman] (VI, 327), as he had in his 'Notes sur *Les Liaisons dangereuses*' (*OC*, II, 69).

This arrival at 'Les Femmes et les filles' brings us to the interferences of Baudelaire's own intertexts, interferences which in the reader's/ translator's mind operate achronically: *Le Peintre de la vie moderne* was written some twenty years after 'Sed non satiata'. It may seem inappropriate to set 'Les Femmes et les filles' alongside the Sixth Satire, simply because while the one explores the 'différences de caste et de race' [differences of class and breeding] of the urban feminine, the other is an unmitigated attack on women and consequently on the present state of marriage. But as Peter Green points out (1967: 25), Juvenal's target is not feminine 'licentiousness *tout court*' but 'the breaching of class and convention'. When noble women consort with musicians, actors and gladiators, when they yield to all their superstitions, when they privilege the Greek over the Roman, then social chaos ensues, and power ends up in all the wrong places; for Juvenal, as for Baudelaire, the appropriation of power has to do with the the appropriation of sexual initiative; but sex is dark, inchoate, a randomly destructive force. Sex is Baudelaire's Africa, his heart of darkness, and the night/midnight which may be the peace of invisibility, or the 'néant' beyond consciousness, or the vast space of associative unity, is equally the 'gouffre', the 'bouche d'ombre' of the female:

> Une riche toison qui, vraiment, est la sœur
> De cette énorme chevelure,
> Souple et frisée, et qui t'égale en épaisseur,
> Nuit sans étoiles, Nuit obscure!
> ('Les Promesses d'un visage', 17–20)

The poet of 'Sed non satiata' has not, perhaps does not want, the sexual flexibility which would make him a 'worthy opponent' of the black Venus, and we may be inclined to believe the last stanza of 'A celle qui est trop gaie', believe that the poet can only consort with the feminine if he creates his own sexual entry:

> Et faire à ton flanc étonné
> Une blessure large et creuse,
>
> Et, vertigineuse douceur!
> A travers ces lèvres nouvelles,
> Plus éclatantes et plus belles,
> T'infuser mon venin, ma sœur!

But what is sexual desire if not the weighing of the psychic anchor? What is the fantasy of insemination if not the release of a journeying imagination? The black of the black Venus's sexuality is no different from the black of 'l'Inconnu' at the end of 'Le Voyage':

O Mort, vieux capitaine, il est temps! levons l'ancre!
Ce pays nous ennuie, ô Mort! Appareillons!
Si le ciel et la mer sont noirs comme de l'encre,
Nos cœurs que tu connais sont remplis de rayons!

Verse-nous ton poison pour qu'il nous réconforte!
Nous voulons, tant ce feu nous brûle le cerveau,
Plonger au fond du gouffre, Enfer ou Ciel, qu'importe?
Au fond de l'Inconnu pour trouver du *nouveau*!

Now we see that the 'Bizarre déité' is indeed Death, and that Hades is a place of possible regeneration, and that the venom, the inseminating poison, might be as much that of the mistress as that of the poet, a point borne out, as all dialectical points are, by 'L'Héautontimorouménos':

Elle est dans ma voix, la criarde!
C'est tout mon sang, ce poison noir!
Je suis le sinistre miroir
Où la mégère se regarde!

Je suis la plaie et le couteau!
…

Now the Megaera is not Death, but Death's most natural form of self-expression, Irony, the unraveller of universal analogy, fanning the flames of destructive self-consciousness. The poison in the veins is now, we note, as black as the power that infuses it and as black as that undefined beyondness into which the imagination ever fares. But what is important for us here is that, in those alexandrines from the close of 'Le Voyage', 'noirs' occurs at syllable 8. 'Noir' occurs most frequently, in Baudelaire's verse, in the second hemistich, that hemistich characterized by falling intonation, by descent into self, by the sotto voce, by cumulative complexity as the line shifts into a new mode of meaning, rhyme.

This short exploration of night and blackness is designed to demonstrate a simple principle: even as unpretentious a word as 'noir' should be translated as a living protagonist in a textuality compounded of text and intertext, not as an element in a system of linguistic equivalences. In line 4 I have maintained it at syllable 10, as in the ST, and, in line 9, to express the intensity it has in the ST, thanks to its structural prominence at the caesura, I have used compounding, but in a suitably banal mode.

What is important is that both occurrences of 'noir' should be translated by the same word.

If Baudelaire ultimately refuses, only flirts with, the darkness of female sexuality, does not enter this 'brûlante Afrique', it is perhaps because he fears, precisely, the disappearance of the mirage, the reduction of the black Venus to her dull self, to the 'femina simplex'. The 'femina simplex' is all that Juvenal has room for. For Baudelaire, the 'femina simplex' is a 'femina complex' by virtue of being 'fatalement suggestive' [fatally suggestive], by virtue of having a life other than her own, a life in the imaginations and fantasies of men. This imaginary other existence is generated, projected, by costume and accessories:

> La femme est sans doute une lumière, un regard, une invitation au bonheur, une parole quelquefois; mais elle est surtout une harmonie générale, non seulement dans son allure et le mouvement de ses membres, mais aussi dans les mousselines, les gazes, les vastes et chatoyantes nuées d'étoffes dont elle s'enveloppe, et qui sont comme les attributs et le piédestal de sa divinité; dans le métal et le minéral qui serpentent autour de ses bras et de son cou, qui ajoutent leurs étincelles au feu de ses regards, ou qui jasent doucement à ses oreilles.
>
> (*OC*, II, 714)
>
> [Woman is certainly a light, a look, an invitation to happiness, sometimes a voice; but, above all, she is a diffused harmony, not only in her carriage and the movement of her limbs, but also in the muslins, the gauzes, the vast and shimmering clouds of fabric in which she folds herself, and which are like the attributes and pedestal of her divinity; in the metals and minerals which wind round her arms and neck, which add their glints to the fire of her eyes, or which softly chatter at her ear.]

If we put this quotation from 'La Femme' alongside an earlier description of woman:

> C'est une espèce d'idole, stupide peut-être, mais éblouissante, enchanteresse, qui tient les destinées et les volontés suspendues à ses regards.
>
> (*OC*, II, 713)
>
> [She is a kind of idol, dull-witted perhaps, but dazzling, enchanting, holding destinies and wills hanging on her every look.]

we see why we must stick with Baudelaire's 'déité', because it falls so neatly between the two terms 'divinité' and 'idole' used here. Equally, I have used 'bewitcher' because it seems to me to lie between the more malignant note of 'sorcière' and the benign note of 'enchanteresse'. And if the lines from 'L'Héautontimorouménos' have not already convinced us that 'Mégère' in Baudelaire's usage does not become the 'Mégère' of 'La Mégère apprivoisée' (*The Taming of the Shrew*), but remains locked in her mythological vengefulness, we should listen to his description of the barmaid in this same 'Les Femmes et les filles':

> cependant que derrière un comptoir chargé de bouteilles de liqueurs se prélasse une grosse mégère dont la tête, serrée dans un sale foulard qui dessine sur le mur l'ombre de ses pointes sataniques, fait penser que tout ce qui est voué au Mal est condamné à porter des cornes.
>
> (*OC*, II 721)
>
> [while, behind a counter stocked with liqueur bottles, lounges a fleshy megaera whose head, wrapped in a dirty headscarf, its satanic points silhouetted on the wall, provokes the thought that everything dedicated to Evil is condemned to wear horns.]

This text gives us the demythicized darkness of 'Sed non satiata', the burlesque of the 'Bizarre déité', what might have been the *Spleen de Paris* version of that 'fleur du Mal'. So, again, we should not let the reference to 'havane' either disappear (Symons 1925: 127), or generalize itself into place of origin (Havana(h)—Wagner 1971: 37; Richardson 1975: 69) or drug (nicotine—Howard 1982: 32), but should keep the insolent image in front of us:

> Comme son joli compagnon, elle a tout l'orifice de sa petite bouche occupé par un cigare disproportionné.
>
> (*OC*, II, 719)
>
> [Like her pretty companion, she has the whole orifice of her little mouth filled with a disproportionate cigar.]

In observations like these, we again hear the sexual rage and frustration of Juvenal, who continues to haunt these pages in more direct ways:

> Il ne rencontrera rien que le vice inépuisable, c'est-à-dire le regard du démon embusqué dans les ténèbres ou l'épaule de Messaline miroitant sous le gaz.
>
> (*OC*, II, 722)

[He will encounter nothing but inexhaustible vice, that is to say the spying eye of the devil lying in wait in the shadows, or Messalina's shoulder gleaming in the gaslight.]

Messalina still plays the prostitute, but now in a Parisian street rather than a Roman stew.

If I have dwelt on pages of *Le Peintre de la vie moderne* as an anachronistic intertext which may teach us something about translating 'Sed non satiata', it is because it cannot be urged too strongly that translation is *reading with hindsight*, like literary criticism; but unlike literary criticism, it invests its hindsight in a creative text. We understand very little about the proper use of hindsight; we understand even less about how it is best expressed, how this afterlife can be fed back into a rendering of the ST. But we should console ourselves with the thought that reading backwards is the principal way in which translation can counter its tendency to 'deaden' origins; it begins to see the ST as that which best encapsulates everything which comes after it. So the TT, as we have said, necessarily subsumes the ST, is necessarily an enlargement, and yet, insofar as the TT is a journey back to the ST, the ST can be projected as the sum of its consequences.

The patterns of temporal survival are complicated by those of spatial survival. In the English consciousness, Juvenal may principally mean Dryden's translation of five of the Satires, or Johnson's 'London' (based on the Third Satire) or his magnificent 'The Vanity of Human Wishes' (based on Satire X), or it may bring A.E. Housman and his critical edition of 1905 to mind. Baudelaire, for his part, necessitates Swinburne and Eliot and Aldous Huxley and Lowell,[2] to mention but a few. And in the translation itself, in its own textuality, the second half of the first line may conjure up A.E. Coppard's 'Dusky Ruth', while 'child of the black midnight' will summon Salman Rushdie as much as Nerval's translation of Goethe's *Faust*; 'Dr', introduced as an accompaniment of 'Faust', lets Marlowe on to the stage; the second half of line 13 takes me to Auden's 'As I walked out one evening'.

The temporality of readerly perception, its collapsing of history, its reorderings of sequence, are themselves complex mechanisms little understood. I have treated extracts from 'La Femme' and 'Les Femmes et les filles' (*Le Peintre de la vie moderne*) as if they were contemporary with 'Sed non satiata', and in that I am imitating the reading mind's drift towards achrony. But there are other instances in which the maintenance of a chronological order is called upon to intensify the poignancy of a perception. Manet's portrait of Jeanne Duval of 1862, again twenty years later than 'Sed non satiata', is for me a pathos-filled commentary on that poem, in that it is both an elegy for, and a revenge on, the 'Bizarre déité'. Here is Jeanne, ill and doll-like, drowning in her dress. Manet's customary distortion of proportions makes Jeanne's head shrunken and her hand large, clumsy. Her feet, in their dainty black shoes, do not belong to her. The passage in 'Les Femmes et les filles' which most closely corresponds to this picture depicts the negative manifestations of 'femmes galantes':

> étalées, vautrées sur les canapés, la jupe arrondie par-derrière et par-devant en un double éventail, ou accrochées en équilibre sur des tabourets et des chaises; lourdes, mornes, stupides, extravagantes, avec des yeux vernis par l'eau-de-vie et des fronts bombés par l'entêtement.
>
> (*OC*, II, 721)
>
> [spread out in display, sprawled on the sofas, their skirts fanning out both in front and behind, or balancing tenaciously on stools and chairs; heavy, low-spirited, empty-headed, grotesque, eyes glazed over with spirits and foreheads bulging with stubbornness.]

In Manet's image of fragile equilibrium, the dress does not occupy the space behind the figure; here an extravagant lace curtain echoes the dress, conspires with the dress to overwhelm, belittle, and disempower the mulatto, to re-establish Western fashion and refinement against the intrusions of the dark; Jeanne is clearly 'dépaysée' and her 'dépaysement' is heightened to a degree which looks like expulsion.

As a final argumentative move, one which continues, however, to explore the reawakening of dead language by cumulative reintegration, and which pursues that process whereby the TT, while maintaining a meta-dimension, re-embeds itself in first-degree meaning by asserting its textuality, I would like to concentrate on the collision of the Western and the African, as an allegory of translation.

I pursue this topic through a sequence of observations about the poem which I hope will make its allegorical value for the translator self-evident:

1.   Baudelaire sees displacement in time and space as an often necessary source of creativity: the exhausted Westerner drinks renewal at the source of the Other. 'Sed non satiata' not only sets a Western psycho-lexicon ('désirs', 'ennuis', 'libertins') against the tropical ('obi', 'savane'), but also sets the geographically distant black against the temporally distant mythological ('Mégère', 'Proserpine').[3] The dominant vocalic sounds /a/, /ɛ(R)/ and /i/ pass between east and west, dark and light, the suffocating

and the refreshing, without hindrance; all are unrounded, inchoate phonemes. In my translation I have tried to suggest both connection and nuanced difference by developing three acoustic manifestations of the grapheme a (/æ/, /ɑ:/, /eɪ/) and in so doing have remembered Mallarmé's praise of Manet's mastery of the different shades of black (1945: 697–8) (and, looking at the portrait of Jeanne, of white, we might add).

2.   But in the act of creative self-renewal, the poet is likely to be as much exhausted or stultified by his subject as recreated by it—the sexual activity here, as we have already suggested, is one way of expressing that paradox. But we might also point out that the virtuoso's production of the lexicon of leonine rhymes in -avane dries up the source: these are the only four rhymes in -avane in the rhyming dictionary. I have taken the process of etiolation and unravelling one stage further: the -avane words retain their conspicuous relatedness, but they are neither in the rhyme position nor do they rhyme. And I have preferred 'Havanese' to 'Havana' not only to avoid the internal rhyme with 'savannah', but also to displace Cuba towards the Orient where the -ese ending is more at home (Japanese, Chinese, Balinese, Javanese, etc.). The poem enjoys a geography /topography which is wide-ranging and scumbled.

3.   If my version of the -avane rhymes pluralizes and disperses, where Baudelaire's is a tight group bound together structurally as well as acoustically, this is only to change the balance of an opposition which animates both the ST and the TT. If the bizarre is what makes the beautiful multiform, the translator or lover may feel bound to try to master it, to reduce the multiform to the single, the feminine (ST) to the masculine (TT), or the 'femina complex' (ST) to the 'femina simplex' (TT), even though he knows that such a reduction would perversely reintroduce that 'vaste unité, monotone et impersonnelle, immense comme l'ennui et le néant' [vast, montonous and impersonal unity, as immense as ennui or nothingness] (II, 578) of the academic and pedagogic, against which the bizarre is such a potent and necessary weapon. I have tried to embody this frustrated attempt to confine the multiform (already evident in the first stanza) by underlining typographically the articulation of the lines, and by alliterating binding elements within the hemistich wherever possible. But this effort is unavailing: the number of syllables per line varies between 13 and 15, and the alliterative mechanism often fails to operate.

4.   Ultimately, of course, this urge towards the masculine and the single is re-expressed as a (regretful?) *inability to become* the feminine and the

multiform—the poet is neither Proserpine nor the Styx. The image of the ST as a product of the TT ('œuvre de quelque obi, le Faust de la savane') is thus reversed ('Ebony bewitcher') and the ST retains its irrepressibly protean nature; and the poet's desire for sexual possession becomes a desire for sexual suicide.

5.   But perhaps this acknowledgement of impotence, however necessary it is, is not total. In his commentary, Arnaldo Pizzorusso (1973: 245–53) asserts that the Furies were the daughters of Pluto and Persephone and that, therefore, while Jeanne is husband (Pluto) to the poet's Persephone, the poet is father (Pluto) to Jeanne's Megaera. What is more, one might notice that in addition to the increased mythological reference in the tercets, there are also increased allusions to the Latin poets. Here, Baudelaire is not quite as well served by his annotators as he might be. In his edition of *Les Fleurs du Mal*, Antoine Adam notes of line 11: 'Il semblerait que Baudelaire avait lu *L'Art d'aimer* d'Ovide, et retenu ce vers: "Et memini numeros sustinuisse novem"' [It would seem that Baudelaire had read Ovid's *Ars amatoria* and remembered this line: 'I remember that, pressed by Corinna, I managed to sustain her assaults nine times in one short night'] (1961: 309). This is not a line from the *Ars amatoria*, but is line 26 of *Amores* III, vii, and it is hardly likely that, in remembering one line, Baudelaire should not remember a whole poem devoted to sexual failure rather than to sexual success:

> I wanted it badly enough, and so did she—
> but could I rise to the occasion?
> > (trans. Guy Lee 1968: 145)

Equally, line 11 points us in the direction of *Aeneid*, VI, 438–9:

> fas obstat tristisque palus inamabilis undae
> alligat et noviens Styx interfusa coercet
> [Fate withstands; the unlovely mere with its dreary water enchains
> them and Styx imprisons with his ninefold circles]
> > (trans. Rushton Fairclough 1916: 537)

But as Pizzorusso points out (1973: 250), to look only at these lines and not further on, to lines 447–9, is to miss a powerful associative impulse:

> ... his Laodamia
> it comes et invenis quondam, nunc femina, Caeneus

rursus et in veterem fato revoluta figuram
[with them goes Laodamia, and Caeneus, once a youth, now a woman, and again turned back by Fate into her form of old]
(trans. Rushton Fairclough 1916: 537)

This is but another taste of that sexual instability, which is a powerful metaphor for translation, that strong transsexual drive that the poem has as a whole and upon which analysts have commented particularly in relation to line 9:

Je préfère *au* constance, à l'opium, *au* nuits [my italics].

At all events, this restoration of a hidden Western agenda acts as a protective and authorizing mantle, even in the poet's apparent surrender. These Roman sources are not a form of dead language which *precedes* Baudelaire's allusions, but are conjured up as living tutelary spirits to protect the poet against the African exotic. Conversely, as Christopher Miller points out (1985: 113): 'On the level of discourse analysis, one can see that the terms such as *bizarre, déité, obi, savane, sorcière,* and *caravane* are so heavily laden with exotic connotations that their denotations of power are undercut.'

Translation is a suicidal art. It is translation which generates and sustains the metaphysics of the untranslatable and the prestige of 'original' creative writing at its own expense. It is translation which, because of its very metalinguistic nature, places the signified outside the signifier, or, to use Meschonnic's term, 'transcendentalizes' it. It is translation which perpetuates linguistic racism and colonialism. There are many ways in which the ST and the TT, it seems, are mutually destructive. And yet, equally, they could be mutually beneficial. Meschonnic's diagnosis (1973: 309)—'Ces notions aboutissent à opposer texte et traduction, par une sacralisation de la littérature. Cette sacralisation est compensatoire par rapport à sa neutralisation politique' [These notions end by opposing text and translation, by a sacralization of literature. This sacralization compensates for the text's political neutralization]—might be reversed: translation can de-sacralize literature by drawing attention to the ST's infelicities, its pretensions, its complacencies, its desire to immobilize itself (we have yet to entertain the idea of a *critical* translation which is something more than a parody); translation can politicize the ST either by 'revealing' its motives and ideology, or by harnessing it to a political activism contemporary with the TT. By making the choice of the text to be translated a tendentious act, the translator can highlight its potentially regenerative contribution to a certain literary status quo—as Meschonnic puts it: 'La traduction, étant l'installation d'un nouveau rapport, ne peut qu'être modernité, néologie, alors qu'une conception dualiste voit la traduction d'un texte comme forme et archaïsme' [Translation, being the implementation of a new relationship, can only be modernity, neology, whereas a dualist conception sees the translation of a text as form and archaism] (1973: 311). We have constructed ample translation theory without sufficiently theorizing the practice of translation—and a theory of the practice of translation is not to be confused with comparative linguistics—because we have no critical account of the TT *as text*. And part of this lack, in turn, is the lack of a fully historicized view of the TT (why at a particular time, by whom, in what guise, for whom, with what intertexts, etc.). History will teach us to see, perhaps, that while linguistic considerations are undoubtedly important in the assessment of translation, they are not necessarily determining:

> Les positions théoriques et les pratiques sont historiquement situées. Cette situation est plus déterminante pour la technique de la traduction, ainsi que la structuration de l'écriture par un sujet, que la connaissance de la langue.
>
> (Meschonnic, 1973: 322)
>
> [Theoretical positions and translation practices are historically situated. This situation is more determining for the technique of translation, as for the way in which writing is structured by a subject, than knowledge of the language.]

Above all, we lack a theory of the reading of translations, a theory which would ensure that TTs, like STs, are points of departure rather than of arrival, subjects of reading, instruments of self-discovery, crucial links in the intertextual chains of which literature is made.

4

Translating and Co-authoring

This chapter continues the task, initiated in the previous chapter, of theorizing the *practical process* of translation. In doing so, it resumes the exploration of a model already outlined above.

Stages

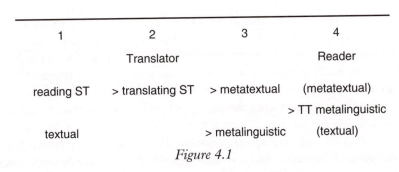

Figure 4.1

The representation in Figure 4.1 indicates that, for the translator, the *textual* is a preliminary activity, which is itself translated into the *metatextual* when the task of written translation is initiated. The bracketing of 'metatextual' and 'textual' at the reader's end indicates not only that, as already mentioned, awareness of the metatextual is smothered by the appetite for the metalinguistic (the need to know what the text means rather than the need to know how it constructs its meanings), but also that the reader does not engage in a textual activity because he assumes that it has been pre-empted by the metalinguistic, and by the metatextual insofar as it survives. The reader is thus as if present, as a disempowered spectator, at a demonstration of the ST's having already achieved its meaning.

Alternatively, the reader may treat the TT as a text which, in the process of translation, has lost its reliability or interest as an autonomously productive text. The consequence of this state of affairs is that the ST becomes increasingly stabilized as a text, over-stabilized in fact; in short, it becomes what I have referred to as a 'dead' text, a hypostatized version of itself. Conversely, the TT finds it difficult to establish any stability for itself. But its instability is not a productive, engendering instability, but a dead-end instability of the transitory, meta-existent and unembedded. We have already seen the means by which the ST can be destabilized in a postmodern version of translation (Chapter 1): the ST, for example, can be regarded as a reconstruction from the TT, something trying to recover itself again, or to be re-originated. We have seen, too, how the TT's stability can be increased, by demoting the metalinguistic in favour of the TT's textuality. If the translator can convince the reader that his intention is not a definitive interpretation of the ST but a self-expressive reformulation, a reformulation by which self-expression can be achieved; or if the translator can convince the reader that his intentions are more fully focused on the metatextual than on the metalinguistic, then the TT might be something more like a relocation of the ST than a pale shadow of it.

But the TT can also achieve a more meaningful textual autonomy by distancing itself from the ST, not as a wilful act of creative independence, but as a measured, systematic, pondered *process* of self-distantiation. More importantly, this process of self-distantiation is not, like the gesture of creative independence, a *terminus ad quem*, but, on the contrary, a *terminus a quo*, a prelude to a new approach to the ST. We are familiar with instances where a translator has had distance imposed upon him by an ignorance of the SL—Auden translating Hammerskjöld's Swedish, Lowell translating Pasternak's Russian, Logue translating Homer's Greek—and where translation has consisted partly of procedural ingenuities by which the TT might draw near—though not necessarily through linguistic fidelity—to the ST. My concern here is slightly different: I wish to investigate the case of the translator who knows the SL, but who wishes to vitalize the relationship between the ST and the TT, and strengthen the status of the TT, by recourse to intralingual translation.

In order to prosecute this purpose, I need first to zoom in on the diagrammatic account of the translation process, and add a little further detail to stages 2,3 and 4. How translators actually go to work will vary considerably, of course, but this is not a reason for leaving this aspect out of the critical reckoning. What I would like to work from is what I take to be a reasonable model, as shown in Figure 4.2.

ST > literal translation > R1 > R2... > TT

Figure 4.2

I do not want to ask what a literal translation is—a thorny problem at the best of times—but to concern myself more with its function. R1, R2, etc. represent a process of progressive *refinement* which leads ultimately to a TT. The first, simple point I want to make is that, even in conventional translation, we often translate a native text, the literal translation, and that, in translating, we are often translating ourselves, our own founding text. The second point, equally simple, is that the texts produced in the process of translation are usually seen as a *progressive* sequence, each superseding the previous one, until the translator is satisfied that an optimal version has been arrived at.

In pursuit of the first point—that a translation is essentially a translation of a native text—I would begin by observing that intralingual translation is often mentioned as a possible dimension of translation but rarely explored. In a pedagogical context, it has increasingly seemed to me a crucial instrument of understanding, for two reasons. First, it allows us to perceive, with graphic clarity, what time and a changed gamut of formal possibility make available to the TT. The last four lines of Henry V's Act 3, Scene 1 'Once more unto the breach...' speech run:

> I see you stand like greyhounds in the slips,
> Straining upon the start. The game's afoot:
> Follow your spirit; and upon this charge
> Cry, 'God for Harry, England, and Saint George!'

I offer the following translation:

1. For me you're
2.   greyhounds
3.   straining at the leash
4.   ready to be off
5.   The quarry's
6. up and running
7.   Go with your will

8. and as you charge   shout

9.   'For King and Country!'

I have not resisted the temptation to introduce, with 'For King and Country', a sobering, undercutting WWI note, permitting the infiltration of Owen's 'Dulce et decorum est' and Joseph Losey's film. Free verse has allowed me visually to dynamize these lines and, at the same time, to maintain a language of resonant cliché. The dynamization has, linguistically, to do with two things: it implies the text's more thorough inhabitation by paralinguistic features, in particular pausing, changes of tempo and intonational variation; and it underlines, indeed polarizes, rhythmic tendencies within the original. Shakespeare's lines are, of course, basically iambic, and more particularly so in the first and fourth lines of the extract; this I have tried to maintain in my lines 1–2 and 8–9. The characteristic of Shakespeare's two inner lines is their reversal of the first foot, to produce a syncopation between the lines and an urgent impulsiveness. I have tried to focus and intensify this impulsiveness in lines 3–7, and at the same time to create rhythmic units which are, as it were, complete psycho-physiological events, both beginning and ending with a stressed syllable, as in lines 3–4 and 7. In my lineation, I have expressly left a gap between 'and as you charge' and 'shout' in line 8, to introduce a pause, so that 'shout' can be performatively uttered with a gathered imperative and hortatory force.

If, in this instance, intralingual translation helps us to identify the formal adaptations and potentialities which time has stored in itself and which unfolding time progressively releases, allowing us, as we proceed, to reimagine the making of a text, so equally intralingual translation dramatizes the translator's personal encounter with the ST, and shows how that ST can be moulded to a different mentality or set of perceptual habits. I recently asked a literary translation class to translate the second stanza of Gray's 'Elegy':

> Now fades the glimmering landscape on the sight,
> And all the air a solemn stillness holds,
> Save where the beetle wheels his droning flight,
> And drowsy tinklings lull the distant folds.

One version which emerged from this ten-minute exercise ran:

> The last light leaves and the world fades away,

Day's dying din yields to holy calm,
The peace is perfect, but for a beetle's whirring rounds,
And now and then, a quiet bell in hillside pens.

What is immediately apparent is that Gray's 'sober wishes', 'sequester'd vale', 'noiseless tenor' kind of elegy of compromise and psychological lullaby is, momentarily at least, put under some strain, and in two ways: first, the writing mentality here gravitates towards the superlative—'last', 'world' (rather than 'landscape'), 'din', 'perfect'—as though the situation needed to be injected with a mystic touch, polarized between an interruptive and restless here and the trance-like spiritual stasis of a there; elegy is characteristically rational and unsublime, a consolation attained by replacing the metaphysical with the universal earthly. Secondly, the translation, in its opening lines at least, uses alliteration and assonance not as a soothing acoustic balm but in order to instress the stress, to gather stress into jagged clusters: 'last light leaves', 'fades away/Day's', 'Day's dying din'. This turmoil of spirit, these vocal eruptions, die down to something temperamentally more even as the writer reconciles here with there: the six-stress lines lengthen, marginally but perceptibly (10. 9. 13. 12), and the stresses become more evenly distributed. In the last two lines, the even-tenored iambic is reinstalled almost without hiccough; and in these last lines, after the first hemistich of the third, there is no obtrusive alliteration, merely spaced assonantal chains ('peace' > 'beetle', 'perfect' > 'whirring', 'then' > 'bell' > 'pen', 'quiet' > 'hillside'). Finally, the heavily adversative, rather irritated 'but for'—more impatient than Gray's reconciled and dispersive 'save where'—softens into an inclusive, welcoming 'And', hardly joined any more to the 'but for' preposition, and followed by an excusing 'now and then' not present in Gray.

These observations perhaps give some indication of how intralingual translation can realize the ST's potentialities in other formal dimensions, and of how the individuality of a translator can find self-expression in drawing an ST towards a new expression of itself. But there are other advantages. Faced with English texts to translate into English, and leaving aside those licences allowed by the need to modernize, students either felt morally obliged to paraphrase (i.e. not to use the same lexical items, even in alternative grammatical forms), or felt that lexical items could be retained, in the same or alternative grammatical forms, only on condition of a radical structural reworking. Even if we overlook the fact that translation has explicit acknowledgement of a source built into it, we must understand that plagiarism, to a greater or lesser extent, is an inherent resource of translation, most importantly because a *sine qua non* of a translator's effective operation is a belief in the right to appropriate language, a belief that language, in all its possible collocations, is a universal possession. Of course, it will be objected that the situation here described never, by definition, obtains in interlingual translation. But what I am here speaking of is the formation of a general attitude. If the intralingual translator should not feel constrained by the anxiety of duplication, so conversely the interlingual translator should not feel constrained by the anxiety of difference.

What I want to suggest, then, is that the literal translation, or whatever we call the first draft, should displace the original as the ST, leaving the original free to function as an alternative text. The underlying direction of my argument inevitably affiliates itself with a tradition of thinking about translation whose roots lie in German Romanticism, a tradition so perceptively explored by Antoine Berman in his *L'Épreuve de l'étranger* (1984)—whose most celebrated inheritor is Walter Benjamin. Benjamin proposes that the ST and the TT are conjoined in a mutual enterprise of self-transcendence, an enterprise whose origins lie not in the ST itself, but in a pre-verbal source where, to use Mallarmé's words, the 'immortelle parole' [immortal word] is 'tacite encore'[still tacit], a tacit word ((TW)) that all languages seek to actualize. As in the Mallarméan sequence, a silence of pure, thought-filled latency begets a poem which tries to re-beget, to communicate, that founding silence which is 'l'immortelle parole' or (TW). We might express this graphically, as in Figure 4.3.

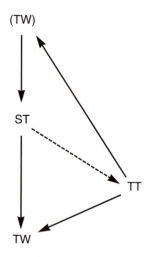

Figure 4.3

Here, the ST deriving from a (TW) reaches beyond itself to reconstitute the TW. The TT uses the ST to intuit the (TW) so that, in its turn, it may reach out towards an unrealized but realizable TW. Since both the ST and the TT are imperfect, the TW must lie at a point of imaginary convergence, not only of the ST and TT, but of all other texts, in whatever language, which might be deemed to have the same (TW). As Benjamin puts it: 'all suprahistorical kinship of languages rests in the intention underlying each language as a whole—an intention, however, which no single language can attain by itself but which is realised only by the totality of their intentions supplementing each other: pure language' (Schulte and Biguenet 1992: 75).

But we must make an adjustment to our model:

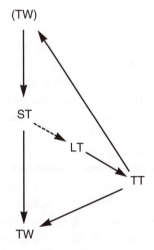

Figure 4.4

Figure 4.4 illustrates that the literal translation (LT) of a text is what defines the difference from the ST and what, by allowing the TT to build on the LT, equally allows the TT to find its way back to the (TW). The important thing for the TT is not simply to be different from the ST, but to be different from the ST by virtue of the LT, that is to say, to be different within the parameters of the LT, a difference enabled but controlled by the LT.

This model is informed by the conviction that the 'progressivity' of translation depends on language being treated as a medium, or 'milieu', rather than as an instrument:

Le langage comme *milieu*, et non plus *instrument*, voilà ce qui est

77

nouveau. Car tout milieu, par nature, est, comme le dit Lacan, 'quelque chose qui dépasse infiniment toute intention que nous pouvons y mettre'.

(Berman 1984: 229)

[Language as an *environment*, and no longer as an *instrument*, that is what is new. For, by its very nature, any environment is, as Lacan says, 'something infinitely greater than any intention we may set in it'.]

Embedded in a language as in a fluid and encompassing medium, a shifting environment, the writer may seek to use it instrumentally, but must do so in the knowledge that it can be shaped but never possessed, that, indeed, the process of shaping, of giving form, is precisely what dispossesses him of it, since form, paradoxically, is what returns language to its multiplicity, to its reverberative continuities and associations. What the translator of poetry often does is pursue, through interpretation, the chimaera first of authorial intention and then of linguistic equivalence; what the translator should do, perhaps, is imagine the author not as a generator of language but as a fellow-swimmer in an inconstant medium of changing reflections, using this medium to propel himself in one of any number of ways (all of which displace the water differently).

It is intralingual translation which is most likely to train us out of instrumental attitudes to language and into mediumic ones. The multiplicity of translations then becomes evidence not of the obstinate resistance (otherwise known as the irrecoverable plenitude) of the ST, but rather of the rich multiformity of the shared medium itself. But we must take care not to throw out the baby with the bath-water: to encourage the perception that language for both ST and TT is mediumic is one thing, but to undermine the predominance of the *textual* consideration (explored in the previous chapter) is another. The TT, like the ST, can only achieve mediumic density, intensity, through textual generation, through that *concerted* linguistic activity which only textuality can ensure. We should treat with the utmost circumspection Walter Benjamin's following words:

> This is a feature of translation which basically differentiates it from the poet's work, because the effort of the latter is never directed at the language as such, at its totality, but solely and immediately at specific linguistic contextual aspects. Unlike the work of literature, translation does not find itself in the center of the language forest but on the outside facing the wooded ridge; it calls into it without entering, aiming at that single spot where the echo is able to give, in

its own language, the reverberation of the work in the alien one. Not only does the aim of translation differ from that of a literary work—it intends language as a whole, taking an individual work in an alien language as a point of departure—but it is a different effort altogether. The intention of the poet is spontaneous, primary, graphic; that of the translator is derivative, ultimate, ideational.

(Schulte and Biguenet 1992: 77)

I have quoted this passage at length because it touches on our present concerns at several points. Benjamin's account, which suggests that the sights of a translator are set on a much larger target than that of the original writer, are set on the whole language rather than on a specific linguistic context or textual development, restores too great a predominance, in the translational process, to the metalinguistic. He assumes that translation, as a supremely linguistic-critical act, involves translators in the sacrifice of spontaneity, directness of contact, viscerality, in the interests of a longer-term, selfless, speculative goal. This sacrifice entails stepping outside language in order to measure, with a keen critical eye, the appropriate equivalence. Of course translation involves the exercise of the critical faculties, as does all creative writing; but I would argue that it can also re-engender, out of its own specific processes, the spontaneity of self-expression. The point I am labouring to make is that translation is not, emphatically *not*, a single act. It is a multitude of acts, in the progressive accomplishment of which the translator's posture towards the ST, and towards the TT, and towards their relationship, changes. What I am trying to imagine is (a) a way of plotting and describing that sequence of changing acts (recognizing that there are many available sequences), and (b) a way of ensuring that I, as a translator, can get back into the language forest and recover some of that surrendered spontaneity. This latter I am chiefly trying to achieve by ensuring that the creative is not pre-empted and inhibited by the critical, and this in turn involves me in an attempt to reverse the standard translational practice (criticism > creation) by relocating the ST, for the moment, in the LT. In other words, I am looking for a way to establish translation as a parallel creative process which leads to a *mutually beneficial* critical appraisal of both ST and TT when they are put side by side.

But what would our evidence be for proposing that the ST and the TT may share a common origin in a (TW)? First, one might argue that one language, by virtue of certain prosodic, grammatical or other linguistic features, can express a putative or reconstituable pre-text or (TW), as well as, if not better than, another, a fact which translation makes visible.

Against the argument that differences of gender, for example, are a cognitive irrelevance, Jakobson sets the view that 'grammatical gender […] plays a great role in the mythological attitudes of a speech community' (Schulte and Biguenet 1992: 149). In translating Rilke's 'Der Panther', Jean-Luc Moreau (Lefebvre 1993: 856–7) must convert the masculine German animal into a feminine French one, the *only* feminine feline (discounting specifically feminine forms such as 'lionne', 'tigresse', 'chatte', etc.). This move is made more significant by the sexual motivations of French rhyme. German operates with masculine and feminine rhymes, but without rules as to their disposition. And the presence of a neuter 'gender' in German makes the binariness of rhyme-gender a less meaningful counter-commentary on grammatical classification. The feminine line-ending in German, as in English, is a metrical syllable, even if superfluous to a verse-design such as iambic pentameter; the line-terminal French feminine syllable, on the other hand, is not reckoned to have a syllabic existence, even though it may be more or less phonated; its exclusive function is to mark 'sexual' rhyme-gender. Thus, while Rilke's panther will not naturally relate to rhyme-words or rhyme-schemes, Moreau's immediately establishes its collusion, in the second stanza of the translation, for example, with the *rime suffisante* 'puissance'/'danse' (/ɑ̃s/):

> Des pas légers l'élastique puissance
> dans le petit espace en mouvement,
> c'est dirait-on de la force qui danse
> et cerne au centre un grand vouloir dormant.
>
> (ll. 5–8)

> Der weiche Gang geschmeidig starker Schritte,
> der sich im allerkleinsten Kreise dreht,
> ist wie ein Tanz von Kraft um eine Mitte,
> in der betäubt ein grosser Wille steht.
>
> (ll. 5–8)

We notice that the masculine rhyme of the French version is indeed a masculine version of the feminine, also *suffisante* (/mɑ̃/), but a reversal (consonant + vowel) of the feminine (vowel + consonant); this is only to be expected, for masculine rhymes in French, by their very nature, tend to be open syllables, which is certainly not true of their German counterparts. We might further notice that the 'vouloir' of the panther is hemmed in by the masculine /ɑ̃/ sounds ('grand' and 'dormant', but also

80

'centre', whose final e is elided). What is peculiar about the feminine rhyme is that, although its syllable is closed (/ɑ̃s/), its very closure implies a following, if latent, feminine syllable /(ə)/: an acoustic leakage is opened up in the closed syllable. In the final stanza:

> Seul le rideau parfois s'ouvre en silence
> de la pupille, et le monde capté
> dans le calme tendu des nerfs s'avance
> et cesse en son cœur d'exister.
>
> (ll. 9–12)

> Nur manchmal schiebt der Vorhang der Pupille
> sich lautlos auf—. Dann geht ein Bild hinein,
> geht durch der Glieder angespannte Stille—
> und hört im Herzen auf zu sein.
>
> (ll. 9–12)

the same feminine rhyme (/ɑ̃s/) persists ('silence'/'s'avance'), but in a slightly stronger form, with reinforcement by word-initial s. In Rilke's version, the relationship between the rhymes of the last two stanzas is only assonant ('-itte' becomes '-ille'), though the '-ille' picks up the 'Wille' of line 8.

This encompassment of /ɑ̃/ by /s/ in the final stanza, in the figure /s…ɑ̃s/, not only imitates the direction of the meaning of 'cerne au centre' (line 8), but *is* the meaning ('sens'). This /s/, with which the poem is saturated, is the being of the panther, both in its 'élastique puissance' and in the 'petit espace' of its cage. 'Silence', a grammatically masculine noun made feminine by rhyme, makes manifest the unvoicedness of /s/: the eyelid opens like a camera-shutter, admitting an image so private that even the poet cannot express it, but can only speak its silence. Rilke's poem, then, perhaps lacks some of the concertedness of Moreau's translation. Rilke's poem is about a panther; Moreau's translation is about a panther, but also suggests, through the play of its gendering, overtones of sexual indomitability and a refusal of the constrictions of a space defined by the masculine ('barreaux', 'petit espace'—but no 'cage'!).

This analysis has necessarily implied that Moreau's poem has gains to offer, thanks to the peculiar resources of the TL.[1] But this need not necessitate a gains and losses argument. An acceptance of difference, of complementarity, would suffice, as long as a principle of a common (TW) were equally accepted. In speaking of *his* translation of 'Der Panther', Beaugrande explains:

Rilke's text moreover uses alternating rime, which alludes to the pacing of the animal back and forth. My text has enclosing rime and thus alludes to the position of the animal inside the cage. In other words, the preservation of sound features demands certain non-equivalences in other areas; but the goal-language exponents of these non-equivalences must themselves be generated by the text in a manner recoverable to readers.

(1978: 104)

We might object to such a manoeuvre if enclosed rhyme were merely a substitute scheme for an alternating one which could not be achieved. But to justify a deviation from the ST's practice on the grounds that the deviation is also allowed for by, inherent in, the ST, implies a situation with which we could readily concur: trading between ST and TT is active, ongoing; in the process of translation, and particularly in its metatextual dimension, ST and TT must come to an understanding which by no means merely ratifies the untouchable status of the ST. Translation opens up the ST to the exploration and reformulation of its surmisable (TW).

Earlier in the argument, I proposed that the LT (or first version) is what defines a difference from the ST and what allows the TT to find its way back to the (TW). The TT is a refinement of the LT, constructed on both an investigative and an enhancing duplication, because the LT is a raw material in which a (TW) is imperfectly embodied. But to achieve our first model (see Figure 4.4) we perhaps need to envisage a substitution: in place of LT read TT(O) (i.e. target text (other), to allow the inclusion of the translation(s) of other translators). Why take this particular detour? For three immediate reasons. First, the translator must be in a position to imagine himself as a native reader, which, with his own version, might prove difficult; there is an inbuilt inclination to read one's own text from the side of the ST. Secondly, the point of departure is no longer the ST or the LT, but another text, so that the translator is more thoroughly turned away from the ST, but is still working within certain parameters of possibility. Third, the TT emerges not from the refinement of an own text, but from a synthesis of other texts, in which self takes account of a native persona, in order to transform it (them) into self. What looks like a profoundly dangerous and irresponsible manoeuvre, starting out from TT(O) rather than the ST, is a way of ensuring that the status of the final TT is more properly equal and complementary to the status of the ST, that the TT can go out to meet the ST on terms of co-authorship; the TT does not refer back to the ST, but stands in *projective* collaboration with it. We should make it clear that a true representation of the synthesis of the TT(O)s is *not* as that shown in Figure 4.5 (where TTs 1, 2, 3 are

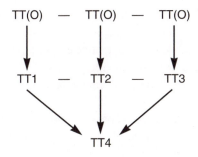

Figure 4.5

'translations', by the author of TT4, of the TT(0)s).

TTs 1, 2 and 3 are not exactly the *linguistic* raw material of TT4, both because they retain their autonomy as versions, and because TT4 does not emerge *directly* from them. TT4 is that mixture of lexis, syntax, tone, rhythm, register, which constitutes the textual integrity which TTs 1, 2 and 3 may not be able to guarantee. TTs 1, 2 and 3 activate a process of multiple assimilation, sketch out parameters, *engage* the translator at different textual points. But, importantly, this process of assimilation is also perspectival; the *other* of TTs 1, 2 and 3 is a way of envisaging the foreign poet in the native language at different times perhaps, and from different cultural positions. Translations exist in order to be superseded, but supersession should not mean erasure, elimination, so much as retranslation or active transformation. They become the necessary intertexts of a process which arrives at TT4 in order that the history of a national perception of a foreign poet may operate cumulatively and inclusively. TTs 1, 2 and 3 liberate TT4, make it possible, not only or principally by lending—although this may be a significant factor—but also by compelling it, by forcing the translator to appropriate his or her own translation.

Benjamin's Mallarméan account of translation is theoretically compelling; it theorizes the function of translation in a way which valorizes translation and gives it a central role in the negotiation of linguistic aspiration. The problem is that this theory exists at the level of the *idea* of translation. How might one theorize its practical application? What processes might it involve? This chapter attempts to produce an answer; not *the* answer, but a way of imagining translational conduct such that

Benjaminian theory might be justified.

Let us now move to our particular example: Baudelaire's 'La Cloche fêlée':

1.	Il est amer et doux, pendant les nuits d'hiver,	4+2+4+2
2.	D'écouter, près du feu qui palpite et qui fume	3+3+3+3
3.	Les souvenirs lointains lentement s'élever	4+2+3+3
4.	Au bruit des carillons qui chantent dans la brume.	2+4+2+4
5.	Bienheureuse la cloche au gosier vigoureux	3+3+3+3
6.	Qui, malgré sa vieillesse, alerte et bien portante,	1+5+2+4
7.	Jette fidèlement son cri religieux,	1+5+2+4
8.	Ainsi qu'un vieux soldat qui veille sous la tente!	(2+4)+2+4
9.	Moi, mon âme est fêlée, et lorsqu'en ses ennuis	3+3+(2+4)
10.	Elle veut de ses chants peupler l'air froid des nuits,	

$$3+3+2+4/3+3+2+2+2/3+3+4+2$$

11.	Il arrive souvent que sa voix affaiblie	3+3+3+3
12.	Semble le râle épais d'un blessé qu'on oublie	

$$1+5+3+3/4+2+3+3$$

13. Au bord d'un lac de sang, sous un grand tas de morts,

$$2+4+4+2/4+2+4+2$$

14. Et qui meurt, sans bouger, dans d'immenses efforts. 3+3+3+3

My first step in distancing myself from this ST has been to produce intralingual translations of other translations (see Appendix I). Now, after these try-outs of various language modes and writerly personae, I can essay my own text, knowing what tone I want to adopt, what lexis, what rhythms, what map of meaning:

The Cracked Bell

1. Winter evenings
2. A fire which can't
   make up its mind
3. whether to smoke or flame
4. and here I am
   listening

straining to hear

5.   vague recollections

coming up for air

slow-movingly

6.   Hear? Yes...in the chiming bells
7.   muffled by mist

sweet

and bitter.

8.   These bells
9.   may have seen better days
10. but their appetite for ringing
11. the faithful to religious offices
12. undiminished
13. tells of sound lungs
14. robust and ready vocal chords
15. like the lusty 'Who goes there?'
16. of a veteran
17. sentinel
18. clapper in a *tente conique.*

19. I too would
20. fill

the dark unpopulated chill

21. with ringing
22. just to lift my spirits
23. but find I cannot strike
24. out of a fissured

and enfeebled self

25. more than a jarring

croak

26. thick as you'd hear from the throat
27. of a wounded soldier

28. suffocating

        buried with the dead

29. dying

        by a pool of blood

30. straining hard and harder still

        for breath

31. forgotten

        and forgetting

32. still

Armed with this TT4 (or rather TT5, since I have 'translated' four TT(O)s), I need to relate back to the ST, and this I do by proposing my text as a companion to Baudelaire's, as the same topos wearing different clothes, half of a married couple. What remarks might usefully be made in a comparison of these poems?

Baudelaire's poem starts with the contradictory pair 'amer' and 'doux' in an order which does not correspond to the order of emotions in the poem but which has another structural justification: 'doux' occurs at the caesura, so that its vowel, /u/, receives the prominence it deserves as it initiates the string 'écouter'—'souvenirs'—'vigoureux'—'sous'—'souvent'—'oublie'—'sous'—'sans bouger'. This sequence is not only the sequence of remembering and forgetting, of health followed by paralysis, it also brings to our attention the reversal of the value of 'sous': 'veille sous'—the sentinel as bell-clapper (made explicit in my version), hidden, protected, but ready to strike—and 'qu'on oublie sous'—the soldier as smothered, obliterated, wiped from memory.

In my version, these two words ('amer' and 'doux') are the final note of the stanza, reversed so that their order prefigures the emotional 'narrative' and so that they create, together, a falling rhythm. I was much tempted by the formulation 'bitter and sweet', merely to sustain a choriambic pattern about which we shall have more to say in a moment, but decided against what would have produced a choriambic saturation of the final lines of the stanza. The /iː/ of 'sweet', picked up immediately by 'These' and 'seen', has a lull, before reappearing in 'enfeebled'. Not a strong suit. The acoustic elements of 'bitter', on the other hand, enjoy a foregrounding which those of 'amer' do not, and take us back to the opening line: 'Winter evenings' not only stands as a metaphor for a mind-state, but is also, and conversely, the phrase which subsumes all events within the poem and of which those events are metaphoric manifestations. It is also the assertion of /I/, and this particular note of 'bitter' encompasses, smothers the /i:/ of 'sweet' in 'evenings'. /I/ then becomes a presiding tonality, particularly in /Il/ ('fill', 'chill', 'still'), and in the participial /Iŋ/. In the second stanza, the /I/ family has an ironically or illusorily positive mien ('ringing', 'religious', undiminished', 'sentinel').

One could spend much time comparing sound worlds. Much attention has already been paid to acoustic patterning in 'La Cloche fêlée' (see Howarth and Walton 1971: 162–74; Lewis 1976; Chesters 1988), but it has tended to overlook that dimension of sound which registers the poem's profound concern with the interdependence of speaking and remembering, speaking and listening (which I have tried to make conspicuous by the repetition of 'straining': 'straining to hear', 'straining [...] for breath'), namely the interplay of voiced and unvoiced. The poet is as much the fire in the hearth as he is bell and soldier, and although the fire alternately smokes and flames, it never quite manages to emerge from the unvoiced, despite the presence of the nasal /m/:

> D'écouter, près du feu qui palpite et qui fume

> whether to smoke or flame[2]

The /f/ goes on to extend its range in 'fidèlement', 'fêlée', 'froid', 'affaiblie', 'efforts', or, in the English version, 'muffled', 'faithful', 'offices', 'fill', 'lift', 'find', 'fissured', 'enfeebled', 'suffocating', 'for breath', 'forgotten', 'forgetting'. But while the French text is more easily able to develop the voiced counterpart, /v/ ('hiver', 's'élever', 'vigoureux', 'vieillesse', 'vieux', 'veille', 'veut', 'arrive', 'voix'), the English version is thwarted on that line ('evenings', 'vocal', 'veteran') and makes more of /b/, which is also important in the French text, particularly in the second tercet. Obviously other voiced and unvoiced consonants are also active, and while the point of application of unvoiced and voiced is frequently loaded and tendentious, it is not always so: the oscillations between the two types of consonant are the way the poem breathes, and acts out the uncertainties of its own voice. One further observation should be made in relation to these patterns: if the fire is the poet, its /aI/ in the English text is 'I' and 'mind' and 'chiming' and 'appetite' and 'strike' and 'dying'.

The English text also picks up the connection between the mist m*uff*ling the bell-chimes and the s*uff*ocation of the soldier, while 'suffocating' distantly echoes 'unpopulated' (/ʌ/ and /eɪt/): to 'fill the dark unpopulated chill' is, in the end, to populate it with the dead.[3] Combinational echoes are also to be found in 'robust' + 'ready' = 'lusty', 'croak' + 'thick' = 'throat', and 'buried' + 'dead' = 'breath'. Resurrecting the past is breathing, and speaking and hearing the self; ringing the past is maintaining the faith, and generating community; forgetting is suffocating under the already forgotten.

Baudelaire's poem is, of course, a sonnet. The English version is a fixed form in free verse, a four-stanza form with a 7-11-7-7 configuration. The typographical lay-out indicates that the second stanza is a centre of confident and continuous discourse, itself gravitating around the twin centres of the monolexical lines 'undiminished' and 'sentinel', centres of sustained energy and alertness to hostile intrusion. The very fact that the English version is in free verse sets the poem in the self-engendering dynamic of improvisation, so that it must be read with an attention to unfolding rhythm rather than to any prior, predicted and predictive metrical structure. Unfolding rhythm registers the temperamental shifts, the notes of obsession, the psycho-physiological vicissitudes of the voice. Of course, regular verse itself allows some degree of improvisatory dynamic within the constraints of metre, no versification more so than French perhaps. But regular verse, by its very regularity, encourages the through-reading of lines, and an elevated style. The sustain pedal of metrical continuity in turn encourages those suspended and suspensive forms of syntax which remove the pressure of time and give one to believe that there is perhaps room for all to be said. The line of regular verse is a great justifier, is what allows 'normal' utterance to be rethought, to achieve an autonomy, a sense of irreversibilty, to become a law unto itself. In free verse, the line can be an instrument of the erosion of elevated style (*pace* Whitman *et compagnie*); it encourages the infiltrations of the paralinguistic, voice having to cope with the unpredictable, the unsupportive, the inimitable and newly discovered. Free verse's appropriacy to translation derives from its 'insistence' on the improvised, on the being-made, on the non-guaranteed and non-predictive; if translation is to make a space of creative and self-expressive spontaneity for itself, if it is to re-enter the language forest and speak out, as it were, from the centre of a language always to be made, reinvented, pushed further along the road of its own development, then perhaps free verse does offer in-built 'sympathies'.

About the rhythm of Baudelaire's poem, I do not wish to speak at any length. My notation of the rhythmic measures demonstrates what seems to me an increasing rhythmic uncertainty, more floating of accent, in the tercets. I should say that Lewis (1976: 9) differs from me in his reading of lines 1 (4+2+6), 5 (3+3+6), 8 (6+2+4), 9 (1+5+6), 11 (6+3+3), 13 (2+4+3+3!), and his options for what I see as ambiguous lines are

3+3+4+2 (line 10) and 1+5+3+3 (line 12). Lewis's favouring of hexasyllabic measures—twice (lines 8 and 9) where my secondary accents are only weak (indicated by bracketing of the hemistich)—is evidence of his perception of a slacker, less wrought-up voice, which I find difficult to discover, particularly in the second hemistich of line 5 and the first hemistich of line 11. Howarth and Walton favour a 4+2+2+4 reading of line 8 (1971: 169), which strikes me as improbable: the conventionally preposed monosyllabic adjective 'vieux' attracts attention (accentuation) neither by semantic/expressive virtue of its position, nor by virtue of its contrastive force—'vieillesse' has already been written into the comparison at line 6. And like Lewis, Walton and Howarth opt for a 1+5 reading of the first hemistich of line 9 (1971: 171); this seems to me to give unjustifiable prominence to the disjunctive pronoun; true, it has a contrastive function, but it does not merit the brashness of this kind of self-projection; its muted shame-facedness, its confessional nature, suggest accentual damping down; and under no circumstances should it be allowed to rob 'âme' of its accentuation—not only does 'âme' have much greater semantic weight, but it is equally contrastive ('cloche' > 'âme'). Otherwise one might argue that the poem engineers a gradual shift from a 2+4 hemistich to a 4+2 one, with 3+3 acting as relatively neutral constant to which the poem periodically returns. The 2+4 hemistich, with its pattern of expansion, enables its 2 to 'carry' into a 4, to establish itself, perhaps against the odds. The 4+2, on the other hand, closes down possibility, is a movement of rhythmic condemnation, where the 2 may seem to brand the 4; the 2's are frequently damning noun complements. A desire to let this latter hemistich establish itself unequivocally in the tercets would encourage me to prefer the 4+2 option for the first hemistich of line 12. And in the second hemistich of line 10, I would prefer the 2+2+2 or 4+2 configurations. The 4+2's in the first quatrain are either an adumbration of the 'grammar' of later 4+2's ('pendants les nuits d'hiver'), or moments of fragile consolation, too fragile, it transpires ('Il est amer et doux'; 'Les souvenirs lointains').

The English version starts with a confident, trochaic 'putting in place'. But this metre then reverses into a more intimate, less potent, rising rhythm, and a syncopation (juxtaposed stressed syllables) leads in the choriambic (/xx/) figure 'make up its mind', which is repeated in 'whether to smoke' before returning to iambic. Another syncopation 'and here I am/listening' heralds a third choriamb 'straining to hear', which, as previously, immediately produces a fourth, 'vague recollections', with an added feminine syllable (or adonic foot). At this point, two remarks should be made: first, the choriamb is a movement of brinkmanship, on the edge of decision or discovery, but suspended, so that no resolution can be generated out of it; secondly, 'vague recollections' lends itself equally to an iambic disposition, particularly if one reads directly on from 'straining to hear'. It is important, it seems to me, not only that the verse should cross back and forth between the rising and the falling, the iambic and the trochaic, as two frames of the same mind, but that the complex feet themselves should be transparent with those underlying duple feet—the choriamb is a perfect clash of the two, falling to rise, unable to 'make up its mind'. The trochaic shape of the second segment of line 5, promising an emergent clarity of definition, dissolves into a second paeon (×/××): 'slow-movingly'. This family of tetrasyllabic measures, the paeons, will have an important role to play later. But immediately a third syncopation, 'Hear? Yes…' introduces another choriamb, this time with added iamb— 'Yes…in the chiming bells'—which, for a third time generates another choriamb: 'muffled by mist'. We have already referred to the rhythmic possibilities of 'bitter and sweet', another choriamb, which I resisted so as to avoid a surfeit of choriambs. As it is, 'sweet and bitter' is at once trochaic and, because of its lineal disposition, an isolated strong syllable followed by an amphibrach, the first appearance of a foot which, like the paeons, will have a further part to play.

I will hasten over the second stanza, stopping only to say that its particular contribution to the unfolding rhythmic drama is the introduction of the extended choriamb, /×××/ (lines 10, 11, 18), and of the third paeon (××/×), 'like the lusty' (line 15). It should be noted that in these scansional remarks I feel able to move from a position in which measures, particularly complex measures, are identifiable because they are independent lineal segments, to one in which a complex foot, embedded in a longer sequence, is made distinctly perceptible by its nuclear function within the line; thus in lines 10 and 11, the extended choriambs 'appetite for ring-' and 'faithful to relig-' delineate the parameters of central semantic units. This seems to me symptomatic of a shift of emphasis in metricality wrought by free verse. Free verse throws questions of segmentation into the melting pot. Ultimately, neither the phrase nor the line/lineal segment has any necessary priority, and, consequently, rhythmic grouping is subject to an unstable criterial base. Free verse is neither unmetrical nor non-metrical; its metricity is a latitude, a field of variation created by a poem. This field is made up of the metres/metrical feet used, which delimit its parameters. Within the field, the metres/metrical feet metamorphose into each other and out of each other, create a multitude of relationships and kinds of dialogue.

This particular principle, if one can call it that, is pertinent again in the third stanza: in addition to the oscillation between iambic and trochaic patterns—an oscillation given special piquancy in line 20 by the isolation of 'fill', as if the trochaic were being expressly sundered in order to reveal its iambic (cf. line 7)—and in addition to the amphibrach at line 21 (echoing the final unit of line 7), we begin to feel, paralleling the ongoing tug-of-war between trochaic and iambic, a competitive vying between choriamb (/xx/) and third paeon (xx/x: 'an enfeebled ...'), which expresses itself in the adonic (/xx/x) feet:

> 24. out of a fissured
> 25. more than a jarring

We realize, too, that the ghost of the third paeon was already haunting some of the choriambic combinations in the first stanza:

> 5. vague recollections (adonic: /xx/x)
> 6. Yes...in the chiming bells (choriamb + iamb: /xx/x/)

In the final stanza, all these forces come together to synthesize doubt, equivocation, fragmentation. Amphibrach (x/x) links with third paeon (xx/x):

> 31. forgotten
>   and forgetting;

first paeon (/xxx) links with extended choriamb (/xxx/):

> 28. suffocating
>   buried with the dead;

choriamb gets caught between dactyl and anapaest: (/xx/xx/)

> 26. thick as you'd hear from the throat;

and embryonic anapaestic/iambic permutates into third paeon + recovered trochaic (xx/x/x):

> 27. of a wounded soldier.

This line, in its turn, is rhythmically echoed, if in slightly abbreviated form (xx/x/), by:

29.…

by a pool of blood

a line which, with the following, separates the trochaic fragment, 'dying', from the iambic one, 'for breath'. The poem ends on the stressed monosyllabic unit ('still'), which has an ancestry running from 'sweet' through 'fill' and 'croak'.

There are many senses, therefore, in which translation is here used to serve an enterprise which is not about translation, or is about translation only in a universalist project. What I give here is not a version of Baudelaire's 'La Cloche fêlée' to be used by a reader ignorant of French; my version does not offer itself to be judged by criteria of accuracy or faithfulness or linguistic equivalence. But I have, it should be said, taken care, in the choice of my source texts, to ensure that my version works within parameters set by an original. My version is a version which I do not wish to be read *as a translation*, but as a parallel or proximate version *derived from processes of translation* (though not, in this instance, interlingual ones). Translation in Benjamin's vision is not a service supplied to the unlearned, but something which a reader of Baudelaire finds it necessary to undertake in order to participate in the expanding life of his poems and in their linguistic/textual aspirations. This is not a translation, in short, in the sense that it does not fulfil George Steiner's dictum: 'The translator performs for others, at the price of dispersal and relative devaluation, a task no longer necessary or immediate to himself' (1975: 380). Here, there is no 'price of dispersal and relative devaluation', and the translator is undertaking something very necessary and immediate to himself, as a reader of the poet in question and as a *practising member* of the linguistic community. Translation does not stand outside literature, as a separate service unit.

The degree to which the process of translation itself can be varied may be much greater than we are inclined to think, as may be the order of events which go to comprise it. The model sequence presented in this chapter attempts to create a situation in which the reader's perception of a movement of convergence rather than divergence might be maximized. In fact, 'movement of convergence' is not an entirely accurate description, because what is sought is not convergence so much as intimate parallelism. In order that 'intimate parallelism' is not simply understood as 'equivalence', I have tried to reduce interlingual translation in favour of intralingual translation—my STs are not versions *I* have derived from the original. My starting point already stands aside from that original, is already a difference which I can then translate into a likeness of my vision of the materials. These, in their turn, will produce, hopefully, a free-standing version whose purpose is fruitfully to interact with the original.

What translation is, or can be, depends very much on our perception of its functioning, and our perception of its functioning depends, in turn, on our understanding of the translational process. At the moment, the evidence on which we base our grasp of the process is little better than anecdotal. It is hardly surprising, then, that the process has not been theorized. This absence of a theory of translational practice means that a large part of translation theory generally hangs in the air of its own invention, as a set of compelling ideas which cannot be brought to ground, enacted, demonstrated. If we are to make sense of the theories of the German Romantics and Walter Benjamin, if we are to salvage them from the decorative realms of quasi-philosophical speculation, then we must be able to describe the specific translational processes which might bring them about. I have tried to suggest one way of making the Benjaminian objective practicable, one version of the translational process which compels us to view the TT and its relation to the ST in a new light.

But an embarrassing question remains. If we proceed to put our parallel texts side by side, what is the *tertium quid*, what the TW, what the pure language? Must it remain something hypothesized, intuited, unrealized? Of course it must, since it is premissed on infinite development in time and space, a process both cumulative and encompassing. The real significance of the *tertium quid* is an attitudinal one: translation no longer serves contrastive linguistics, balance sheets of gain and loss, a linguistic ethos of competition, of the faithful and the free, no longer seeks to arrive at a handbook of characteristic problems and characteristic solutions. It removes the stigma of translation from translation; it looks upon the relationship between the TT and the ST not as contrastive but as combinatory, as a means of spanning space and time in a perpetually more fruitful and diverse series of relationships. The translator translates in order to become a participant in this enterprise, in order to contribute to textual survival and interaction.

5

Translation and Trans*form*ation

Two considerations introduced in the previous chapter are the basis of this one. First, the ST begets many possible translations, many possible versions of the translator's view of the ST. In other words, the ST frees the translator into a multitude of texts, the translator is as if provoked into, irritated into, self-proliferation, and into the challenges of self-synthesis, translation as self-portrait. The translator is a negotiator between these conflicting impulses: the impulse to multiply translations as manifestations of a range of critical (and creative) personae; and the impulse to produce a single translation as a version of a *self*, a translation which may be revised in its detail but which maintains the demands of its wholeness, of its continuities. In a sense, this negotiation is a reformulation of the free/faithful debate, but now centred in the translator's creative psyche rather than in questions of linguistic equivalence. Indeed, it is time to affirm that translation is not a linguistic matter so much as an existential one, and the translatability of an ST depends as much on an intertextual bridge, on the possiblity of a psychic continuity, as on the mechanics of language systems.

The second consideration relates to the (TW)/('tacit word') or 'third text'. It is possible to 'force' the ST into an admission of a (TW) merely by affirming, or instituting, *indirect* equivalences. That is to say that the ST, by virtue of not being *directly* translatable, naturally implies translation via a third party. The originating text (TW) says: 'Translate me by means appropriate to your own particular language'. However, a stringent *caveat* must be attached to this manoeuvre: an appropriate equivalent of the (TW) must not be confused with an appropriate equivalent of the ST.

One all too frequently encounters the argument that formal features of the ST can be transferred to the TT either by a process of *relocation* or by *alternative structures*, so that the overall effect of the ST will be maintained.[1] The misconception which underlies the strategy of relocation (of the same figure) is that the expressive force of the figure in question is something generalized and consistent, and therefore can be applied at any point in the TT with the same effect. But the figure of repetition, for example, cannot be said to mean in a general way; its potential meanings—emotional paralysis, constancy, obsession, tedium, determination, linguistic alienation—are multifarious, and which one of them is realized, and in what way, depends entirely on the specific verbal and structural context. Similarity of figure does not guarantee similarity of effect.[2]

The drawbacks of the alternative structure are twofold: first, the chances are that, unless alerted, the reader will make no connection between the ST feature and the TT's substitute; secondly, the appropriacy of the alternative structure is wholly dependent on our 'proper' interpretation of the device in the ST. Alistair Elliot, for example, explains his translation of Verlaine's 'Nevermore' (texts provided in Appendix II) in the following terms:

> Verlaine's poem rhymes AAAA (all feminine), then BBBB (all masculine), and the usual mingling of masculine and feminine rhymes only comes in the sextet. This is certainly a deliberate effect and presumably symbolizes the separateness of the two human figures at the beginning of their walk and their joining at some point during it. The effect can be pointed out in a note, but is it not better to refer to it indirectly, as the odd rhyme-scheme of my version tries to do?.
>
> (1993: 69)

Elliot has felt it necessary to supply us with the note which the note itself eschews, and not surprisingly: only a reader with a sixth sense would intuit, unaided, the connection between Verlaine's *aaaa/bbbb/ccb/dbd* and Elliot's *abba/cddc/eff/geg* (in half-rhymes). And what if his structural transposition is based on a false premise? Verlaine's *a* rhymes are *riches*, in /tɔn/, and are all, bar 'automne', concerned with sound: 'atone', 'monotone', 'détonne'.[3] Autumn is the season of the unmusical. As in other poems (e.g. 'Mon rêve familier'), the poet is in search of a music, and, more specifically, the music of a voice: /(t)ɔn/ becomes the first element of 'sonore' (line 9), where it combines with /ɔr/, itself an echo of line 8: 'sa voix d'or vivant'. The woman's voice is also 'douce' (/dus/), where /us/ is a mirror of /suvəniR/ and the poet's own /suRiR/. The *b* rhymes (masculine) are only *suffisantes*, in /vɑ̃/, and, apart from 'vent', are, not surprisingly, present participial ('rêvant', 'émouvant', 'vivant'); this particular note (/ɑ̃/) is struck again in the final masculine rhyme, 'dévotement'/'charmant', but is more immediately audible, in a countertonic position, in 'angélique', and as the accentuated vowel of 'blanche' in the trimetric line 11. But the sestet not only picks up the acoustic threads of the octave, it contributes its own: /i/ ('angélique', 'sourire discret', 'lui', 'réplique', 'bruit'). This sound-string fittingly culminates in the 'ou*i* qu*i* sort de lèvres bien-aimées'. In other words, the voice itself is produced by the combination of an unpromisingly tuneless autumn (first quatrain) and an initially uncommunicative couple. But it is a voice which, once created, operates as the source of tunefulness and profound communicativity. For this latter to resolve itself into a word, however, it first needs the insertion of /i/, the phoneme of confidently wordless communication ('sourire discret'). If this is the particular 'plot' which the poem pursues, then it is difficult to see how either Elliot's half-rhymes or his odd rhyme-scheme promote it.

Bearing in mind what we have already said about the paramountness of maintaining the TT's integrity as text, the search for alternative but equivalent structures might more usefully jettison the notion of equivalence as both an impediment and a mirage, and let the alternativity of the TT play itself out to its fullest extent. The most obvious way to achieve this is by opting for alternative ready-mades, fixed forms which, as it were, *compel* a textual integrity, and entail a change of approach to the ST's material radical enough to keep the dangerous lure of equivalence and relocation firmly at bay. There is a concomitant pair of prices to be paid, however: first, the ability of the Romance fixed forms to sustain poetic discourse at credible levels of gravity has not really been established: the virtuosity required to fulfil the structural demands of the form in question generate a self-consciousness, a meta-critical awareness in both poet and reader, which interposes itself between expression and its formulation, ironizing receptivity. The fixed forms, in their nineteenth-century revivals, were particularly associated with the ingenuities of *vers de société*, the ingenuities of epigram, amorous urbanity, and wry pastoralism. The second price is, then, condemnation to persona, with no option on self-expression. This may suit some. But, for others, little satisfaction is to be derived from the production of a successful rondeau, say, at the expense of a successful translation. The way to avoid both these prices is to extend the range of the fixed forms and, in doing so, to open their availability to unpre-empted lyric utterance. And the extension of the range of the fixed forms might be engineered by loosening their fixity, by experimentation in freer versions, consonant with their updating, a possibility we shall explore in our first example. More important still, perhaps, the process of translation itself provides the opportunity to put these forms under much greater expressive pressure, to oblige them to carry more emotional freight, and ultimately to test their capabilities, or to discover what moves are necessary if their flexibility is to be significantly increased. How well will a villanelle withstand the stresses and strains of a Baude-lairean sonnet? And what counter-claims will the villanelle wish to make on that sonnet, and will they be justified, and could they be enhancing?

Without further ado, I would like to offer a villanelle version of 'A une passante' (standard definition of an English villanelle: *A1bA2/abA1/ abA2/abA1/abA2/abA1A2*, where the capital letters denote refrain lines):

> La rue assourdissante autour de moi hurlait.
> Longue, mince, en grand deuil, douleur majestueuse,
> Une femme passa, d'une main fastueuse
> Soulevant, balançant le feston et l'ourlet;
>
> Agile et noble, avec sa jambe de statue.
> Moi, je buvais, crispé comme un extravagant,
> Dans son œil, ciel livide où germe l'ouragan,
> La douceur qui fascine et le plaisir qui tue.
>
> Un éclair…puis la nuit!—Fugitive beauté
> Dont le regard m'a fait soudainement renaître,
> Ne te verrai-je plus que dans l'éternité?
>
> Ailleurs, bien loin d'ici! trop tard! *jamais* peut-être!
> Car j'ignore où tu fuis, tu ne sais où je vais,
> O toi que j'eusse aimée, ô toi qui le savais!

> Her motion elastic, her furbelows Stygian—
> Marooned on a refuge, by the din of the street,
> My whole self convulsed as she passed callipygian,
>
> Her figure as svelte as her cadence was Phrygian
> And legs statuesque and galbous and fleet.
> Her motion elastic, her furbelows Stygian,
>
> An hypnotic *douceur* and Salome's religion
> Were locked in her look which I drank till replete;
> My whole self convulsed as she passed callipygian,

Her eyes full of storm and so hauntingly strygian.
Was she grieving *grande dame* or a whore on her beat,
Her motion elastic, her furbelows Stygian?

And then she was gone, slick-fast as a widgeon,
To beyond all beyond, to where none ever meet.
My whole self convulsed as she passed callipygian,

Too late, but she knew, this canny Parisian,
That love at last sight puts the city on heat,
Her motion elastic, her furbelows Stygian.
My whole self convulsed as she passed callipygian.

On what grounds has the initial choice, to transform this sonnet into a villanelle, been made? Well, there may be grounds for hoping for a potential improvement. This poem is one whose importance is owed substantially to its appearance in Benjamin's account of the poet (1973: 44–6, 124–5); and I have tried to incorporate this cultural fact, in my translation, by including the Benjaminian 'love at last sight'. It tells us about the street's hand in fashioning a creativity dependent on the nerves rather than the imagination ('crispé comme un extravagant'); it tells us about the city's eroticization of brief encounters; in the Baudelairean canon, it alerts us to the co-extensiveness of widow and streetwalker, the one accompanied by the empty space of loss and the possible aestheticization of co-suffering, the other accompanied by the empty space of possible transaction, and mutual degradation, the surgery of sex intensifying confinement in the here and now ('ennui'). But here is where the problems begin: the transition from widow to streetwalker (first stanza > second stanza) is covert, and left unconfronted, as the poet swings into the cliché of romanticized encounter as it is to be found in, say, Nerval's 'Une allée du Luxembourg' or Rilke's 'Begegnung in einer Kastanienallee'. Nor is the accompanying physical shift—from emphasis on gait (first stanza) to emphasis on eye/look (second stanza)—picked up or alluded to in the sestet. Nor does the sestet make any sense of the deconstruction of the sonnet by the urban environment: the street's opening one-line intrusion produces a discrepancy between syntactic units and development of the subject on the one hand, and verse-form on the other, at its most pointedly awkward in the trimetric fifth-line hangover from the first stanza. A comparison of lines 5 and 8 underlines a rhythmic and stylistic friction whose possibilities are not pursued. Additionally, one may feel that lines 10 and 11 have a certain hollow amplitude which, far from intensifying the sharp drama of the encounter, disperses its dynamic, undoes its complex specificity.[4] Opting for another form, then, may offer an opportunity to put these things 'right'—to better integrate prostitute and widow, sanctioned form and novelty, and to achieve greater tonal insistence, not to sacrifice troubling urban incident to rhetorical romantic convenience.

But more important still, this transformation allows us to test the capacities of a form to bear certain messages and modalities, or to discover their innate tendencies to take material in certain directions. This will never be an unprejudiced investigation, of course, because one has to make choices among other variables (rhyme, rhythm, etc.) which inevitably affect the outcome.

I should say immediately that what I felt the villanelle made necessary was the projection of the encounter, not, as in the sonnet, as a unique, once-and-for-all event, but as something repeated, habitual, as a kind of Muybridgean cinematic sequence, a series of frames slightly differentiated from each other, where the repetition itself takes the woman away, confirms her in an otherness. It is in this sense that I imagine the villanelle as something new, as a traditional Renaissance fixed form reborn as minimalist music, a kind of Nymanian experience designed to accompany the theatrical spectacularity of Greenaway cinema. For, after all, the villanelle is better able, perhaps, to convey that theatricality of the street which we associate with post-1860 urban writing and painting (Impressionism) than the sonnet. The sonnet has a dangerous gift for mythicization, while the villanelle, for its part, can imitate that patient historicization of musical process enacted by minimalism.

I have chosen an English villanelle, that is to say, the nineteen-line variety popularized by Joseph Boulmier (*Villanelles*, 1878) and based on the work of Jean Passerat (1534–1602) (and specifically Passerat's 'J'ay perdu ma tourterelle'). It is this stipulation of nineteen lines which makes the English version a fixed form, rather than a stanza-type as it is for the French.[5] But I have not taken up Passerat's heptasyllables—few English villanelles do—although I do take the calculated gamble of opening, as the French so often do, with a feminine rhyme, calculated because a saturation of feminine rhymes in English is likely to push verse towards doggerel, particularly if the feminine rhymes are all on the same sound. If anything, the gamble is increased by the rareness of the rhymes, partly a move suggested by the leonine rhyme 'majestueuse'/'fastueuse' of the ST's first quatrain, partly a response to Baudelaire's own comment: 'pourquoi tout poète qui ne sait au juste combien chaque mot comporte de rimes est incapable d'exprimer une idée quelconque' [why any poet who does not

99

know exactly how many rhymes each word has is incapable of expressing any idea whatsoever] (*OC*, I, 183). But the choice of rare words allows the lexicon to shift across a whole range of items, from the explicitly French ('*douceur*', '*grande dame*'), implicitly French ('svelte', 'strygian') and neo-implicitly French ('galbous') to crude English ('din', 'on heat'). This text also attempts, through the ongoing consistency of the form itself, to reconcile a lexicon which is 'historical' ('furbelow', 'replete'), 'Baudelairean' ('elastic', 'strygian', 'cadence'), anachronistic in terms of specific reference (the 'refuge', the traffic island made necessary by Haussmannization, has, as its date of first use in this sense, 1875. The word makes one think particularly of Caillebotte's *Un refuge, boulevard Haussmann* (1880)), and anachronistic in more general terms ('on her beat', 'slick-fast', 'canny').

These latter observations lead to two general reflections. The villanelle has a special historical appropriacy to 'A une passante'. Both the villanelle and the sonnet are forms which, in France, emerged in the sixteenth century, and the villanelle's rustic origins (from Italian *villanella*, a rustic song or dance, *villano*, a peasant) remind us that pastoral is essentially an urban dream; in Baudelaire, this pastoralism is, rather, an exoticism, evidenced in forms of urban ill-adaptedness, an ill-adaptedness which, paradoxically, finds expression in the quintessentially urban profession, prostitution:

> Il te fallait glaner ton souper dans nos fanges
> Et vendre le parfum de tes charmes étranges,
> L'œil pensif, et suivant, dans nos sales brouillards,
> Des cocotiers absents les fantômes épars!
>
> ('A une Malabaraise')

> Je pense à la négresse, amaigrie et phthisique,
> Piétinant dans la boue, et cherchant, l'œil hagard,
> Les cocotiers absents de la superbe Afrique
> Derrière la muraille immense du brouillard;
>
> ('Le Cygne')

The widow of 'A une passante' may parade all that is 'le dernier cri' in fabric, 'soulevée, balancée par la crinoline ou les jupons de mousseline empesée' [lifted, set swinging by crinoline or the petticoats of starched muslin] (II, 695), but the undulating, flexible rhythms of her gait announce something more tropical, more 'natively' harmonious, the very subject of her mourning perhaps, a loss which is presented to us as existentially isolating.[6] Then, and not surprisingly, occurs the sudden transformation into the streetwalker of the second stanza, the degradation of a 'sainte prostitution de l'âme' ('Les Foules') into a prostitution of the body. If the 'passante' has caused a rebirth in the poet, it is perhaps not so much a rekindling of sexual desire as a resurrected nativity, and the 'bien loin d'ici' of line 12 is not a temporal and spatial distance of the future, but rather of the past—'le vert paradis des amours enfantines' ('Moesta et errabunda'). Perhaps the two are not to be put apart: impatient sexuality is a longing for a paradisal past—'L'innocent paradis, plein de plaisirs furtifs'—and the only way in which that longing can embody itself.

But if I want to suggest that the rustic villanelle is, in a sense, buried in, and redeemable from, the urbane and cultivated sonnet, it also has, as we have seen, the consistency of surface which permits the cohabitation of heterogeneous items. One might argue that the villanelle can accommodate a postmodern fragmentation of tone, register, style, can operate as a patchwork of texts and intertexts, under cover of its trompe l'oeil consistency, calling on the intractable difficulties of its fixity to excuse a certain catholicity. The villanelle might then, as other fixed forms, become, ironically, the vehicle of a postmodern translational mode in which personae could be multiplied because held together by the overriding identity of the form itself.

One final reflection is called for. In the Introduction, we claimed that translation is not an intenser form of literary criticism, but is one of the few ways we have of making manifest what reading has released in us, not in the way of interpretation, so much as in the way of unbidden associations, memories, the desire to speak ourselves in a TT generated by the ST. Looking at this translation, we realize that translation has an option on anachronism, or achronism, in a way that literary criticism has not. Literary criticism tends to polarize itself between historicity and contemporaneity, either reconstituting the text in its context as best it can or assessing the work's significance in contemporary thinking. Of course, literary criticism can review reactions to a work as they have unfolded over the years, but this history cannot really be written into an interpretation, much less written *back* into the text itself. My TT contains references to the years following 1860, and has historical commentary ('love at last sight') assimilated as part of its own textuality. This can only happen, it is worth reiterating, because one text (ST) has become another *text*, has been reconstituted as an other text which makes available, by allusion, all that has taken place in the time that has elapsed between itself and the ST.

The villanelle tries to be true to itself by an appropriate translation of the sonnet's materials into an optimal response to its own formal demands.

I have borne in mind Pound's comment on Dowson's villanelles: 'the refrains are an emotional fact which the intellect, in the various gyrations of the poem, tries in vain and in vain to escape' (Pound 1954: 369n)—the refrain lines ineluctably call each other up, in a mutually intensifying oscillation, so that, even when the machine has finally stopped, a reflex, a set of muscular convulsions, must play itself out. Even the corpse is not at peace.[7]

I have also borne in mind Banville's general comment on the villanelle: 'On dirait une tresse formée de fils d'argent et d'or, que traverse un troisième fil, couleur de rose' [It is rather like a plait made of threads of silver and gold, interwoven with a third, rose-coloured thread] (1909, 215). The 'troisième fil' [third thread] is presumably the villanelle's *b* lines, and it is these which endow the form with its peculiar poignancy: in attempting to withstand the conspiracy, the foregoneness, of the *A/a* lines, they are likely only to aggravate their own vulnerability. Through their masculine rhymes, which normally and naturally will entail monosyllabic rhyme-words, these *b* lines try to maintain a certain clear-headedness, a certain unfussy and confrontational rationality. But again and again they are engulfed by the irresistible tide of refrain lines which cannot stop to heed them. The isolation, and glimpse of safety, in the 'marooning' and 'refuge' of line 2 are, then, only seeming; the *b* line is certainly cleaved to as a sanctuary, as the last resort of sanity. But even though it is a *b* line, the last, which attempts to generalize erotic capitulation to the city as a whole, it is also a *b* line—'Were locked in her look which I drank till replete'— which reveals the breaking down of the dykes, with a clarity of mind which is also that of the self-executioner.

If anything, the villanelle has, among the lesser fixed forms, shown itself to be the most adaptable. It had already shown itself capable of handling serious and metaphysical materials in the hands of Leconte de Lisle, and its relatively healthy survival in the twentieth century has depended on its continuing to explore its darker potentialities: one thinks particularly of Auden's 'If I could tell you', Dylan Thomas's 'Do not go gentle into that good night'[8] or Empson's 'Villanelle' and 'Missing Dates'. And American poets have, as Ronald McFarland points out (1982a; but see also McFarland 1982b and 1982c)), exploited the form to even greater advantage, and examples are to be found in the work of Sylvia Plath, Theodore Roethke, Richard Hugo, Barbara Lefcowitz, Marilyn Hacker, Gilbert Sorrentino. If Leconte de Lisle's lyricization of the villanelle is aided by structural idiosyncrasy, so these American poets, too, have loosened the form by introducing metrical variation, by exploiting enjambement, and by complicating the music of the rhymes. Philip Stevick and Barbara Lefcowitz have experimented with a prose villanelle, 'nineteen sentences written with the same pattern of repetition one finds in the conventional villanelle, but without rhyme' (Lefcowitz quoted by McFarland 1982a: 125). These experiments owe something perhaps to Ezra Pound's 'Villanelle: The Psychological Hour' of 1915.

Many, like Ruthven, would like to argue that Pound's 'The Psychological Hour' 'is a villanelle in name only' (1969: 242). But, at the very least, Pound's poem indicates what the liberation of fixed forms might mean, and what kinds of spectral existence they might lead. First, Pound's text is evidently an unstable one: the 1952 *Personae* has a stanza-ending after 'the rain, the wandering buses', where the 1959 *Selected Poems*, edited by Eliot, has none. On the strength of the first printing in *Poetry* (vol. 7, 1915), and of the first, unabridged *Lustra* (London, Elkin Mathews, 1916), one must opt for the stanza-break. There are also variations in punctuation, after the two appearances of the line '*Beauty is so rare a thing*'. In *Poetry*, there are *points de suspension* in both cases; in *Personae*, a full-stop and no punctuation; in *Selected Poems* and the 1916 *Lustra*, full-stops in both cases. Another problem is the treatment of indented margins. In most instances, one feels that these signal a caesura rather than the beginning of a new line, but in the poem's second section such an interpretation is evidently inappropriate. To create a liberated fixed form is to create an unfixed text, a text no longer able to call upon the prefabricated authority of its givenness. Conversely, we may feel that we are reading a free-verse text in which the fixed form is an embedded allusion, a distant formal modality. One might argue that Pound's poem formally dramatizes the loss, or memory, of that authority: the psychological hour, the hour outside time, 'between the night and the morning', is the hour, if we trace this allusion back to its context in Yeats's 'The People' (see Ruthven 1969: 243), when a man loses his reputation, or, as here, when a poet loses confidence in his own powers. What relates the treatment of this theme to the villanelle are the triadic structures—the poem is in three parts, the middle one being bracketed, parenthetic, in the way that a *b* line might be, the majority of the stanzas are tercets—and the intermittent appearance of refrains. This villanelle exists only in its 'psychological hour', in an indeterminate state between being and non-being.

My own free-verse villanelle version of 'A une passante' is not so extreme:

1. The street. Pandemonium. Hell let loose in the ear.
2. Tall and slim and regal,

all in black, a woman grieving
3.   What loss? Her cultured hand

raises her dress's hem.

4.   My dazed eyes will not let

her go, cling
5.   To *her* eyes, pale with a coming storm
6.   Which breaks. The street crashes round me.

7.   What did I see? Of course the tenderness

which holds you very still
8.   And the headlong suicides of the flesh.
9.   Her hand reveals a lithe, well-moulded leg.

10. Then she was gone. Nowhere to be seen.
11. Yet I've been jolted

back to life.
12. Somewhere the traffic rumbles on and on.

13. Missed trains, missed friends,

and other chances missed.
14. These little pains disturb,

whip up the blood,
15. And still the street-noise dins inside my head
16. And still her hand lifts up her swinging hem.

This abbreviated, sixteen-line villanelle uses topic as its refrain principle, rather than the textually repeated: *A1* is Baudelaire's first line explored, the changing ways the street strikes the poet's ear, and *A2* Baudelaire's fourth and fifth lines, but here tracing variations of focus and response. This is a rhymeless version, apart from the assonant /ɛ/ on the *A2* lines, echoed, complicated in the 'flesh' of line 8 (a *b* line) and the 'tenderness' at the caesura of line 7. The relative insistence of /ɛ/ in this central stanza marks this as a point of fixation, of being 'held still'. The choice of the topics for *A1* and *A2* is designed to enact the poet's attempt to transform a set of aural pressures and disorders into an exclusivity of the eye, a concentration which wills a revelation. This revelation may sound sexual, and is, but it is also that to which we have already referred, a nativity of the body, a primal harmonious dynamic. But this is the dynamic of the streetwalker, can only be born and lost in a dialectical relationship with the street itself; and correspondingly, the optical therapy, the stillness of optical fixation, associated also with tenderness, cannot but exist in counterpoint to the torment of the other senses, the tireless aural suicides. In a version like this, the separation of functions between the *A/a* lines and the *b* lines will not be so vivid, both operating as part of the same continuum. The *b* lines still have a certain distinctive ability to see clearly, to bring things home; and the 'refrain' lines have not, for all the variation in their formulation, lost their obsessiveness, which I have not scrupled to underline with the 'still' of the final lines. But the greater feathering together of the two 'rhymes' helps voice to maintain itself as voice, to sustain a tonal continuity across the relative syntactic independence of *A1* and *A2*.

This syntactic independence of *A1* and *A2*, warranted, if not justified, by the independence of 'La rue assourdissante autour de moi hurlait' and 'Agile et noble, avec sa jambe de statue', reflects the general independence of refrain lines in the Romance fixed forms. It is the separation of the fifth line of each of the stanzas of 'Le Goût du néant', both syntactically and typographically, and the fact that it is built on two rhymes only (/dœR/ and /yt(ə)/), each alternating as the stanza's leading rhyme, which suggest a fixed-form treatment in translation. And the shape of the five-line stanza, *abbaa*, makes one naturally think of the rondel, and particularly of its final quintet:

> Morne esprit, autrefois amoureux de la lutte,
> L'Espoir, dont l'éperon attisait ton ardeur,
> Ne veux plus t'enfourcher! Couche-toi sans pudeur,
> Vieux cheval dont le pied à chaque obstacle bute.
>
> Résigne-toi, mon cœur; dors ton sommeil de brute.
>
> Esprit vaincu, fourbu! Pour toi, vieux maraudeur,
> L'amour n'a plus de goût, non plus que la dispute;
> Adieu donc, chants du cuivre et soupirs de la flûte!
> Plaisirs, ne tentez plus un cœur sombre et boudeur!
>
> Le Printemps adorable a perdu son odeur!
>
> Et le Temps m'engloutit minute par minute,
> Comme la neige immense un corps pris de roideur;
> Je contemple d'en haut le globe en sa rondeur
> Et je n'y cherche plus l'abri d'une cahute.
>
> Avalanche, veux-tu m'emporter dans ta chute?

'Rondel', the early form of 'rondeau', is used in modern prosodic parlance to designate those types of rondeau current before 1500, and to distinguish these from the 'modern' rondeau, which came into being in the sixteenth century, and was revived in the seventeenth century by Vincent Voiture. The rondel standardized by Banville and other nineteenth-century poets, such as Maurice Rollinat and Albert Giraud, derives from the *rondeaux quatrains*, with abbreviated refrain, of Charles d'Orléans, and has the structure *ABba/abAB/abbaA* (where the capital letters denote refrain lines). This structure was a dominant one in Charles's work while he was in England (1415–1440), though on his return to France he also came to favour a twelve-line form (*ABba/abA/abbaA*) (see Fox 1969: 119–20). Although there are later 'respectable' variations on the thirteen-line model to point to—Corbière's *Rondels pour après* (1873), three of Mallarmé's four rondels, Rollinat's experiments in *Paysages et paysans* (1899)—my version of 'Le Goût du néant' does not noticeably deviate:

1.   Silent the bugle-calls and fluted sighs,
2.   At last by avalanches swept away.
3.   Once, gloomy spirit, you enjoyed the fray,
4.   Now hope, your spur, looks elsewhere for its rides.

5.   Love has, for sullen kill-joys, lost its spice,
6.   For broken-winded nags and old roués
7.   Deaf to the bugle-calls and fluted sighs,
8.   To be by avalanches swept away.

9.   Second by drowning second, the swell of time
10.   Engulfs my carcase in its whirling spray;
11.   From out in space I view this ball of clay
12.   And find no comfort in a place to hide.
13.   Quite gone, the bugle-calls and fluted sighs.

I say 'noticeably deviate' because in one area of its operation, rhyme, the thirteen-line rondel is less sure of itself. Charles d'Orléans, as other poets of his age, had not felt bound by any principle of the alternation of rhyming gender, and Banville, in his turn, perpetuated a somewhat cavalier attitude to the alternation of masculine and feminine rhymes. Eighteen of his twenty-four rondels 'composés à la manière de Charles d'Orléans' (1875) are of mixed gender, but three are exclusively masculine and three exclusively feminine. Two of Giraud's rondels are single-gender (feminine), as are thirteen of Rollinat's (ten feminine). In one sense, all my rhymes are masculine (on stressed syllables alone), but in another sense they are mixed: in French, masculine rhymes will tend to coincide with open syllables (consonant + vowel), while feminine will coincide with closed (vc + mute e); my *B/b* rhymes are open, in /eI/, while the assonant *A/a* rhymes (/aI/ + c) are closed, except for *A* itself. By this mechanism I have attempted to achieve three effects: the gendering of the bugle-call/fray topos as masculine, and the fluted sigh/love topos as feminine; the sense, nonetheless, of a close collusion between *A* and *B* refrains (both cv); and the suspicion of a drift to the masculine, where the masculine is the syllable without that closure which would prevent waste of sound and dispersal of energy.

One might argue that this last effect would have been heightened had I adopted the form of the rondel favoured by the English, the fourteen-line form in which the refrain is repeated in its entirety, *A* and *B*, at its close; in my version this would have necessitated a slight adaptation in line 13:

13   If no more bugle-calls and fluted sighs,
14   Let's be by avalanches swept away.

My objections to this manoeuvre are essentially threefold. First, it tends to generate a refrain even more conscious of its status as ritual utterance, as the presiding source and justification of the poem, to which too much formal variety has to be sacrificed. It should be added that the English version usually entails the adoption of alternating rhymes as the prevalent structure—thus *ABab/abBA/ababAB*. This greater structural continuity and single-mindedness leads to my second objection: the French rondel has a curious oblique relationship with the sonnet, in that something like a 'turn' , or *volta*, or *bascule*, is frequent after the eighth line, generating a different kind of expressive energy, or tonality, in the final five lines. In both the English and French versions, the 'octave' begins and ends with the refrain (its second appearance inverted in the English model); this self-completion helps to establish the autonomy of the eight lines. The French model then embarks upon a final movement which does not end in reiteration and confirmation, as the English model does, but may be a journey to the heart of darkness, a deepening of experience. The tripartite structure of 'Le Goût du néant'—stanza I: no more appetite for conflict (political? philosophical? military?) ('chants du cuivre'); stanza II: no more appetite for love ('soupirs de la flûte'); stanza III: existential self-evaluation—seems to me to be better suited to reformulation in the three stanzas of the French rondel, not least because it can structurally mark the change of psychological and lyrical temper which occurs after the first two stanzas, underlined by the shift from second-person critical, not to say derisive, self-address to a disabused first-person declarative mode. And this leads on to my third objection: the lyric thrust of the third stanza is crucially dependent on the jettisoning of the refrain's second line. Henri Morier describes the function of the refrain in the French rondel thus:

> On devine les condition requises au rondel pour sa pleine réussite: 1° les deux vers du refrain doivent être poétiquement assez liés pour que le premier appelle ou suggère le second; 2° le second doit néanmoins pouvoir être syntaxiquement détaché; 3° le contenu sensible du vers mental ou sous-entendu doit offrir une substance sensuelle ou savoureuse, susceptible de se dissoudre lentement.
>
> (1975: 931)
>
> [One can guess what conditions the rondel must fulfil if it is fully to succeed: 1. the two lines of the refrain must be sufficiently linked poetically for the first to summon or suggest the second; 2. the second, nonetheless, must be syntactically detachable; 3. the recuperable content of the mental or implied line must have a sensual substance, or a substance to be savoured, and likely to dissolve slowly.]

Is the absent *B* line as inexorably conjured up as it is manfully suppressed? In 'Le Goût du néant', does the regretted loss manage to outweigh the urge for self-annihilation? Or do the dramatics of the wish for oblivion suddenly fall away to reveal the banality, the 'average' pathos, of a premature no-hoper? Curiously, the repetition of the *B* line at the end would strike a dissonant note, would make too stentorian, too throw-away, an ending, and mask the suddenly more intimate operation of the *A* line, both self-consoling and self-justifying, after the grander metaphysics.

If 'Le Goût du néant' naturally offers itself as a candidate for transformation into a rondel, one might expect other poems with five-line stanzas, and particularly those in which the fifth line repeats the first, either exactly—'Le Balcon', 'Moesta et errabunda', 'Réversibilité', 'Lesbos'—or with variation—'L'Irréparable', 'Le Monstre'—to constitute potential fixed-form material, although their length is a significant obstacle. I have tried rendering 'Le Balcon' (text supplied in Appendix II) as a rondeau, reducing its thirty lines to thirteen (*aabba/aabR/aabbaR*, where *R* stands for *rentrement*, the special term for the rondeau's refrain, which consists of the first word(-sound) or words(-sounds) of the first line; I do not count the *rentrement* as a line):

The Balcony

Mother of memories, mistress of pleasure,
Evening embraces, the enfolding of leisure,
Coals burning bright in the darkening sky,
Rose-misted balconies, silk of your thigh
And words that survive, in a space beyond measure.

The weight of your breasts is your heart's subtle pressure,
Your breath has more venom when its savour is fresher,
The smell of your blood is as black as the sky,
                      Smothering memories.

The dark makes me guess at the site of the treasure,
As I curl up again in the lap of your pleasure.
Why look elsewhere for the pearl that's close by?
Vows, perfumes and kisses, wherever they lie,
May well be submerged at depths we can't measure,
                    Salvaging memories.

To begin with, 'rondeau' was the generical term for all three forms (rondeau, rondel, triolet) originating in dance rounds with singing accompaniment, in which the refrain was sung by the chorus—the general body of dancers—and the variable section by the dance leader. Although dance and music disappeared in the fourteenth century, as did the distinction between soloist and chorus, I have tried to suggest the movement of song lyrics; there is, as a result, some drift towards vulgarization, which the poem may deserve. I have taken liberties with the text designed to point up the occlusion of memory by a sensuality which draws one to the present, the immediate, the short-term, and to focus this threat in the second stanza. Accordingly, the final stanza has an opportunistic sexual cynicism which is not (so) present in Baudelaire's final two stanzas. Instead of a sensual surface beckoning one to depths, instead of erotic contact generalizing itself in spiritual beatitude ('douceur', 'beauté', 'charme', 'soleils rajeunis'), the contrary movement occurs: the poet, attempting to dive into the depths of an accumulated, therapeutic experience, to find solace, is thwarted, buoyed up, kept on the surface, by the invitations and opportunities of the flesh.

The modern form of the rondeau, as we have it here, is the one popularized by Banville and derives from the practice of Voiture. The *rentrement*, like the shortened final refrain of the rondel, is probably the result of copyists' habits of abbreviation, and not surprisingly, given that it is a rhymeless element among forms which seem to exist expressly for their rhymes, became the rondeau's distinguishing expressive resource. But Banville's account of the *rentrement*, as 'plus et moins qu'un vers, car il joue dans l'ensemble du Rondeau le rôle capital. Il en est à la fois le sujet, la raison d'être et le moyen d'expression' [more and less than a line, for it plays the principal role in the Rondeau's overall effect. It is, at once, the Rondeau's subject, its *raison d'être* and its means of expression] (1909 [1872]: 207) makes it the focus of more attention than it can bear. And this pressure accounts for the fact that punning was an integral part of the aesthetics of the *rentrement*:

> Le refrain ne compte pas comme vers; il ne rime pas avec le reste, et rien n'est plus piquant que de lui faire répéter les premiers mots de la pièce avec une acception différente, ou même de les rappeler seulement par une identité de son formant calembour.
>
> (Dorchain 1933: 367)
> [The refrain does not count as a line; it does not rhyme with the rest, and nothing is more piquant than to make it repeat the first words of the poem with a different meaning, or even to recall them merely by an acoustic similarity, in a pun.]

This way of approaching the rondeau seems fraught with danger, condemning it to flippancy and arch ingenuity, asking it to over-exploit a phrase or phonemic sequence which is quickly exhausted. Much better to imagine the *rentrement* as an echo, beyond the pale of the text, reminding the reader of unassimilable truths. In my version of 'Le Balcon', I have nodded in the direction of pun, but have tried to make of the *rentrement* something marginalized, something like a confession that the poem does not wish to make, something like the comment of a bystander beyond the reach of illusion.

In a rendering of 'Bien loin d'ici', a variety of 'sonnet renversé' on two rhymes, I have pushed the *rentrement* unequivocally towards the pun, but tried to maintain its relative marginality:

> C'est ici la case sacrée
> Où cette fille très parée,
> Tranquille et toujours préparée,
>
> D'une main éventant ses seins,
> Et son coude dans les coussins,

Écoute pleurer les bassins:

C'est la chambre de Dorothée.
—La brise et l'eau chantent au loin
Leur chanson de sanglots heurtée
Pour bercer cette enfant gâtée.

Du haut en bas, avec grand soin,
Sa peau délicate est frottée
D'huile odorante et de benjoin.
—Des fleurs se pâment dans un coin.

A Long Way From Here

Flowers swooning in a corner. It's the hut
               (A sacred place!)
Where this girl, over-bangled but
Serene and always at her best,
Using an idle hand to fan her breasts,
Listens to water dripping in the butt.

Here's where our Dorothy can strut
Her stuff, while the distant sob-song, whole, uncut,
Of breeze and water lulls to rest,
             With 'Flowers swooning',

This spoilt child, whose skin's a glut
Of aromatic oils, including coconut
And benjamin (or benzoin), caressed
Into every last pore. With that, she's dressed,
As the cat tucks into sly-filched halibut
             aux fleurs qui se pâment.

I have written about the formal intricacies of Baudelaire's original elsewhere (1980: 178–80) and about its mixture of mockery and compassion. I have chosen the last line as the *rentrement*, largely on the strength of the letter of 29 March 1866, addressed by Baudelaire to Catulle Mendès on receipt of the proofs for *Le Parnasse contemporain*, in which the poem appeared:

Le dernier vers de la pièce intitulée: *Bien loin d'ici* doit être précédé d'un tiret (—), pour lui donner une forme d'isolement, de distraction. (*Correspondance*, II, 630)

[The final line of the poem entitled *Bien loin d'ici* should be preceded by a dash (—), to isolate it, to make it more abstracted.]

This function seems to me to be echoed by the rondeau's *rentrement*. I have increased what is condescending and derisive in Baudelaire's poem, and used the swooning flowers as a subversive taunt, as something Dorothy is not allowed to forget; these flowers, looking for a way of usefully filling their time, become the title of a romantic song, or the accompaniment with which the cat eats the fish.

My general intention here has been to create a tropical and downmarket reminiscence of Manet's *Olympia* (1863). Although Dorothy is without a maid, she has Olympia's flowers (but what kind of tribute?) and, as the translator's gift, her cat, whose role in the household is, however, less clearly defined. I have depastoralized Baudelaire's 'Écoute pleurer les bassins', supposing that Baudelaire is already gilding the lily. Pichois calls the structure of the sonnet 'aussi libertine que le sujet' [as dissolute as the subject] (*OC*, I, 1119), and I have tried to convey something of the 'esprit libertin', or the simply careless and disrespectful, in my treatment of an underlying iambic tetrameter (lines 2, 3, 6 and 8), whose syllabic quantities increasingly err: the overall configuration of syllabic quantities—excluding the two standard *rentrements* and the false one ('(A sacred place!)')—runs 11.8.8.10.10./8.11.8./7.12.10.10.11.

On the whole, I have in these transformative exercises, maintained the shape of the ST's arguments, even if these latter have been subjected to some local distortions. I have not been systematically pursuing that translational policy of 'extension' promoted by Frederic Will:

Translation can be considered an extension of an original work. I mean by extension something entirely different from translation as variation or imitation (in Robert Lowell's sense), in which latitude is provided for interpretation. (Extension and interpretation are very different kinds of metaphor for the work done in translation). The notion of interpretation flirts with returning us to the duller aspects of equivalence, its too open sense of balancing counters. I mean at this point to consider translation as a continuation of the impulse latent in an original.

(1993: 8)

It is true that I have developed hints which, I believe, are given by the texts I have translated. But my overall design is not dictated by the notion of extension, so much as of negotiation. I have not chosen the fixed forms I have chosen because I felt that the Baudelairean texts were somehow struggling, but too tentatively, to become them, that I was merely completing a process which is latent in the text, realizing a formal ambition that the poem has. True, there are elements of refrain to be found, and rhyme-schemes reduced to two rhymes. But these are certainly not sufficient to justify claims of having 'extended' Baudelaire. I have negotiated with him on behalf of the forms I have sought to represent. Certainly, I have chosen these forms in the belief that some fruitful accommodation could be arrived at, and, arrogantly perhaps, I have believed that the benefit might be mutual: that the fixed forms might learn new uses, might return to circulation, thanks to handling Baudelairean material, and that Baudelairean material might, in the reconfigurations offered by fixed forms, discover unexploited expressive resources in themselves, be located in their historical contexts differently, marshal their forces in more economical ways. This has inevitably entailed my omitting certain elements and adding others: the 'thigh' in line 4 of 'The Balcony', for example, is designed to introduce that directness of erotic contact which will threaten and supersede the pervasive generalities and pluralities of spiritual solace; while without the cat in 'A Long Way From Here', the Olympia connection might be too shadowy.

It may then seem strange to resist the clear indication of the presence of the pantoum in 'Harmonie du soir', particularly as it strikes an historically remarkable note. Pichois draws our attention to the publication of the first French pantoum by Charles Asselineau in 1850 (*OC*, I, 920);[9] Banville claimed his 'Monselet d'automne' (dated September 1856, published in *Odes funambulesques*, 1857) to be the second French example; 'Harmonie du soir' was first published on 20 April 1857 (*La Revue française*). The most celebrated pantoums of this period, Leconte de Lisle's chiefly octosyllabic 'Pantoums malais', were published only in 1882 (and afterwards in *Poèmes tragiques*, 1884). In this Malay verse-form, composed of quatrains in alternating rhyme, the second and fourth line of each stanza form the first and third lines of the stanza following, there being no limit to the number of quatrains. To draw the poem to a close, the fourth line of the final stanza repeats the first line of the opening stanza.[10] I find Pichois's comment on 'Harmonie du soir'—'Pantoum, ont prétendu certains. Mais pantoum libertin [...]' [Pantoum, some have claimed. But undisciplined pantoum (...)] (*OC*, I, 919)—unjustifiably disparaging. It is true that Baudelaire uses only two rhyme-sounds (no such constraint applies to the pantoum), and *rimes embrassées* rather than the expected *rimes croisées*; it is also true that none of the lines of his first stanza is taken up in the last. But Baudelaire observes the pattern of repetitions and, more unusually, incorporates that convention of pantoums, insisted on Banville (1909: 243–8), whereby each pair of lines of the quatrain (i.e. first and second, third and fourth) pursues, through the length of the poem, a different thematic thread:[11] the first two lines of each stanza are devoted to the vicissitudes of the heart, while lines three and four trace the fortunes of the dying light, the poem's final line reaching across into the world of the heart.[12] This feature is the more surprising in that late nineteenth-century practitioners of the pantoum tended to treat it rather carelessly and draw their effects from the form's repetitiousness alone.

Harmonie du soir

1. Voici venir les temps où vibrant sur sa tige
2. Chaque fleur s'évapore ainsi qu'un encensoir;
3. Les sons et les parfums tournent dans l'air du soir;
4. Valse mélancolique et langoureux vertige!

5. Chaque fleur s'évapore ainsi qu'un encensoir;
6. Le violon frémit comme un cœur qu'on afflige;
7. Valse mélancolique et langoureux vertige!
8. Le ciel est triste et beau comme un grand reposoir.

9. Le violon frémit comme un cœur qu'on afflige,
10. Un cœur tendre, qui hait le néant vaste et noir!
11. Le ciel est triste et beau comme un grand reposoir;
12. Le soleil s'est noyé dans son sang qui se fige.

13. Un cœur tendre, qui hait le néant vaste et noir,
14. Du passé lumineux recueille tout vestige!
15. Le soleil s'est noyé dans son sang qui se fige.....
16. Ton souvenir en moi luit comme un ostensoir!

A crucial indicator of Baudelaire's formal intentions is to be found, perhaps, in the punctuation of his penultimate line. In *La Revue française* (1857), this ends with a semi-colon followed by a dash, as if Baudelaire were caught in a dilemma. Does line 15 lead directly into line 16, as two clauses of the same sentence, as coterminous experiences (semi-colon)? Or do these two lines pull apart from each other, in a relationship of tension, so that line 16 seems to be a breaking free from, a transcendence of, line 15? In the 1857 edition of *Les Fleurs du mal*, there is only the semi-colon; the two lines seem to share a single isotopic concern, and to occupy the same semantic plane. The 1861 edition, on the other hand, has *points de suspension* (but why five rather than the customary three?), which not only allow the final line to float free and to attach itself to the heart theme, but also increase its finality, its ability to act as a destination, the attainment of a light that never dies. Conversely, the *points de suspension* at the end of line 15 imply the infinitely self-reiterating gestures of time at evening, despite the immobilization and definitive atrophy insinuated by 'se fige'. In preparing my own version, I looked for a form which, like the pantoum, was stanzaic rather than fixed, and had the same principle of *perpetuum mobile* built into it, but which would give me greater freedom in structural handling and allow me to be just as equivocal about endings. Inevitably I found terza rima:

Evening Harmony

1. Like censers, flowers give up their fragrant ghosts.
2. Eddies of sound and perfume stir the air
3. At evening; and like a monstrance host

4. Your memory shines in me. So I lay bare
5. A heart vibrating like a tautened string,
6. A heart abominating bleak despair,

7. Which hoards from distant years their everything,
8. Their every trace of luminous largesse.
9. The sky's a makeshift altar, saddening,

10. Its rich sun drowning, drowned, the blood congealing.

11. Slow-wheeling waltz and giddy heaviness.

As in the pantoum, terza rima's concatenated rhymes give it a powerful forward momentum, an inexorability difficult to withstand. It may seem that things are being taken away from themselves, taken from a point of inner identity, singleness (the middle line), to an outwardness which both doubles and disperses (outer lines following). At the same time, each of these movements outwards reveals a new inwardness. Terza rima balances on the very cusp of time lost and time regained, time regained within time lost, losing as an inevitable consequence of regaining. But this verse-form, by its very impetus, creates difficulties of closure. The pantoum, as we have seen, comes back on itself, elegantly reversing the mechanisms of propulsion: instead of a second and fourth line becoming a first and third line, first (and third) line(s) become(s) fourth (and second) line(s). And as this closure is brought about, so the third and first lines (rhymes) of the first stanza, which, to begin with, looked like orphans, without parentage, themselves become parents of the final stanza and find their repetitional function. Terza rima is altogether untidier. The standard mode for completing a sequence of terza rima stanzas is recourse to a single final line which rhymes with the inner line of the tercet preceding it, yzy/ z. This final line can look extremely awkward, can seem to have all the desperation of a guillotine abruptly resorted to, or all the *invraisemblance* of a *deus ex machina*. And its braking power often depends a great deal, too much perhaps, on the resonance of its image or the lapidariness of its formulation. Looked at positively, however, this single line can halt the processes of inwardness > outwardness, time regained > time lost. The final line stabilizes the inner line of the final tercet, marks it, refuses its dispersal. In my version, the fragile traces of 'luminous largesse' are given substance, arrested in presence, by the rhyming 'heaviness'. But the ending is complicated by another single line, which relates to the larger structural arrangements of the piece.

Resorting more than previously to the pliability and moveability of 'refrain' lines, which in terza rima, of course, cease being repeated, I have shifted the consolation of Baudelaire's last line to lines 3–4, and by slinging it between 'l'air du soir' and 'un cœur qu'on afflige', I have tried to construct an immediate bridge between the two thematic threads. Roughly speaking, I have placed the concerns of the heart at the centre of the poem, flanking it before and after with the dying evening (this is not entirely accurate since the first line, to be exact, belongs to the heart thread). In this way I have tried to suggest the threat of an engulfment—memory, and the heart which abominates oblivion, are besieged by the rising tide of moribundity. What is more, I have created a temporary 'figement' of the /Iŋ/ rhymes and an alternative mode of ending—yzy/y—whereby, by sheer insistence and incontrovertibility, the y rhyme works to erase any trace of z, to break its will to survive. In the event, this alternative ending turns out to be a false one, a corruption of the terza rima structure. The 'true' incumbent, z, comes to confirm its divine right.

The only fly left in the ointment is the fact that this second final line— 'Valse mélancolique et langoureux vertige!'—belongs to the topos of the setting sun. The circularity of the waltz implies a suspension of animation, endorsed by ideas of slowness and lassitude, a running down of energy, a loss of consciousness. But, equally, the line may present a pair of oxymoronic collocations where the light-headed animation of 'waltz' and 'giddy' try to pull 'slow-wheeling' and 'heaviness' out of their torpor. These ambiguities remain to unsettle the poem's dearly bought repose.

If we return to our point of departure, to what we said in the opening paragraph about the tension between persona and self activated by translation, it might seem that, in undertaking fixed-form translations of certain Baudelairean poems, we have cut off our nose to spite our face. Given that the central components of poetic persona are register, tone, genre, form, we have apparently, in locking our versions into fixed forms, deprived Baudelaire of his voice, but necessarily and perversely at the expense of our own. Put another way, we have subjected Baudelaire to the kind of formal manhandling which, by virtue of the very conspicuousness of the form chosen, and of the way in which this formal interference reflects back on, makes self-conscious, the formality of the ST, increases the metatextuality of both ST and TT, and thus seems to condemn both poet and translator to persona existence. Ultimately, I hope, this fear has proved unfounded, largely because forms themselves need to find their way back to textuality, to 'first-hand' expressive capacity; and translation is one of the ways in which this lyric re-potentiation of conventionalized forms can take place. The more the TT has been able to redeem self from persona, the less chance there is that the ST will see its own self suppressed by persona-text.

In the case of 'A une passante', the threat was never very great; the sonnet is so fully naturalized as a lyric mode that it is unlikely that its formality will ever intervene between the text and our digestion of it (unless a new environment—the city street—throws the appropriacy of that formality into question). But here certain formal decisions I had made in adopting the villanelle did nothing to conceal artifice and ingenuity, and I felt bound to essay a parallel free-verse villanelle in an attempt to recover something of my own voice and to give myself the opportunity to inhabit Baudelaire's poem on my own terms.

In the account of 'Le Goût du néant' which followed, I felt more at home in a 'straight' rondel rendering, simply because the rondel's structure itself invites a turning to the self (after line 8) and because, by 'reducing' one of the rhymes to assonance, I had frayed the edges of the form, removed some of its capacity for poised complacency.

Similarly, in the transformation of 'Le Balcon' into a rondeau, I allowed myself the liberty of repeating two of the rhymes, and encouraged the *rentrement* to retreat from the text, to sacrifice its virtuosic turns to a cooler, self-distancing function, but with more vocal presence.

117

'Bien loin d'ici', on the other hand, starts as a highly idiosyncratic confection, a two-rhyme 'sonnet renversé', whose tercets are monorhymed triplets, and whose quatrains are more like tercets, in that, besides themselves being in essence interrupted monorhymed triplets, their interrupting 'fourth' lines make them rhymally interdependent. The rondeau version can thus more easily afford its cleverness, and can parade a metatextuality consonant with that of the ST. At the same time, a certain metrical freedom again allows the translator's voice to relax into its own expressive impulses.

In all these instances of fixed-form transformations, apart perhaps from the opening villanelle, I felt no need to radically liberate the form in question in order to discover self in persona, and this for reasons I have already adverted to: the theory of translation is, on the whole, happy to discuss the ways in which translation adds to, or extends, the capacities of the TL— this is the principal justification for 'foreignizing' translation. What theory rarely discusses is the way in which translation can contribute to the expressive expansion of particular forms, can accustom forms which have become fossilized in conventional uses to new handling capacities. I did not feel obliged to produce free-verse versions of all the forms I used, because the forms themselves found it necessary to liberate themselves within their existing parameters, in order to accommodate a Baudelairean material which would not tolerate translation into *vers de société*. In their new exploratory guise, in these moments of defamiliarization, the forms provided me with ample flexibility to pursue my own expressive agenda. Formal translations of these kinds, not capriciously undertaken, since certain indications within the Baudelairean originals seem to warrant them, are too often treated as pieces of virtuosic exhibitionism which do the ST no service. We should, however, remember that, however much these forms have fallen into disuse in this century, however anachronistic they seem (but do not need to seem), the appropriacy of fixed forms to the Baudelairean enterprise is historically endorsed. The revival of the fixed forms in later nineteenth-century French and English poetry owed much to Banville's enthusiasm as a practitioner and to his authority as a poetician (*Petit Traité de poésie française*, 1872). But the cultivation of these forms was not confined to a group of minor Parnassians, at least in France—Leconte de Lisle (pantoums, villanelles), Verlaine (ballades, pantoums), Mallarmé (rondels, rondeaux, triolets), Rimbaud (triolets), Corbière (rondels), Maeterlinck (triolets) all had their brush with them, and it is clear from Baudelaire's work that intricate verse-forms, or acrobatic versions of commoner species (the sonnet especially), were an integral part of his creative practice. Perhaps one of the reasons why recognizable fixed forms, apart from the sonnet, did not emerge in Baudelaire's work relates to an inveterate habit of formal embroidery and variation; his handling of the pantoum, for example, when described by Cornulier, sounds like sheer perversity:

> au lieu d'opter pour la solution la plus naturelle ou directe—des quatrains rimés en (*abab*)—, ou pour des quatrains rimés en [*aabb*], il opte pour le schéma (*abba*), moins commun que (*abab*), et qui implique, par sa conjonction avec le schéma de répétition, que tous les quatrains soient sur les mêmes sonorités de rime, permutées de l'un à l'autre, en l'occurrence -*ige* et –*oir*.
>
> (1989: 70)

> [instead of opting for the most natural or direct solution—quatrains in alternating rhyme (*abab*)—or quatrains rhyming *aabb*, he opts for enclosed rhyme (*abba*), less common than alternating rhyme, and implying, in its conjunction with the pattern of repetition, that all quatrains have the same rhyme sonorities, alternating from one quatrain to the next, in this case -*ige* and –*oir*.]

Our rendering of 'Harmonie du soir' as a short sequence of terza rima with a 'double' ending, does not raise the same questions, perhaps, as the properly fixed-form translations, although the endings of these stanzaic forms are themselves sites of intensified formal attention and varied practice. In the event, my doubling of the last line is no different in degree of gravity from the terminal variations to be found in, say, Shelley's 'Ode to the West Wind' or Hofmannsthal's 'Ballade des äusseren Lebens'. But, more importantly, this particular translation confirms what is implicit in all the fixed-form translations: that translation is a crucial instrument in the comparison of forms and the revelation of their distinguishing expressive potentialities. Our understanding of forms is still remarkably crude, but translation provides us with the opportunity to set Baudelaire to another tune, to listen to terza rima alongside the pantoum, to discover how close the rondel is to the sonnet—even though 'Le Goût du néant' is neither sonnet nor rondel—to measure the different organizational pressures at work in the sonnet and the villanelle; and our sense of the rondeau's expressive range is helped by the translation of two very different kinds of poem into it. A chapter like this may remind us how unhelpfully narrow the albeit necessary question about the possibility of translation can be. The more fruitful questions are: what can translation do, what ends can it serve, how can it improve our understanding of verse? And entailed in these questions is another: what does the translator need to do if he is to safeguard, indeed justify, his part in the process, as a creative writer?

6

'Shot' and 'Reverse Shot' Translation

A principal fear of translation is that it operates as a process of fragmentation. Source texts are dealt with as sequences of separable problems; the claims of various aspects of a poetic text (rhyme, rhythm, figures of speech) are assessed *against* each other, and decisions about translational priorities made. We speak piously about the importance of maintaining the integrity of the text (both ST and TT), without stopping to ask how it is to be identified, and yet tolerate a criticism of translation which picks and chooses its tally of felicities and infelicities. About the criticism of translation we shall have more to say in Chapter 8. One defence of the trans*form*ations we have undertaken is that they *compel* an 'integrization' of the text: for a translator looking to transform a six-quatrain poem into, say, a thirteen-line rondel, the entirety of the ST has to be absorbed into the mind so that the optimal redistribution of the material can be evaluated; it is as though one took a model in soft clay of, say, a tree-loving leopard and reshaped that clay, but the same clay, into a plains-loving cheetah. Such trans*form*ations may entail changing the order of poetic events (reconstructing the poem's skeleton), and redistributing emphases (redefining the poem's musculature), but the point of departure for this anatomical metamorphosis must inevitably be the whole ST. This is a formal solution to the integrity problem.

I want now to look at a form of translation which seeks to ensure integrity by the construction of a point of view which subjects the language of the ST to the integrative influence of a presiding consciousness, which is not that of the poet, simply because the poet's consciousness is either irrecuperable, because of distance in time or space, or because, even if it does seem recuperable, it is by definition inappropriate to the TT. One might think that the consciousness of the translator would be sufficient to the task, and so it might, were the business of translation itself not so dispersive of consciousness, so manifold in the ways it projects the translator's role and the nature of the TT. Is the translator a self, a vividly imagined persona, or some kind of neutral cultural representative? Is the translator a reader of the ST, a critic, an educator, an authority, a writer? What kind of mix of the textual, the metatextual and the intertextual is the TT? When we speak about generating a consciousness to inform the translational process, we may be speaking about a consciousness which assumes the voice of the poet (shot), or a consciousness which speaks out of the text, the voice of the subject (reverse shot), or something in between.

It is curious to observe how few of Baudelaire's translators have been women.[1] One thinks of the edition of translations from *Les Fleurs du mal* which Edna St Vincent Millay co-authored with George Dillon (1935); one thinks of Joanna Richardson's selection (1975) and of Carol Clark's plain prose translations (1995). There are versions by Frances Cornford in her *Fifteen Poems from the French* (1976). Louise Varèse produced an edition of translations of Baudelaire's prose poems in 1951, as did Rosemary Lloyd in 1991 (with *La Fanfarlo*). From this fact one might derive two possible conclusions: that Baudelaire's work is antipathetic to women and that therefore, for women, little reward is to be had from translating him; or that translation is an ungendered activity, and that to observe that few women have translated Baudelaire is to observe a coincidence without further significance. Martin Sorrell's experience in his translations of modern French poetry by women, *Elles* (University of Exeter Press, 1995), adds a further nuance to this latter argument:

> And now there was another issue, ideologically more fraught. Could and should a man translate and publish a selection *he* had made of women's poems? My affirmative came about only after discussion with women colleagues, friends, acquaintances and with the poets themselves and their publishers. One person was wholly opposed; a few had certain reservations, but most, including colleagues involved in women's studies, were in full support. On Bancquart's and Yaguello's principle of re-joining the sexes, the consensus was that the way men read and translate women ought to be no more of an issue than the way women read and translate men, and should be as instructive. To debar translation on the grounds of gender difference was to beckon the demon of censorship.

(p. 6)

In this quotation, we begin again to feel the speciousness of arguments about the necessary authority of the translator, if taken to its logical end. If a man is not qualified to translate the poetry of a woman, who is qualified to translate 'Homer', who to translate the work of negritude poets? If a man is not qualified to translate a woman, beware the automatic acceptance of the corollary, that a woman is. Besides, are there not, among the profound functions of translation, the following: to explore and express difference; to understand the other as the self; to transform one mode of consciousness into another; to make intercultural, intersexual, interethnic journeys possible?

It is clearly unreasonable to argue that translation is an ungendered, or otherwise 'unmarked', activity, that the translator does not create perspective, modality and so on. In assessing choices made by the translator, we too easily suppose that the criteria of judgement are supplied by the ST; we too infrequently ask about the appropriacy of choice in relation to a translating psyche which can be reconstructed from the evidence of the TT. If we believe that translation is valuable not only as an interpretation of the ST, but as a response to it, then the translator must be allowed to register those modal shifts, those adjustments of perspective which best convey reactions and associations generated by the text. But perhaps, in pursuit of moral or psychological integrity, and ostensibly at the expense of aesthetic integrity, the translator must also be allowed to register those modal shifts as they occur, without obligation to an uninspected valorization of consistency as a stylistic virtue; montage is a methodology available to translators.

If I translated the first stanza of Baudelaire's 'Une nuit que j'étais près d'une affreuse Juive'—

> Une nuit que j'étais près d'une affreuse Juive,
> Comme au long d'un cadavre un cadavre étendu,
> Je me pris à songer près de ce corps vendu
> A la triste beauté dont mon désir se prive

—by the lines:

> Last night I fucked a fucking awful yid,
> Two stiffs laid out together, side by side,
> And thought about my girl, great tits, sad-eyed,
> Next to this lump of meat, cost thirty quid

and claimed it to be the voice of National Front punk, my reader might well repine and tax me with not so much having assumed Baudelaire's voice as hijacked it, and with having degraded translation to creative piracy. I might retort that a Baudelaire of modern Britain would probably have been a street-corner racist and crypto-sadist, and would justify the view by recalling Baudelaire's admittedly undeveloped comment in *Mon cœur mis à nu*:

> Belle conspiration à organiser pour l'extermination de la Race Juive.
> Les Juifs, *Bibliothécaires* et témoins de la *Rédemption*.
>
> (*OC*, I, 706)[2]
>
> [A nice conspiracy to organize for the extermination of the Jewish Race.
> The Jews, *Librarians* and witnesses of the *Redemption*.]

I might also argue that since we can never satisfactorily *know* the original, and since a central task of translation is to translate (in the theological sense) the original to another culture, in order, among other things, to define that culture to itself, by making visible the lens through which it views other cultural material, then, like the native speaker of a language, the translator is never wrong.

But translation has quickly become politicized. And we cannot entirely sweep the open clashes or covert seditions of conflicting ideologies under the benign carpet of cultural difference. However much he protests his innocence, the translator will not be able to wash his hands of linguistic fifth-columnism. Translation is the political arena where motives are difficult to unravel and even more difficult to trust. Suddenly, in this rendering of 'Une nuit que j'étais près d'une affreuse Juive', I no longer evaluate the iambic pentameter in terms of its metrical 'equivalence' to the alexandrine, but rather as the vehicle of a voice which is trying to persuade me of an authority borrowed from someone else. Iambic pentameter acts as an ideological sedative, here placing in a national order, as part of the property owned by the culture, a fornication motivated by disgust and murderous intention. The very regularity of iambic—first-foot inversions included—the rhythm of aggressive intercourse, suggests compliance with something learned by heart, from the home culture, and a speaker whose outrageousness can be forgiven in the name of his obedience to metrical imperatives. Another way of putting this, of course, is to say not just that the establishment condones such behaviour, but that we have no right to extirpate these words from the poem since they are not unmetrical. Readerly impotence is itself a powerful politicizer peculiar to translation. And the arguments for free-verse translation gather strength, simply because they imagine a mode of translation in which the translator is inescapably responsible for his own words.

This image of the translator as infiltrator, usurper, politically motivated con-man, has its obverse in the image of the translator as guardian of public morals, right-thinking and political correctness. Feminist translation might be cited as an example, particularly where it seems to use translation as an opportunity systematically to cleanse the ST's active sexism or involuntary linguistic patriarchalism, by interferences of various kinds (sexually neutral or inclusive forms of reference, transformations of passive to active, modifications of lexical colouring, etc.). This does not seem to be an activity which necessarily requires foreign texts, and the distinction between translation and editing becomes muddied. But sense of purpose brings the translator out of the shadows, helps to establish a meaning for translation and justifies those prefaces, caveats and translators' biographies which translation increasingly needs. Additionally, it revives the sense of the irresolution and mutability of the ST, of a text that we can reach back into and inflect. The difference between re-interpreting and re-writing a text is not a large one, and, to use Lori Chamberlain's terms (1992: 58), the original can be shown to be as guilty of infidelity as its translation.

Feminism in translation studies has followed many routes—deflecting masculine or masculinized works back into bisexual operation, recovering lost women writers and lost woman translators, translating experimental feminist texts, revising the metaphorics of the translation process (see, e.g., Simon 1996, and Flotow 1997). In the context of this last, Chamberlain's 'Gender and the Metaphorics of Translation' (1992: 57–74) leads us from an *embattled* view of translation as feminine (reproductive not productive, derivative not original, treasonous not lawful), as a writerly equivalent of the marriage contract, to one in which the feminine of translation is the destruction of difference between the creative statuses of ST and TT, so that both are original and secondary, uncontaminated and transgressed or transgressive. In this sense, the feminine is as much a figure of the postmodern as it is of translation; in this sense, translation finds its true home in the postmodern. And perhaps in the way that a postmodern text sees itself evacuated of an author and not to be extricated from the continuum of intertexts and deferred meanings, with the voice of the text diffusing and multiplying, so translation might make easier the coexistence of its many facets and functions by embracing a multivocality which would leave the TT profoundly unsettled, and the translator's voice a kind of putative point of convergence. As a 'poème-conversation', or as Eliot's Dickensian 'He do the police in different voices', the first stanza of 'Une nuit que j'étais près d'une affreuse Juive' might look like this:

When was it then?
A Jewish woman, yes,
enough to turn your stomach.
Special exotic offer, so they said...
Or was it another 'Rachel, quand du Seigneur...'?
(We might as well have both been dead—
stuffing the mummy)
I don't suppose I'll ever again...
'Again,' I told her, 'and none of your lip.'
Her lips apart, cash down and none to go,
            I thought of someone else,
beautiful,
            if in a melancholic vein.
Someone my desire keeps me from,
someone my blood too readily forgets.

Words, textual fragments, collocational possibilities, rhythmic variations, flit endlessly across the mind in an unresolved state of writeability. The translator's claims to privilege are an authorial construct which has no place in this fluid, uninterrupted, verbal *in medias res*. From the point of view of a Walter Benjamin, translation's role in the unfolding of ideological history is fundamental. The language of translation, an inevitably intertextual (if only because metatextual) medium, is like that other intertext, the quotation, constitutive of the cultural debris out of which we constantly re-read history, to find in it directions and designs which will reveal our intentions to us. But translation is also itself a reading of history, in which the ST becomes a quotation, a fragment of a larger cultural canvas, other fragments of which, anterior and posterior to the ST, can be put together in the TT. In the multivocal 'poème-conversation' version of translation, consistency is abjured, and the pieces that make up the jigsaw display their joins, insist that they are only temporarily on loan and might find a more fitting place in some other jigsaw. Point of view, if one emerges, is as fragile, as vulnerable to modification and break-up, as authorship is tenuous. Successive translations become the stuff of dialectic. And poetry has a special relevance, simply because, relative to prose, its linguistic structure can be so variously adapted; because of the distance from the original that the translator can create, because of its formal measurability, because of the visibility of its formal consequences, so the coordinates of the original can be radically redrawn and the original can be made to operate in unforeseen arenas.

This 'postmodernization' of translation begins perhaps with Ezra

Pound. His work, and specifically *The Cantos*, establishes the links between copying (close translation), remaking (editing and reshaping the ST) and, indeed, direct quotation; it makes translation and original creation coextensive with each other; it unravels distinctions between English and other languages (see Alexander 1997: 23–30). The proposal that direct, verbatim quotation is a kind of extremely close translation (see also Edwards 1997: 48–65) has two important implications: first, in an intensely cosmopolitan view of cultural production, translation must have a very different function from that of *liberating* cultures from hermetically sealed isolations; already liberated and available to a polyglot audience, texts look to translation to increase their capacity to fertilize, to metamorphose, to enter into dialogue with other idioms and sentiments; quoting a text verbatim may now be a way of alluding to the totality of its survivance. Secondly, to treat verbatim quotation as translation is to acknowledge that any recontextualization of a text, and particularly of a piece of text, is to make it something new (when it did not have any 'origin', in any meaningful sense of that word, in the first place). In other words, an 'original' text does not need to be translated in order to be 'translated'; it simply needs another environment. A text is a piece of writing looking to pass on its genes in as many forms as possible; the genes are the phonemes and graphemes of the ST; in quoting a text we activate a sexual display which is already also a mating, because the act of quotation itself is a transference of the text, a move in the direction of metatextuality (a quotation represents, is a comment on, itself, or the whole text from which it has been taken), the cultural reinsertion of a text not simply as meaning differently, but as *being* differently; a quotation is not a text, or does become a text-in-itself; it is perhaps an intratextual epigraph, or an allusion rather than itself; it has a certain degree of familiarity, or unfamiliarity, which may not square with the familiarity, or unfamiliarity, of its parent-text at all.

For Steiner (1970: 34), Pound is the watershed in the development of translation and of our perception of what it is:

> [...] the fact of radical change is no longer in doubt. The contemporary translator and even reader of classic verse comes after Pound as the modern painter comes after Cubism. Inevitably, much of the translation in this book [*Poem into Poem: World Poetry in Modern Verse Translation*] implies and was made possible by Pound's enlargement of the term.

It is surprising that so much modern translation still feels like a branch of literary archaeology, of preservation, or, to use Lowell's term, 'taxidermy', rather than like a process of projection, or deflection, or even cosmetic surgery.

It is one thing to imagine a translation of 'Une nuit que j'étais près d'une affreuse Juive' as a multi-image single-screen 'poème-conversation', and another to imagine a series of screens, to be put together in the reader's mind, over a longer period and with potentially greater degrees of inter-image tension. But this is what emerged from Nicholas Moore's entry in a 1968 *Sunday Times* Baudelaire translation competition, judged by George Steiner: thirty-one versions of Baudelaire's 'Spleen' poem 'Je suis comme le roi d'un pays pluvieux'. Roy Fisher's explanation of the venture questions the sagacity of any single-version objective for translation:

> The knowledge that each version is one of many lets him off the hook of a service-translator's convergent caution and frees him from what would otherwise have been a deadening task, the attempt to reproduce in any one version what I take to be the steady, contained tone of the original.
>
> (Moore 1990: 8)

There is no doubt that Moore's work is extremely instructive about attitudes to translation more generally. Moore is ostensibly entering a competition in which his own versions have no interest in competing, particularly with each other. And as readers of these versions, we certainly do not feel that our task is to judge their comparative merits, and extract from the sequence our preferred account. Our real task is to find ways of putting them together, not only to find a poem but also to find a poet. Why is it that we set so much store by the single version? Is there a moral good in it (choices have to be *real* choices, once-and-for-all)? Is it meant to echo the struggle for singleness of the ST (but why)? One of the principal functions of translation, one might argue, is to ensure that the ST recovers, both internally and externally, some of its dynamic as a work-in-progress. And why is it that we are always more inclined to compare different versions of the same ST *at the expense of* comparing a rendering of an ST with other renderings of other STs in a particular translator's *œuvre*? The translator's visibility should not be dependent on having come first (i.e. on making other translators invisible); a translator's visibility should derive from the public's being prepared to interest itself in the totality of his/her work. Moore himself was momentarily caught in an 'old', unregenerate view of translation, before being released into his own translations; but even so, the old view hung on:

> But then it occurred to me that—paradoxical as it might be—by
> doing several completely different versions I could in effect illustrate
> my own thesis of the impossibility of translation. Why I eventually
> did so many is simply that one thing led to another. It became clear,
> if it wasn't from the start, that there were many different ways of
> translating almost every Baudelairean phrase into Mooreian English
> (as well as into other people's English); that the nearest in literalness
> was not necessarily the nearest in tone; so too with metre and the
> transmutation of idioms and references to fit different situations.
> [...] All I have against translation is that it can't be done!
>
> (Moore 1990: 12–14)

Untranslatability is a pre-translational perception of inevitable loss if an
ST is reproduced in any form other than itself. But translation has never
pretended to repeat the ST; this would probably, in the play of temporal,
spatial and cultural relativities, constitute a bad translation anyway. As we
have already observed, untranslatability is what makes translation possible.
Translation is when 'one thing leads to another', is about the multiplication
of choice and the proliferation of possible permutations. Only when a
translating self, as opposed to a set of translating personae, is seen to be at
stake, will it become imperative to a translator to stem the flood of
multiplication and 'come home' to a single version. But this is an
existential, not a translational, decision, a decision not dictated by the
ST.

Moore's translations might seem, at first sight, to be at pains to
differentiate themselves one from the other. Many of the 'entrants' provide
their addresses, many of the versions bear dedications, and titles chosen
are punctiliously distinctive: 'For the Tomb of a Press Baron', 'Sonnet
117', 'A Bad Dream Recurring', etc. And even though the majority of
versions stick to the ST's nine stichic couplets, there are free-verse
versions, versions in quatrains (sometimes with a closing couplet), song-
lyric versions and the telegraphic 'After the Deluge':

> Not riches, power, advisers, pets, sport, gold
> Nor even naked women cheer the old
> In heart. Bones will be bones. All that remains
> Instead of blood, green water, clotted veins.

Additionally, many of the translations have epigraphs. But all these factors,
far from installing water-tight boundaries between the poems, create
bridges, the common ground of garrulous dialogue between versions, an

urge to compare notes and be promiscuous. The names of the poets, where they are not anagrams of 'Nicholas Moore', are clearly caricatural, fronts for pastiches—W.H. Laudanum, H.N. (Helga Neverdotoomuch). And the commonness of (light satirical) purpose is helped by the network of references to popular music and jazz, and by shared attitudes or themes in the epigraphs.

Moore's recourse to titles other than Baudelaire's own, to epigraphs, to dedications even, deserves some comment, simply because of its general significance as a translational resource. In his book on various kinds of paratext (peritext, epitext), Genette sums up their function thus:

> Cette frange, en effet, toujours porteuse d'un commentaire auctorial, ou plus ou moins légitimé par l'auteur, constitue, entre texte et hors-texte, une zone non seulement de transition, mais de *transaction*: lieu privilégié d'une pragmatique et d'une stratégie, d'une action sur le public au service, bien ou mal compris et accompli, d'un meilleur accueil du texte et d'une lecture plus pertinente—plus pertinente, s'entend, aux yeux de l'auteur et de ses alliés.
>
> (1987: 8)
>
> [In fact this fringe, always bearing an authorial commentary, or a commentary more or less legitimated by the author, constitutes, between text and off-text, a zone not only of transition, but also of *transaction*: the privileged site of a pragmatics and a strategy, of an effect on the public in the service, however well or ill understood and carried out, of a better reception of the text and of a more appropriate reading—more appropriate, of course, in the eyes of the author and his allies.]

Justifiably, we bemoan a situation in which there is little criticism of translation from a reader-response point of view—translation criticism to date has been preoccupied with the relationship between ST and TT. True, questions of reception, in the sense of horizons of expectation and the ideological positions of texts, are central to a growing body of recent criticism (gender, post-colonial/ethnic, cultural). There is still, however, much progress to be made in understanding not what is read in a translation, but how to affect the way in which a translation is read, how to affect the uses to which a TT is put. Paratextual input, in the form of explicit authorial intervention (prefaces, annotations), has long been a concern of translation studies, but titles (and particularly what Genette calls 'intertitres' [intertitles], epigraphs and dedications) have received relatively little attention. As I proceed, I would like to assimilate this latter class of 'hidden persuaders' into my argument.

In approaching a translation of another of the 'Spleen' poems, 'Quand le ciel bas et lourd pèse comme un couvercle'—

> Quand le ciel bas et lourd pèse comme un couvercle
> Sur l'esprit gémissant en proie aux longs ennuis,
> Et que de l'horizon embrassant tout le cercle
> Il nous verse un jour noir plus triste que les nuits;
>
> Quand la terre est changée en un cachot humide,
> Où l'Espérance, comme une chauve-souris,
> S'en va battant les murs de son aile timide
> Et se cognant la tête à des plafonds pourris;
>
> Quand la pluie étalant ses immenses traînées
> D'une vaste prison imite les barreaux,
> Et qu'un peuple muet d'infâmes araignées
> Vient tendre ses filets au fond de nos cerveaux,
>
> Des cloches tout à coup sautent avec furie
> Et lancent vers le ciel un affreux hurlement,
> Ainsi que des esprits errants et sans patrie
> Qui se mettent à geindre opiniâtrement.
>
> —Et de longs corbillards, sans tambours ni musique,
> Défilent lentement dans mon âme; l'Espoir,
> Vaincu, pleure, et l'Angoisse atroce, despotique,
> Sur mon crâne incliné plante son drapeau noir.

—I had initially wanted simply to re-author it, and do so by adopting a free-verse rendering which would allow me, with greater ease, to 'ornament' the ST, to generate a margin, a supplement, of myself in the text. But it occurred to me that re-authoring the text might leave me with the problems of an unconvincing rhetoric, of a language insufficiently warranted. So I decided to try to move from authoring the text towards the text as author; or, put another way, instead of the text being the I's subject, the I would be the subject of the text. My chosen method of doing this was to activate the text by a minimal dialogue, by the presence of an enquiring voice, rather like the voice which addresses the travellers in 'Le Voyage'. This voice might well sound to some like the voice of a therapist, and thus quite clearly cast spleen as a pathological condition. But it might equally serve as the voice of an interested acquaintance, fearful of 'infection', or a curious bystander looking for gothic anecdotes. In this way, the poet/text is thrown back into him/itself, hemmed in by a saner externality, confronting an inevitable incomprehension. This sense of the imprisoned and powerless text might be increased by an epigraph. Certainly an extract from Baudelaire's description of one of his worse splenetic attacks in a letter to his mother (30 December 1857)[3] would increase the sense of clinical case-history and further empower the voice of enquiry. But, in the end, I chose an epigraph taken from one of the 'Dimanches' poems in Laforgue's *Des Fleurs de bonne volonté*, in the translation of Peter Dale (1986: 275). The title of this collection, which supplied much of the material for the *Derniers Vers* and was published posthumously with them in 1890, reflects ironically on Baudelaire's title and on itself, given the poet's mischievous, and often apparently willed, maladjustment. Laforguian spleen is a gentler, suburbanized and quotidianized version of Baudelaire's, permeated with wry self-mockery rather than with bitter self-derision, and the lines chosen are, fittingly, a small-scale echo of the din in Baudelaire's skull (stanza 4). Laforgue, more than Baudelaire, generates the modernism of the likes of Pound, Eliot and Huxley.[4] And what I wanted to achieve rhythmically was to create a sustaining iambic, which might turn trochaic, or at least become stress-led, when it came to the erratic and collisional flight of the bat, and which would briefly polarize its stresses and non-stresses at the poem's close, betokening the encounter of the despotic and the subjugated. The relative monotony of the rhythm is designed to express the drift towards the mechanical, towards the automatic pilot, towards the featureless self-alienation, of spleen. Within this grey state is a febrility, a paradoxical sense of being out of control, subject to all invasions, and this texture of panic can be conveyed by a free-verse lay-out, with its unpredictabilities, its abrupt ruptures, its intonational vagaries and mixed tempi. In short, it appeared to me that the very verse-form of free verse might embody and enact the splenetic state, as a particular disturbance of the psyche, as a particular combination of elements, in a way that quatrains in alternating rhyme cannot. This is what I mean by the I speaking out of the text, as the text's subject. The free-verse rendering would also, of course, take me in the direction of Laforgue's *Derniers Vers*:

Spleen

> Oh that piano's groans so clear!
> Headstrong, they are, against my head.
> (Dale/Laforgue)

How does it begin?

A low-slung sky
Pressing down on me
    like a heavy lid
Doubling the weight
    of things that plague my life
And through its length and breadth
It sheds a murky light
    gloomier than the night.

And so the world darkens
    to a dank dungeon
Its only inmate, hope, a bat
Flitting here and there
    rapping its head on
Rotten ceilings, flapping
Its frightened wings
    against the walls.

And then
It's raining stair-rods
Thick as prison bars
God get me out of here
And deep inside my brain
Noiselessly
A mass of spiders, nauseating spiders
Spin their patient webs.

Then, suddenly, a furious
Clatter of bells
A howling hurled
    in Heaven's face
Just like the plangent wail
    unprompted

Of lost nomadic souls
En route, like me, to nowhere.

And then?

And then? Ah, then
With neither drums
                              nor music
Long files of hearses move
                              in slow procession
Through my soul.
Hope's routed, broken,
And anguish, angst, angoisse—
                              call it what you will—
Malicious, cold, or genially unforgiving,
Drives its black flag
Into my submissive skull.[5]

The real importance of the epigraph, for translation, is, then, twofold. First, it introduces a third voice into the perennially difficult dialogue between poet and translator; this third voice defuses a fruitless confrontation. Can it really be so easy to intrude? The voice of the epigraph is an exhortation to give no voice the final word. Secondly, the epigraph is an invitation to let both ST and TT expand, across time, across space, backwards or forwards, without worrying too much about the plausibilities of chronology and geography. And it should be emphasized that it is *expansion*, rather than interpretation, which matters in this particular move; it matters more that the epigraph will activate an associative process (which may go well beyond the range of the epigraph) than that it will tendentiously interfere with the reader's understanding of either the ST or the TT. In my translation of 'Obsession' (see note 5), I had first thought of using something from Hopkins as an epigraph: 'O look at all the fire-folk sitting in the air!' But although 'The Starlight Night' (1877), from which this line is taken, is a long way from what is expressed in the tercets of 'Obsession', Hopkins's celebration of starlight is too symmetrically contrary to Baudelaire's treatment, and the epigraphic line itself too conveniently and restrictively close. Instead, the closing line from Auden's 'Woods', in the 'Bucolics' cycle, is no more than something to break the frames of both ST and TT, and to encourage the reader to wander in their shared 'blind field', a 'blind field' which all kinds of epitextual material, including other translations, are trying to enlarge. The kind of distance that an epigraph creates between itself and its texts must be sufficient to take the reader off at oblique angles, but not so great as to imply that it is some kind of cryptic, but total, solution to the poem's problems and thus attract to itself more strenuous efforts of decipherment than the ST and TT put together. But once again we should insist: it is not merely the epigraph which inflects the meanings of the texts it serves; those texts in return inflect the meaning of the epigraph. This is what we have meant by the translational dimension of quotation.

I would like to consider, in greater detail, one further example of the translation which attempts to locate point of view somewhere between what I am calling 'shot' (consciousness in poet) and 'reverse shot' (consciousness in subject), namely 'A une dame créole':

> Au pays parfumé que le soleil caresse,
> J'ai connu, sous un dais d'arbres tout empourprés
> Et de palmiers d'où pleut sur les yeux la paresse,
> Une dame créole aux charmes ignorés.
>
> Son teint est pâle et chaud; la brune enchanteresse
> A dans le cou des airs noblement maniérés;
> Grande et svelte en marchant comme une chasseresse,
> Son sourire est tranquille et ses yeux assurés.
>
> Si vous alliez, Madame, au vrai pays de gloire,
> Sur les bords de la Seine ou de la verte Loire,
> Belle digne d'orner les antiques manoirs,
>
> Vous feriez, à l'abri des ombreuses retraites,
> Germer mille sonnets dans le cœur des poètes,
> Que vos grands yeux rendraient plus soumis que vos noirs.

I have chosen 'A une dame créole' simply because it raises some interesting questions, the first two pairs of which I leave in a rhetorical state:

1. This poem is an early one: the manuscript, not much revised later, was part of a letter addressed to M. Autard de Bragard, 20 October 1841. Does the translator feel that earlier work is more open to creative 'revision' in translation than later? When a poet's output spans a relatively large number of years, should the translator think first and foremost of imposing on it the temporal consistency of his own voice?

2. The translation by Walter Martin (1997, 165) opens with the line:

> I met, among the amber tamarinds

which does not correspond with anything we find in the 1861 French edition which Martin uses. However, in the manuscript, and in the version of 1845 (*L'Artiste*, May 25), we find reference to 'tamarins ambrés' in the second line. How far should variants remain a source of alternatives for the translator? Do they help, in Martin's case, retrospectively to generate a (TW), a single experiential source, which has multiplied in writing? The manuscript version may well seem to have a certain primal veracity, the quick of first impressions, and in this instance that feeling may be enhanced by the manuscript letter's subsequent loss.

3. The third set of problems relates to semantic drift. In English, the word 'creole', when applied to people rather than language, has basically two meanings: (a) a native-born person of European, especially Spanish, ancestry; and (b) a native-born person of mixed European and Negro ancestry (who probably speaks a creole). In French usage, 'créole' means unequivocally 'une personne de race blanche, née aux colonies' [a white born in the colonies]. The probable etymology of the word sheds no further light: < Portuguese 'crioulo' (Spanish 'criollo') = slave born into one's household; < 'criar' = to nourish, bring up. I suspect that most English speakers—partly because of its meaning in relation to language—assume 'creole' to mean as in (b). Baudelaire's poem is addressed to Mme Autard de Bragard (née Emmeline de Carcenac, mother of the comtesse Ferdinand de Lesseps), whom Baudelaire had met in Mauritius on his abortive voyage to Calcutta (June 1841–February 1842). An anonymous portrait of *c*. 1840 (Bibliothèque Nationale) leaves one in no doubt as to the pallor of Mme Autard's skin and the darkness of her hair ('brune').

As one looks through the English translations of this poem, one can find evidence of a will, voluntary or involuntary, to let the English understanding of 'créole' have its way. I cite a sample of examples:

(i) 'A creole woman'; 'brown-skinned Enchanteress [*sic*]/Has languors' (Symons 1925: 169);
(ii) 'that dark enchantress' (Scarfe 1964: 5–6);
(iii) 'a creole's haunting mysteries'; 'enchantress brown' (Richardson 1975: 119);
(iv) 'This brown enchantress' skin' (McGowan 1993: 129—despite an explanatory note);

(v) 'Alluring sorceress'; 'You were to loll by verdant banks' (Shapiro 1998: 107—despite an explanatory note which begins: 'Contrary to common belief, "creole" in this sense refers to an individual of European ancestry born in the colonies' (p. 198)).

These may seem to be no more than a matter of connotative tints—'loll', for example, indicates tropical indolence and unselfconscious posture; 'sorceress' opens on to voodooism and other black arts—but under the influence of 'creole', these connotations will be active. And this raises a delicate question: on the evidence of these translations, English renderings of this poem make possible for Mme Autard a dual personality: she has the European graces and accomplishments of a white colonist, unfortunately born to blush unseen, but aware of her ethnic dominance, and the sexual electricity and enigmatic 'darkness' of a creole (English sense (b)), she can more than hold her own in the company of a rakish, if poetic, French aristocracy. This potent mix is, it seems, a product of a translation process in which 'literal' translation begets misunderstanding, because the popular acceptance of a term, 'creole', no longer corresponds with the meaning to which the dictionary still gives priority. Is it the intention of the translators that this should be so? Should we as translators following on perpetuate this English tradition, this fruitful licence? Or does this ambiguity invite the reader of the translation to a kind of prurience, to the transformation of a perfectly respectable woman into an ethnic image of sexual availability ('chasseresse' nicely balances this ambiguity between a chaste Artemis/Diana and a predatory Amazon perpetuating her race through casual commerce with men). Rich though this 'English' juxtaposition may be, it also victimizes or exploits the text, in sexist and racist ways. And the reader/translator is really in no position to excuse this on the grounds that it is already inscribed in the ST. Certainly, Baudelaire is no innocent writer, but to read this poem as an ethnic equivocation is to do an injustice to it in relation to other poems of Baudelaire's, namely 'A une Malabaraise', 'La Belle Dorothée' and 'Bien loin d'ici'.

Part of my 'project' for this translation, therefore, was to remove all possibility of ethnic crossover by simply removing any reference to 'creole' and assigning 'brune' directly to hair. I also changed the grammatical category of 'enchanteresse', because the noun, with its drive to encapsulate and designate, did not coincide with my desire to 'free' Mme Autard; the adjective 'vaporizes' substantivality, produces an unstable dynamic, not quite steady enough to be firmly defining. Besides, 'enchantress' has, in English, to my ear, something cumbersome and baroque about it which Mme Autard has not. And I have gravitated towards the Diana/Artemis pole, being careful to endow Artemis with an indefinite article, to give the subject some option on the choice, to avoid isolating her, to de-amplify the mythological reference:

A Lady in the Colonies

Quel passe-temps prends-tu d'habiter la vallée
De Bourgueil où jamais la Muse n'est allée?
Quitte-moi ton Anjou, et viens en Vendômois.

(Ronsard)

The sun lays a caressive hand on that
Rich-scented country. I remember you,
Your charms sequestered overseas,
Beneath a canopy of trees, their leaves touched
With crimson, and of palms
Weighing heavy on the eyes.

A pale complexion, but still
Strangely warm; dark-haired, enchanting,
You held your head with nobly mannered poise
And walked as tall and slender
As an Artemis,
With steady eyes and cool
Untroubled smile.

If your beauty, Madam—fit to grace
The country seats of quality—were to migrate
To France (where people make the most
Of their repute), to the Loire's lush banks
Or to the Seine,

It would,
In shady bowers,
Set sonnets freely flowing
Through the hearts of poets, more mastered
By your large eyes
Than your blackamoors at home.

Another part of the project concerns gender. Baudelaire's poem is a tributary sonnet which refers to tributary sonnets: 'Vous feriez

[...]/Germer mille sonnets [...]'. In other words, in flattering mode, Baudelaire is happy to throw in his lot, so powerful are Emmeline's 'grands yeux', with the bevy of love-sick poets. But there are two troubling factors here: (i) the title has a vocative dimension, which the poem does not let surface until the sestet (compare with 'A une Malabaraise'); in the octave, the 'dame créole' is a third person, absent, at the poet's descriptive disposal, her charms recalled for the benefit of (male?) others (with an arch wink perhaps in 'J'ai connu'?); (ii) the tributary love sonnet is a peculiarly transfixative and manipulative form; it uses the desire to immortalize as its pretext; it is a courtship display whereby the servant is turned into the master, and whereby sexual harassment takes place under cover of compliment. Commentators have often remarked that this poem, particularly in its first tercet, betrays traces of Ronsard, and it is perhaps with Ronsard that the brow-beating amatory sonnet first came into its own. I have taken two steps to counter these ills: first, I have maintained my free verse habit, here for political as much as expressive reasons—it seemed vitally important not to write a sonnet, but to leave that to the others. Secondly, I have consigned Ronsard to the epigraph; it behoved me to point up this textual reminiscence, but I did not wish to identify myself with it in my writing; the epigraph I have chosen, from 'Le Voyage de Tours' (1560), works on a different geographical scale, and is drawn from a sequence of lines which culminate in conceited soft soap:

> Quel passe-temps prends-tu d'habiter la vallée
> De Bourgueil où jamais la Muse n'est allée?
> Quitte-moi ton Anjou, et viens en Vendômois.
> Là s'élèvent au ciel les sommets de nos bois,
> Là sont mille taillis et mille belles plaines,
> Là gargouillent les eaux de cent mille fontaines,
> Là sont mille rochers, où Échon alentour
> En résonnant mes vers ne parle que d'Amour.
>
> (ll. 289–96)

My solution to the first problem—temporarily suppressed vocativity—was the introduction of the second person from the outset, and the removal of the preposition of address from the title: where Baudelaire broadcasts address and then delays using it, I wished to do the opposite. The effect of the presence of the second person in the octave is, I think, considerable: it makes the description of shared experience notionally revisable by the interlocutor (unlike reports to third parties); it is a mutual testing of, and agreement about, the appropriacy of the language (not the one-sided lingo of club or bar); it removes any insinuation of voyeurism. The octave, then, is part of an essentially private memory, which seemed to require a consistently used past tense. In the sestet, on the other hand, my poet adopts a public voice, a voice to be overheard, applauded, and accordingly the complicity between the first and second persons shifts from an intimate to a covert and ironic mode—the parentheses in the first tercet are designed to remove all innocence from the remarks made, and in the second tercet, I have sought a corresponding effect which I will shortly come to.

But first, I must comment on one further general change. Part of my reason for consigning Ronsard to an epigraph, and part of the reason for ironizing the first tercet, is my adoption of an English point of view (while eschewing the 'Englishing' of 'créole'). This Englishness necessitates the naming of France, because the 'vrai pays de gloire' is obviously no longer 'here', which might in turn suggest that Mme Autard, though French, does not belong in a country which has too high an opinion of itself and where, symptomatically, the poets all suffer from 'sonnetorrhoea'. It is also a *crypto*-nationalist move on my part, in that an appropriation of Baudelaire's poetic voice, and of Mme Autard, echoes the taking of Mauritius from the French by the British in 1810. I take it that 'fit to grace the country seats of quality' will also strike a properly British note. In this way, I can alert my readers to the depredations of domesticating translation.

The explicit Englishing of the poetic voice in the second tercet is focused on 'blackamoors'. This might be considered an infelicitous choice—'blackamoor' is an archaic word hatched in the seventeenth century, redolent of all that is worst in liveried black children serving the British gentry. But I hope that it serves its purpose in four respects:

(i) It bespeaks racial hybridization, or a desire to lump races indiscriminately together ('black' + 'Moor') which is as insulting to sonneteering poets as it is to black servants, and reflects challengingly on English assumptions about 'creoles'.

(ii) It suggests a relationship between white woman and black native men which is more intimate and equal—'black amours'—than the relationship between white lady and white male poets.

(iii) It opens acoustically not only on to 'black amour' but also on to 'paramour'. I spoke earlier of the 'bevy' of love-sick poets, mindful that 'bevy' is gender-marked 'female' and is intended to conjure up a group of chattering, high-spirited women engaged in some frivolous pursuit. 'Paramour', if it is gender-marked at all, is also 'female' (= 'mistress'); but whether this gender-marking operates or not, the word is about illicit sexual relations. The public acceptability, respectability, of poets offering sonnets of fruitless longing to 'la dame' conceals a private wealth of transgressive affairs.

(iv) Neither 'blackamoor' nor 'paramour' have direct French equivalents, though the latter clearly derives from French ('par amour'); these words constitute an English language which, as it were, keeps its secrets, conceals its connotations and acoustic insinuations.

A final part of this project, already adverted to, was to remove all ethnic blurring in the interests of other poems by Baudelaire addressed to women in tropical climes: 'A une Malabaraise', 'La Belle Dorothée' and 'Bien loin d'ici'. These four poems (including 'A une dame créole') are related by more than theme and setting. 'A une Malabaraise', not included in *Les Fleurs du Mal*, is also an early poem: it was first published in *L'Artiste* on 13 December 1846. Although dated 1840 (reliably?) by Baudelaire in *Les Épaves* (i.e. as predating his voyage to the Indian Ocean), Solange Rosenmark, grand-niece of Mme Autard de Bragard, declared in 1921 that Baudelaire had known the 'Malabaraise' at the Autards', where she was a servant. It seems that the 'Malabaraise', whom Rosenmark calls 'Dorothée', shared the same wet-nurse with Emmeline, and later, in her turn, became wet-nurse to Mme Autard's children. Pichois, who provides this account (*OC*, I, 1159–60) points out that the claim that the name of the 'Malabaraise' was 'Dorothée', is very doubtful: Baudelaire met Dorothée in La Réunion, and she was a prostitute rather than a servant. Whatever the facts of the matter, we can imagine that this trio of women formed, in Baudelaire's mind, a triptych of conditions, which reflected poignantly the one on the other. The white mistress of the house can be recalled to a traditional rural France à la Ronsard, where values are stable and achievement properly recognized, to receive sonnets from admiring poets; the servant girl, the 'Malabaraise', on the other hand is urgently discouraged from going to an urban France, Paris, of perpetual winter, where, prostituted, she will receive the insults and cash of her clients. The colonial prostitute, Dorothée, is caught, unnervingly, in a peculiarly vacant space, between opportunism and innocence, the colonist client and the tropical hut, the exploitative master, out of whose slavery she wishes to buy a younger sister—'et qui est déjà mûre' ('La Belle Dorothée')—and the exploited/exploitative native (herself), who will no doubt prostitute that sister. And about these relationships between the metropolitan French and the colonial, one should have no illusions; to make free with them, to blend them, is to refuse to see them, to indulge in an involuntary racism, a wilful sexism.

In my treatment of 'A une dame créole', I have tried once again to combine shot and reverse shot, both to reformulate the poet's consciousness and to take up a position within the text, in the mind of the subject, so that a negotiation between the two consciousnesses is necessary, so that one can feel in the text something of the dialectical relationship between those different angles of vision.

I now move on to construct a version of 'Les Aveugles' which is entirely reverse shot, espousing the blind men's point of view. Here I have followed an overtly oppositional line, and tried to re-establish the identity of those whom poets turn into images. It is all very well for Baudelaire to say, in 'Le Cygne': 'tout pour moi devient allégorie'. We can certainly sympathize with the mind that cannot escape into other, which constantly encounters figures who turn into mirrors of his own soul. But looked at from the point of view of the figures themselves, this requirement constantly to become an exemplar, to serve the purposes of poetic despair, is a theft of civil rights against which they might well rebel. This sense of the deprivation of identity is exacerbated by an awareness of the probable contribution of another image, Brueghel the Elder's *Parable of the Blind Men*, to the poem's elaboration. Images of images, parabolic or allegoric, the blind men, with all individuality erased by their physical condition, might at least seek to recover some group solidarity:

> Contemple-les, mon âme; ils sont vraiment affreux!
> Pareils aux mannequins; vaguement ridicules;
> Terribles, singuliers comme les somnambules;
> Dardant on ne sait où leurs globes ténébreux.
>
> Leurs yeux, d'où la divine étincelle est partie,
> Comme s'ils regardaient au loin, restent levés
> Au ciel; on ne les voit jamais vers les pavés
> Pencher rêveusement leur tête appesantie.
>
> Ils traversent ainsi le noir illimité,
> Ce frère du silence éternel. O cité!
> Pendant qu'autour de nous tu chantes, ris et beugles,
>
> Éprise du plaisir jusqu'à l'atrocité,
> Vois! je me traîne aussi! mais, plus qu'eux hébété,
> Je dis: Que cherchent-ils au Ciel, tous ces aveugles?

The Blind

> I who have sat by Thebes below the wall
> And walked among the lowest of the dead.
> (T.S. Eliot)

1.   They watch us with derision and distaste,
2.   compare us
3.   to tailors' dummies
                and sleepwalking freaks.
4.   What can the movements of our eyeballs mean?
5.   What do we look like, we who cannot see?

6.   Is sightlessness a curse? Is it redemption we're
7.   trying to make out
                somewhere up there
                        far off?
8.   At any rate we're
9.   streetwise enough to know
10. that dreamers
                staring at their shoes
11. get shortest shrift from passers-by.

12. What clever metaphysics can account
13. for our condition? While the city crowds
14. laugh or sing or bellow, clawing
15. at pleasure's
16. tattered
17. shreds,

18. one of the unblind comes to say
19. 'See! I, too, have lost my way;
20. and drag along,
21. more dazed than you.'

22. But what does he
23. really want?
24. To give us walk-on parts
25. in a fancy masque of his
26. about the *deus absconditus*?

My particular approach once again makes it easy for me to abandon the sonnet for free verse. The sonnet's *volta* is a formal warrant to turn to Pascalian metaphysics, to plumb the meaning of the image, to pose the resounding question, to assume the mantle of responsible poet. This change of perspective and scale is signalled in the text by the shift from the lower case 'ciel' of line 7, to the capitalized 'Ciel' of line 14. Both of these occurrences of 'ciel' are structurally dramatized by their position as *rejets* (as is 'au loin' in line 6), first after the line-ending ('restent levés/Au ciel;'), and then after the caesura:

Je dis: Que cherchent-ils//au Ciel, tous ces aveugles?   2+4+2+4

Faithful to my oppositional strategy, I have used the lineational flexibility of free verse to create a sequence of *contre-rejets* which lift out the personal pronouns of the blind ('us', line 2; 'we're', line 6; 'we're', line 8) and set these against the 'he' of line 22 (backed up by 'his' of line 25) of the poet. The blind have no desire to prosodically project a sky they cannot see, but rather express a vulnerability, a state of suspension always threatened, which, for a moment, they wish on to the poet. And it is not the confrontation of the physical ('ciel') and the metaphysical ('Ciel') which interests them, but, rather, the social, and the way in which individuals are 'concentrated' into groups by some shared infirmity, so that other individuals can stand off from them.

My version does not allow the poet to put the final question, largely because the blind have, in their subversion of sonnet-structure, already put it (lines 6–7). At the same time, the blind's habit of looking skyward—picked out by connoisseurs as a curious, distinguishing feature of blind people[6]—by which the poet's question is justified, is explained by the blind as a strategy for physical survival in a city subject to 'pavement rage'. But I have, in my treatment of this last tercet, maintained the poet's exclamatory imperative 'Vois!' In the version of the poem published in *L'Artiste* (15 October 1860), this penultimate line runs:

—Moi, je me traîne aussi, mais, plus qu'eux hébété.

In other words, the poet, thanks to the buffer of a dash, is able to turn suddenly into a quiet space of his own, to reflect, in soliloquy. The rhythm of this line is wonderfully equivocal from a tonal point of view; one might read it either as

—Moi,/je me traîne aussi,//mais,/ plus qu'eux hébété,   1+5+1+5 or as

—Moi, je me traî/ne aussi,// mais, plus qu'eux/hébété;   4+2+3+3

that is, either as moments of jarring realization, in a repeated rhythm of illumination, or as the confession of a knowledge arrived at much earlier, in a rhythm whose modulations express an existential discomfort. The line that we have from the second edition of *Les Fleurs du Mal* (1861) is, to my ear, altogether less satisfying: the poet amplifies his voice, as if to outshout the noisy, pleasure-seeking throng, in an appeal for sympathy. The rhythm of the line tends more certainly towards 1+5+1+5, at least in the first hemistich. But the 1861 version does introduce the notion of seeing, a resource which can be put to several uses. In the ST, the imperative is addressed to the city, which is sighted, but is subject to its own kinds of 'aveuglement'.[7] In the TT, it is addressed to the blind men, and it looks either like a moment of thoughtlessness (but with the blind, one can afford to be thoughtless); or it expresses an exasperation, not with the crowd so much as with a Western tradition which requires *visible* evidence of any ill, pain, or misfortune, if sympathy is to be deserved; or it is some messianic desire to work a miracle in a world deserted by the divinity.

We have made mention of the dash in the 1860 version and something further should be said about the punctuation. First, in the ST, only one question is asked, in the final line, a rhetorical question which will get no answer. This question, perversely and peculiarly, is not addressed to the blind men, though if anyone were to know the answer, they would. In fact, the blind remain in the third person throughout the poem. The poet only communicates with the sighted, with the city, even if it is addressed in a contemptuous 'tu' form. The poet's rather covert way of justifying this ostracization of the blind is to render them mute as well, by passing them, in lines 9–10, through Pascal's 'Le silence éternel de ces espaces infinis m'effraie' [The eternal silence of these infinite spaces fills me with fear]. This muting of the blind makes them look like the scapegoats of the city's pleasure—the uninterrupted din of the crowd is punished by a visitation of dumbness and blindness on a selection of its members. Part of the TT's purpose, therefore, is quite simply to restore to the blind a voice which the ST, under false pretences, robbed them of. The blind then use their voice to ask many more rhetorical questions than the poet has the presence of mind to pose, preoccupied as he is in monumentalizing their symbolism. I have tried to point up this matter of enforced muteness, a little too heavily perhaps, in my reference to 'walk-on parts'.

Secondly, to judge by the degree and force of the punctuation in the first quatrain, Baudelaire wanted to imprint the blind men's unsteady, staccato gait and the erratic movement of their eyes on the body of the text, by resorting to a telegraphic style of random abuse. If we turn to the variants to be found in *L'Artiste*, we shall find increased punctuational activity in the first stanza, with additional commas after 'singuliers' and 'Dardant' and 'où'. As the poem proceeds to its close, no sign of remorse for this opening appears, apart from the self-punishment which the poet inflicts on himself, by identifying himself with the subjects of his derision. My version restores continuity and easy fluency to the blind men, at least to their speech: I have kept the punctuational interruptions as few as possible. This has the added advantage of putting their knowledge at some distance from the here and now; the detemporalizing effect of the removal of punctuation gives a restful equanimity to their elucubrations. That Baudelaire, for example, is haunted by the idea of the *deus absconditus* is no new revelation—for the blind this is to be treated as old hat. And free verse helps to reinforce the impression that they are not performing to the poet's tune, as in some circus sideshow, but that they are able to improvise their own destiny, their own rhythms of speech, their own emphases and pacing. Free verse stands here against any suggestion of the robotic. Conversely, however, I have littered the 'unblind's' words with as much punctuation as I can manage; this is not intended as a gesture of vengefulness, so much as an unmasking of the poet's bad faith; this is, on his part, an act of hammy imitation, which, precisely, necessitates 'See!', for otherwise it will not be believed; by aping the broken and staccato, by making it graphically visible, in signs, he will not, however, convince a blind man of its truth.

Finally, I would like to comment on the epigraph. These two lines from Eliot's 'The Fire Sermon' ('The Waste Land') relate, of course, to Tiresias, who, 'throbbing between two lives', has 'foresuffered all' and is a guide to lust in the city. Tiresias is the figure who would see Thebes in Paris, who turns the poet into the wily Odysseus visiting the Underworld. But more important still, he is the point of convergence of all experience, and thus the one who sees the poem in its entirety; as Eliot puts it in his own footnote:

> Tiresias, although a mere spectator and not indeed a 'character', is yet the most important personage in the poem, uniting all the rest. Just as the one-eyed merchant, seller of currants, melts into the Phoenician Sailor, and the latter is not wholly distinct from Ferdinand Prince of Naples, so all the women are one woman, and

The Route through Prose

It is difficult to know what the ambitions of the prose translation of a verse poem should, or can, be. Easy assumptions about the inferiority of its status are already confirmed by habits of layout: in bilingual editions, instead of boldly standing alongside the ST, on the facing page, prose versions are 'relegated' to the page's foot. One cannot, in fact, imagine an edition of prose translations which is not bilingual (I leave aside 'special cases' such as Jouve's translations of Shakespeare's sonnets, or Bonnefoy's of 'Venus and Adonis' and 'The Rape of Lucretia'): prose translations usually make no claims to ontological independence, but instead gladly embrace their role as textual aids. Are the majority of prose versions, then, inevitably cribs?

This is certainly the function that Carol Clark seems to accept for her prose renderings in *Baudelaire: Selected Poems* (1995):

> This translation does not pretend to be anything but an aid to reading the poems in French. It does not (and, I believe, could not) aspire to convey the rhythms and melody of the originals, but at most to avoid outright cacophony [*sic*]. To help the reader whose French is not strong, I have followed wherever possible the grammatical constructions of the original; where I have not, it is because I judged the order in which words appear in the line more important than the precise syntax.
>
> (1995: xxvii)

Here, quite clearly, translation is envisaged as a supplement and a convenience. It helps the reader through those tricky patches where his knowledge of the SL is insufficient, and removes the need to search out the dictionary. These translations are lifeboats which plan to put the reader back aboard the abandoned ship of the ST with all speed. To facilitate these transitions back and forth, the TT tries to shadow the steps of the ST as closely as possible, tries to manage the word-for-word translation of an interlinear rendering.

Clark calls her work 'plain prose translation'. It is not entirely clear whether this means a translation in plain prose, that is, a prose without pretension, unfussy; or a plain translation in prose, that is, a translation looking to be 'literal', imitative, without interpretative liberties or connotational elaborations. Perhaps both ideas are included. At all events, the translator must embark on a programme of self-denial, where prose is a discipline of privation which guarantees against obfuscation. Francis Scarfe's 1964 *Baudelaire* also offers a plain prose translation of each poem, and J.M. Cohen's 'General Editor's Foreword' confirms what we have so far supposed: foot-of-page prose translations accelerate the reading of a text in a language which the reader still finds difficult, and, in so doing, accelerates the process which leads to the ability to do without the translation:

> In this way, if they [adventurous readers] are willing to start with a careful word-for-word comparison, they will soon dispense with the English, and read a poem by Petrarch, Campanella, or Montale, by Garcilaso, Gongora, or Lorca, straight through.
>
> (1964: v)

But Scarfe himself is not altogether happy with these constraints:

> In translating these poems of Baudelaire's into prose, I have tried to compromise as well as possible between the necessity, in this popular series, of giving word-for-word equivalents for the original, and a desire to render them into something like a prose-poem.
>
> (1964: lx)

Unfortunately, he does not go on to say what this might entail.

Let us then briefly compare Clark's and Scarfe's accounts of the first stanza of 'Confession', a poem addressed to Mme Sabatier:

> Une fois, une seule, aimable et douce femme,
> A mon bras votre bras poli
> S'appuya (sur le fond ténébreux de mon âme
> Ce souvenir n'est point pâli);

Once, just once, lovable and gentle woman, on my arm your
polished arm leaned (on the dark ground of my soul that bright
memory has never faded);

(Clark, 1995: 47)

Once and once only, lovable and gentle woman, you leaned your
smooth arm on mine: the memory of it has never faded from the
dark background of my soul.

(Scarfe 1964: 134)

Clark is true to an intention which makes comprehensible potentially
controversial choices. 'Polished' read without the French alongside might
seem odd (prosthetics?), but as it is we understand this as a translation
which alerts us to a word favoured by Baudelaire both, interestingly, as a
quality of verse ('A une Madone', 'L'Avertisseur') and as a grace of
different parts of the female anatomy—Baudelaire writes the female body,
and tattoos it with punctuation—often made more assimilable by simile:

> Sur ton beau corps poli comme le cuivre
>
> ('Le Léthé')

> Polis comme de l'huile, onduleux comme un cygne
>
> ('Les Bijoux')

It also warns us against thinking that 'poli' here means 'polite' (this negative
function of literal translation can be extremely important). The possible
awkwardness of 'on my arm your polished arm leaned' is to be explained
by Clark's determination to keep to the order of the words in the line and
to pursue the strange feelings of disjunction and transferred agency that
go with the reflexive verb ('S'appuya'). But these moves give Clark's
account altogether move expressive energy, more potentially dark corners
and devious turns, than Scarfe's version has. Scarfe has, if anything,
dispersed the energy of the verse by lifting the 'hidden' parenthesis into
the open air, increasing its transparency, by omitting one of Baudelaire's
commas and by straightening out all the inversions. And two things must
immediately be said about prose: (i) punctuation is a crucial agent of
rhythmic tensility; and (ii) 'normal' word order is more likely to de-
rhythmicize language at the phrasal level than a syntax complicated by
inversions and *incises*. My own version would run:

Once, and only once, lovable, solicitous, you laid your smooth arm

149

on mine (against the darkened backdrop of my soul, the memory
still burns bright);

Here I have tried to intimate 's'appuyer' in 'solicitous', and turned what
appears, in the French, to be an absolute evaluation ('lovable and gentle
woman') into responses prompted by the mood of that particular evening
('lovable, solicitous'). Furthermore, by treating the adjectives disjunc-
tively, I have tried to imbue them with some of the force they have by virtue
of their pre-positioning in the French: intimate, infused with tonal
innuendo. With 'darkened backdrop', I want an inner theatre where the
dark is the result of some process, the gradual losing of light or a strategy
of progressive self-concentration.

If we started this translation on another prose tack, a prose tack which
had no mindfulness of poetry, that just wanted to be prose, then we might
arrive at something rather different:

> Do you remember? I do. As clearly as if it were yesterday. You leant
> against me, your arm on mine. It was late, with a full moon bright
> as a new coin… and Paris asleep. The night had a kind of solemnity,
> like a very slow-moving river. Cats were on the prowl, along the sides
> of the houses, under the coach-gates…sometimes listening,
> sometimes keeping us company, like familiars.[1]

What prose of this kind, at a lower and more colloquial temperature, does
is sharpen our sensitivity to linguistic 'invraisemblance'. Poetry's lineation,
and suspensive, sustaining music disarm our assessment of probabilities;
poetry can thus indulge in the kind of syntactic accumulations and
embeddings, the shifts in tense and liberties of expression, that would raise
eyebrows in prose (Scott 1998: 57–9). With the kind of prose utterance
purposed here, 'aimable et douce femme' seems an improbably
condescending interpolation, as improbable as describing her arm to her
as 'smooth', or as anything else. Nor would such a voice have wanted to
linger over 's'étalait'. Prose translations, and prose poems, may want to
root out those plausible implausibilities with which verse is littered. And
when David Scott points to that 'apparent lack of poetic self-confidence
and relative decline in lyrical energy' which 'was to become a characteristic
of Baudelaire's prose poems of the 1860s' (1984: 66), we may believe that
Baudelaire was growing weary of the self-delusions perpetuated by verse's
bag of tricks.

As a way of turning to the rhythmic features of prose translation, I
would cite from one further preface to a recent anthology of French verse,

William Rees's *French Poetry 1820–1950* (1990). He describes his aims as translator in the following terms:

> The main purpose is to provide access to meaning by removing semantic barriers, and thus to accelerate the penetration of the poem itself by the non-French reader. My translations are, I hope, neither woodenly literal nor pretentiously literary. They seek neither to efface themselves nor to blur criteria by competing with the original for attention.
>
> (1990: xxiv)

Once again the emphasis is on comprehension and speed of access. And rather like Scarfe, Rees wants to find a fruitful compromise between promoting the original and avoiding the pedantically punctilious. His own assessment of what takes them beyond the latter is as follows:

> Even so, if my translations are successful they are a step above the literal. They have decided rhythms and sound-patterns that please the ear, or at least do not displease it. They may occasionally even have a certain equivalent musicality.
>
> (1990: xxiv)

There are rather too many let-out clauses here; and there is too yawning a gulf between 'decided' and 'may occasionally'. But what might words like these mean? Let us look at Rees's account of the first stanza of 'La Musique':

> La musique souvent me prend comme une mer!
>   Vers ma pâle étoile,
> Sous un plafond de brume ou dans un vaste éther,
>   Je mets à la voile.

> Music often takes me like a sea! Towards my pale star, beneath a misty ceiling or in a vast ether I set sail;
>
> (Rees 1990: 151)

and compare it with Scarfe's version:

> Music often carries me away like a sea, and under a canopy of mist or through the vast ether, I set sail for my faint star.
>
> (1964: 93)

I do not wish here to investigate the lexical differences, which are relatively insignificant, but rather to focus my attention on their rhythmic divergencies. Rees's translation is 30 syllables long and has the following rhythmic configuration, where // marks a major juncture, and / a minor one:

6   3   5

/ × / × /   × / × /   × /   × / /

Music often takes me/ like a sea!// Towards my pale star,//

7   6   3

× / × / × / ×   / × × / / × × / /

beneath a misty ceiling// or in a vast ether// I set sail;

Against this sequence of five major units, Scarfe has four, adding up to 34 syllables, rhythmically disposed thus:

9   3   9

/ × / × / ×   / × / × × / × / × ×

Music often carries me away/ like a sea,// and under a

6   3

/ × × × / ×   × × / / × × / /

canopy of mist// or through the vast ether,// I set sail/

4

× × / /

for my faint star.

What is fascinating in this comparison is the way in which different rhythmic environments apply different pressures on identical words. Preceded by a weak syllable, Rees's 'like' tends to attract a stress, to maintain the run, despite the juncture. Similarly his 'or', in a context of weak syllables, will perhaps seek to re-establish the principle of alternation with a stress. Rees's version then is proportionately more stressed (16 stresses in 30 syllables) than Scarfe's (15 in 34 syllables), and the stresses are more evenly distributed. Scarfe's account is a more 'climactic' one, in two senses: (i) the movement of the first clause, from broad gesture to dramatic point (9 > 3), is repeated in the second clause, but now in paired measures (9 + 6 > 3 + 4); (ii) paired stresses create a 'destinational' sequence in the final three measures, as 'vast ether' leads into a bacchic measure (×//) followed by an ionic one (××//). This kind of concerted drive is not to be found so markedly in Rees. His version ends with a bacchic which also picks up the double stress of 'vast ether', but these double stresses now *echo* 'a pale star', which is part of the first measure of the clause; in other words, Rees's design is more about closing a circle than about providing unrelenting and frame-breaking forward propulsion. And Rees's mirroring effect is repeated in the way that the trisyllabic close of the first clause ('like a sea') is answered in the trisyllabic close of the second clause ('I set sail'). Finally, the syllabic lengths of his measures seem to be less polarized: it is the more nuanced nature of the syllabic fluctuations which provide his particular music.

The different kinds of rhythmic pleasure we can take in these two versions perhaps transcend questions such as 'Is "ceiling" a better or worse choice than "canopy"?' Indeed, without differences of lexical and syntactic choice, we would have no differences of music. Furthermore, because prose is our material, rhythmically variable readings of the same lexical sequence are more available to us.

In describing what takes place when a verse poem becomes a prose poem, it is usual to propose that rhyme and metre are removed. The removal of rhyme reminds us that prose has little interest in mnemonicity: it remembers, but does not itself ask to be remembered, at least in its textual specificity. Mnemonicity is ultimately about textual survival, that is, the survival of a text in its non-interpreted, or pre-interpreted, integrity. This is perhaps to argue that prose is under greater readerly pressure than verse, the pressure of comprehension, of consumption. In the moment of reading, metre's presence in verse is pre-interpretational; it preserves the existence of the verse poem and, at the same time, maps out/stakes out its textuality. Rhythm in prose does not map out textual space, cannot work as a textual cadaster, but instead constantly questions itself, improvises itself, interrupts itself and, more important, creates no continuity between textual organization and the process of being remembered by the reader.

The kind of rhythmic presence we have just described is one in which the linguistic is constantly being appropriated by the performative. In regular verse, the function of metre is to confirm the 'linguisticity', the text-determined nature, of rhythm; metre requires certain stress promotions and demotions for its fulfilment. But for the reader of prose, as we have seen, promotions and demotions are made according either to guessed-at probabilities or to the conveniences of the voice. English is ostensibly an accentuated language, but whose accentual flexibility prose is interested to maximize. It is common to treat the rhythm of a poem as the linguistic matrix of all possible scansions (i.e. what is said, the *énoncé*, precedes the saying of it, the *énonciation*). The prose version of this relationship would rather be that the rhythm of any passage is the sum of all possible scansions (i.e. what is said coincides with the saying of it) (see Meschonnic 1982: 275).

We might suppose that each genre of written language defines, to a degree, the status of the speaking/reading voice, and solicits the voice in a distinctive way. Genres are different kinds of theatricalization of the voice. Furthermore, we might propose that the 'natural' voice of a poem is the poem's own, the intonational patterns peculiar to stanzaic structure, the respirational spans peculiar to line and caesura, the phonic materiality of its language. In other words, we acknowledge that verse, partly at least, disembodies the voice, makes it abstract. This is the diction of verse; this helps us see that rhythm in verse is established elsewhere, is generated by *what is to be said*. Rhythm is both part of the poem as shared experience, its trans-subjectivity, and part of its futurity, and to be these things it must be coded. Prose is highly uncoded. Without the express purpose of keeping open trans-subjective channels, the rhythmic world of prose is open to all kinds of vocal solipsism. But this solipsistic solitude cannot maintain itself, however much it may protect itself with paralinguistic differentia (of stressing, stress-degree, pausing, pace, tone, etc.); other voices, vocal multitudes, intervene. And perhaps, after all, the prose translation's yearning to pull itself into something aesthetic, something shaped, is motivated by a desire to escape from the chaos of the paralinguistic into the linguistic, from the rhythms of idiolectal saying into the rhythms of the said.

The 'literalness' which the plain prose translation pursues has two meanings: 'word-for-word' and semantically 'close'. The absence of verse constraints is meant to make both tasks easier. But if the plain prose translation is not read interlinearly, but simply as a prose translation, then it might be argued that its 'word-for-wordness' does not survive. Word-for-word memorability, as part of mnemonicity, is made possible by verse structure. What advertises itself as a word-for-word translation (prose) does not asked to be remembered word-for-word, but in the totality of its accumulated but transitory effects, that is, as a *paraphrase*; in other words, this purportedly faithful translation is not faithful in the way it imagines, because we apprehend it in a different way. And yet paraphrase is not an ST in a fallen state; our general contempt for paraphrase is born of an inability to treat it as a transposition. And this inability relates, in turn, to a misunderstanding of the notion 'literal'. The literal is not the neutral, but a mode of utterance motivated by the laconic, or the anti-rhetorical, or the trivializing, or the plain-dealing, i.e. a well-understood code. All in all, it seems that the plain prose translation both falsifies, even if unwittingly, its own capacities, and does a disservice to prose translation in general, by giving its audience the wrong kinds of expectation. The simple fact of the matter is that a plain prose translation would rather not have to exist;[2] its being a kind of extended, continuous glossary dangerously encourages it to remain inert at the textual level. A glossary, continuous or not, brings us back to the evils of bilingual translation (as opposed to bi-monolingual translation): when Baudelaire writes 'plafond', we may tell ourselves 'ceiling'; we do not ask what 'ceiling' means, because it is assumed we already know, as if the TT had no ambition, indeed no ability, to revitalize its own language.

As a first step to gathering up these complex and often conflicting genetic impulses, I would like to inspect an example of a prose translation which grew up alongside a verse translation. In 1860, Baudelaire produced his translation of passages from Longfellow's *Song of Hiawatha* for Robert Stoepel's symphony/oratorio (the partnership came to nothing), and we are lucky enough to have his prose versions of his own fragmentary verse accounts. The fourth 'paragraph' of Longfellow's 'The Peace-Pipe' runs:

> And the smoke rose slowly, slowly,
> Through the tranquil air of morning,
> First a single line of darkness,
> Then a denser, bluer vapour,
> Then a snow-white cloud unfolding,
> Like the tree-tops of the forest,
> Ever rising, rising, rising,
> Till it touched the top of heaven,
> Till it broke against the heaven,
> And rolled outward all around it.

The unrhyming paragraphs in trochaic tetrameter are rendered by Baudelaire into sixains of alexandrines, rhyming *aabccb*, thus:

> Et lentement montait la divine fumée
> Dans l'air doux du matin, onduleuse, embaumée.
> Et d'abord ce ne fut qu'un sillon ténébreux;
> Puis la vapeur se fit plus bleue at plus épaisse,
> Puis blanchit; et montant, et grossissant sans cesse,
> Elle alla se briser au dur plafond des cieux.

The omission of the line 'Like the tree-tops of the forest' is to be attributed to the process of abbreviation: Baudelaire had to reduce Longfellow's 800 lines to some 300. The same omission occurs in the prose version:

> Et la fumée s'élevait lentement, lentement, dans l'air tranquille du matin; ce ne fut d'abord qu'une simple ligne de ténèbres; puis la

vapeur s'épaissit et bleuit, puis se déploya comme un vaste nuage
d'un blanc de neige, et montant, montant toujours, alla se briser
contre les cieux, où elle s'élargit et déborda de tous côtés.

There are things here to be expected as natural 'freedoms' of the prose
version: the removal of the inversions to be found in the verse; the use of
repetition to generate rhythmic awareness and continuity; the avoidance
of adjectival decoration ('divine', 'onduleuse', 'embaumée'), apparently
designed to hold the verse rapt; a lack of embarrassment about multiplying
pronominal verb-forms (which the verse diminishes, partly by recourse to
adjectives).

A comparison of these two versions may seem to bear out a comment
made by Bonnefoy on the desirability of verse as a medium for the
translation of verse:

> S'il y a poésie, c'est parce qu'on a voulu que la part sonore des mots
> soit écoutée, se fasse élément actif dans l'élaboration d'une forme,
> et cela pour que la signification ne soit plus seule à décider de la
> phrase, et que l'économie des concepts en soit brouillé, leur autorité
> affaiblie, leur voile déchiré, tant soit peu, qui nous prive de
> l'immédiat.
>
> (1993: I)
>
> [If there is poetry, it is because the writer wanted the acoustic
> dimension of words to be listened to, to play an active part in the
> elaboration of a form, so that meaning is no longer the only factor
> dictating the phrase, and that the organization of its concepts is
> muddied, their authority enfeebled, their veil, which deprives us of
> the immediate, even if ever so slightly, rent.]

In prose, it would seem, language sinks its materiality into its conceptuality.
While in verse the signifier always exceeds the signified, and verbal
presence, or presence within words, exceeds meaning, or denomination
exceeds identification, in prose the reverse shift takes place. We might
argue, for example, that the reflexive verb (e.g. 's'élevait') 'translates' the
intransitive verb (e.g. 'montait') into the auto-transitive, and in so doing
increases the sense of intentional and *responsible* agency. The intransitive
verb mystifies action and wraps the agent in something private and
engrossed. A reflexive verb exhibits the self, while the intransitive verb
reveals very little and leaves the relationship between the agent and the
surrounding world unrealized and unresolved. The cultivation of
adjectives in the poem obviously increases our sense of qualitative

investigation and response, of the evaporation of nouns/facts into bodiless and elusive experience. In this respect, poetry, however grammatically third-person, will be first-personalized to a degree that prose cannot achieve; prose will always tend to report things which have lost a certain proximity (of time, space and memory). The adjectives also add significantly to the dominant sound-patterns: /ɑ̃/ and its modulant /ɔ̃/; the punctuation of /ø/, and most oddly perhaps, /d/ and /y/—I say 'most oddly' because 'dur', a rather pointed choice, the result perhaps of the sudden installation of Baudelaire's Christian God, acoustically grows out of the sequence '*d*ivine f*u*mée' > '*D*ans l'air *d*oux *du* ... on*du*leuse' > '*d*'abord ... f*u*t' > 'pl*u*s' (bis) > '*du*r'.

Another more speculative point that Bonnefoy makes is that while in prose time leaks away, in poetry the instant is dammed up, not in such a way as to stop time, but to give time a sense of direction, to enrich time:

> Mais cet instant ne sera pas pour nous détourner de la temporalité, bien au contraire: de tels débouchés sur l'indéfait, sur la plénitude, ne pouvant que donner un but à notre existence, et donc enrichir— d'un contenu, de désir, de recherche, d'égarement, de retour—le temps qu'on consacre à la vivre.
>
> (1993: II)
>
> [But this instant will not have the effect of turning us away from temporality, quite the contrary: such openings on to the unfragmented, on to fullness, can only give a goal to our existence, and thus enrich—with a content, with desire, with searching, with distraction, with return—the time spent living it.]

The syntactic and narrative cohesion is provided in the poem by the changing activity of the smoke: 'd'abord' (black line) > 'Puis' (bluer, thicker) > 'Puis' (white). But these line-initial notations of sequence become, at the line-endings, a set of rhymes: 'ténébreux' > 'épaisse' > 'sans cesse', which distribute meaning differently, more problematically. What this rhyme-sequence also begins to tell us is that the experiential value of a sequence of changing colours is a transition from qualitative adjective, through verbal activity (represented by the adverbial 'sans cesse'), to a substantival destination or anchorage ('plafond des cieux'). Progressive changes of colour in the smoke, in unilinear time, produce variations in modality which remain unresolved as a sequence until the full-stop. The prose covers the fourth stage—the smoke rising to the 'top of heaven'—at a consistent speed, and we are again encouraged to see the two participles as consecutive, one on top of the other ('montant, montant toujours'); the verse, on the other hand, creates an experience of teasing, self-amplifying delay, and of increasingly intolerable imminence, by the acoustic means of rhythmic juncture and phonetic organization:

Puis blanchit;/ et montant// et grossissant sans cesse.   3+3+4+2

This line is the second of an enclosed couplet in *rimes embrassées*, and so has a highly suspensive intonation, before the dramatic arrival of the final, clinching line. It is a line which, after closing off the colour changes in a trisyllabic measure, two of whose syllables are /i/, the phoneme of the past historic, picks out the other phoneme, /ɑ̃/, and develops it relentlessly. Here the repetition of 'et' (/e/) not only increases pressure, but transforms the consecutive into the simultaneous. The rhythmic regularity of the first hemistich overrides the syntactic juncture: the semi-colon after 'blanchit' cannot really install interruption, in the face of the metrical drive of the two trisyllables—/pɥiblɑ̃ʃi/emɔ̃tɑ̃/. And no sooner is the upward movement of 'montant' mentioned, than it is momentarily stalled (the caesura helps to create Bonnefoy's 'instants'), and then released in a broader tetrasyllabic measure, before being confined again in a dissyllabic measure which, however, tells of anything but confinement. In other words, while the prose version uses syntax to organise information about a sequence of events to which the reader has not been privy, the verse re-animates the events as a sequence of psycho-modal responses which invite the reader into the experience, if not the action.

One further and connected observation, which grows out of the syntactically 'anachronistic' or 'achronic' positioning of 'onduleuse, embaumée' also relates to Bonnefoy's comments on verse's temporality. Elsewhere (1998: 97–101), I have argued that the temporality of verse has four levels: the 'temps désigné' (the time denoted for any events in the poem, whether external or internal) and 'le temps existentiel du poète' (the poet's own experience of time); the 'temps de la lecture' (the time it takes the reader to 'speak' the text) and the 'temps du lecteur' (the existential time of the reader, including memory, fantasy, association, and the reader's experience of language). Crudely put then, two kinds of time which relate to linguistic output, and two that relate to readerly input. 'Onduleuse, embaumée' are the way in which the poet translates the 'temps désigné' ('lentement montait') into the 'temps existentiel du poète': the poet, fascinated, creates rhythms in the smoke's unfurling ('onduleuse'), willing time to be frozen in this moment, even as he breathes in the smoke's fragrance. And it is likely that the 'temps de la lecture', equilibriated at 3+3+3+3, will encourage the 'temps du lecteur' to associate the mood of the adjectives with the pervasive 'air doux du matin', to read this smoke as a feminine presence, whose initial phallicity ('sillon ténébreux'), is belied by her widening, whitening canopy, which is bruised as it collides with the patriarchal limits ('dur plafond des cieux'). This temporal complexity, this layering of writerly and readerly textures is something that verse, peculiarly, can achieve.

So far, all we have said implies that prose experience is somehow flattened and unilinear, that the quality of the reader's attention is less intense, less shaped, more distant. It is likely that, without the urgings of verse-structure, accentuation will decrease both in strength and frequency. It is likely that, given the longer perceptual spans, the reader's mind will wander, be more selective, be more passive. But these negative arguments have their positive counterparts, most of which remain invisible to us simply because we are unpractised readers of prose. And as we have already remarked, it is one of the functions of translation to energize, and sharpen critical awareness of, the forms it puts to its uses.

As a way of approaching the expressive resources of prose, I would like offer a rendering of 'Correspondances', which tries to push prose as close to a verse landscape as it can, while still enjoying benefits peculiar to prose:

> La Nature est un temple où de vivants piliers
> Laissent parfois sortir de confuses paroles;
> L'homme y passe à travers des forêts de symboles
> Qui l'observent avec des regards familiers.
>
> Comme de longs échos qui de loin se confondent
> Dans une ténébreuse et profonde unité,
> Vaste comme la nuit et comme la clarté,
> Les parfums, les couleurs et les sons se répondent.
>
> Il est des parfums frais comme des chairs d'enfants,
> Doux comme les hautbois, verts comme les prairies,
> —Et d'autres, corrompus, riches et triomphants,
>
> Ayant l'expansion des choses infinies,
> Comme l'ambre, le musc, le benjoin et l'encens,
> Qui chantent les transports de l'esprit et des sens.

1. Nature is a temple:/ from time to time,/ its living pillars,/ sibylline,/ let slip bewildering words.// We pass along these

/   ×   / × / ×   /   / ×   × /   ×

aisles,/ through symbols forest-thick,/ followed by eyes that

/ × /

know our minds.

× / × / ×   /   × / × /   / × × /

2.   Like vibrant echoes which,/ from far away,/ blend in a dark,

×   / × / ×× × / × / ×   / × / × /

deep-reaching unity,/ as vast as night,/ immense as light of day,/

/ ×   / ×   /   × / × /

colours, perfumes, sounds to each reply.

×   ×   / ×   / × / ×   /   × / ×

3.   There are perfumes fresh as children's skins.../ as sweet as

/ ×   / ×   /   ×   / ×   / × /   ×/ ×

oboes.../pasture-green,/ and others over-ripe/—elusive,

/   ×   / ×   / ×

dense—/ and domineering:

×   / ×   / ×   / ×   / × /   / ×   ×   / ×

4.   like musk and amber,/ incense, benjamin,/ radiant with untold

/ ×   /   × / × ×× /×/ ×   /   ×   / ×

space and time,/rejoicing in exhilarated soul and senses.

First and foremost, I wanted to create a text with a firm bearing rhythm, but with an equally strong phrasality, the sense of independent units developing, within the iambic pattern, their own leitmotivic connections and variations. The achievement of the first of these designs presented no problems: iambic is always ready to insinuate itself into voice. Punctuation can help to give relief to phrasal structure, and, in its turn, often needs the motivation of syntactic displacement (e.g. inversion) or an insertional syntax (apposition, adjectival and adverbial phrases). I have tried to use punctuation in a crudely modal way, too: the youthful, 'candid' perfumes are accompanied by concessive, dreamier, recollective *points de suspension*, which invite the intrusions of readerly subjectivity; while the power-based, mature perfumes have the peremptory interjections of the dash, generating impatient energy. I have also used the colon in both a conventional, grammatical way, and, an expressive one. On both occasions in the text, the colon introduces, in traditional manner, an explanation, elucidation, exemplification. But we would do well to remember what Gracq has to say: he calls the colon 'ni tout à fait ponctuation, ni tout à fait conjonction' [neither wholly punctuation, nor wholly conjunction], and goes on:

> Tous les autres signes, plus ou moins, marquent des césures dans le rythme, ou des flexions dans le ton de voix; il n'en est aucun, sauf lui, que la lecture à haute voix ne puisse rendre acceptablement.
>
> (1980: 258)
>
> [All the other signs, more or less, mark junctures in the rhythm, or

inflections in the tone of voice; all of them, save the colon, can be acceptably rendered when read aloud.]

Behind our confidence in ascribing to the colon a 'conjunctival' value which relates to 'because' or 'such as', lies our sense that many other conjunctival values are available. The colon loads syntactical and semantic relationships with invisible motive and intention; by concealing these motives, the colon engages readerly intuition, suspicion, interpretivity. Similarly, because the voice is unsure of 'conjunctival' function, so it is intonationally unsure. What it is doing is introducing a suspension: it may be the suspension of normal discourse or time, as the poem creates its own space, generates its own duration(s)—this is certainly what I intend with my initial colon: a sequence which is essentially unmetrical (although with trochaic potentialities), a bare statement ('Nature is a temple') discharges a poem which pursues its own rhythms and meanings, rather in the way that 'A sudden blow:' discharges Yeats's 'Leda and the Swan'. An originating, perhaps banal, metaphor, activates an exploration of implications which lie dormant within it. As we cross the colon, we cross into another layer of consciousness, into the play of another kind of mental energy. Even in the second example, after 'domineering', the sign of elucidation might be the sign of revelation, of a sharp upheaval of consciousness. The colon is a force of ellipsis, of implicitness; it creates a fertile tension between clauses/phrases which seem to have equivalent status. These rich perfumes are, it seems, duplicitous, or self-contradictory; exemplification is here not a mode of confirmation, but of possible redefinition, or of re-immersion.

Once phrasal structure is given prominence, then one can attend to the rhythmic relations between phrases, and to a music peculiar to prose, the music of junctures. The phrasal structure of the translation, assuming underlying iambic, might be tabulated thus:

1. $\neq$Tr 6 */4/5 */$\neq$Am 3/6//6/6/$\neq$In 8 ($\neq$In 4+4) = 44 syll. = 3$\neq$, 2*
2. 6/4/$\neq$In 10 */4/6/$\neq$Tr 9 ($\neq$Tr 5+4) = 39 syll. = 2$\neq$, 1*
3. 9 (4 * + $\neq$Tr 5)/5 */$\neq$Am 3/6/4/5 * = 32 syll. = 2$\neq$, 3*
4. 5 */$\neq$Tr 5/$\neq$In 8/13 * (3 * + 10 * (7 + 3 *)) = 31 syll. = 2$\neq$, 3*

[where * means that the measure ends with an unstressed syllable
$\neq$ means that the measure begins with a stressed syllable
Tr means that the measure has a trochaic pattern
In means that the measure has an inverted first foot
Am means that the measure is an amphimacer (/$\times$/)]

Number of different lengths of measure per 'stanza':

1.   6 = 4, 5 = 1, 4 = 3, 3 = 1
2.   6 = 2, 5 = 1, 4 = 3
3.   6 = 1, 5 = 3, 4 = 2, 3 = 1
4.   6 = 0, 5 = 2, 4 = 0, 3 = 2

A casual glance at this tabulation tells us that hexasyllabic measures set out strongly, but gradually die away, to be replaced by pentasyllabic measures; while 6 is accompanied by ≠ and ⋆ only once in the first (prose) measure, 5 has an opposite tendency to attract either ≠ or ⋆. Tetrasyllabic measures remain significant up to the final tercet, where they abruptly disappear. Trisyllabic measures constitute a thin, but, as we shall see, important thread through the poem. Where junctures are less marked, I have noted them as intraphrasal rather than interphrasal—thus, ≠In 8 (≠In 4+4), ≠Tr 9 (≠Tr 5+4), for example—but counted the subordinate, rather than the superordinate, measures. As far as these longer measures are concerned, I should observe three features immediately:

1. The only long measure which is 'simple' (single-unit) rather than 'composed' (a compound of units)—the 10 in 'stanza' 2—is so for a particular and self-evident reason ('blend in a dark, deep-reaching unity'). In many senses this is the heart of the poem, the achievement of organic wholeness by universal analogy. It is worth noting that the line to which this corresponds:

Dans une ténébreuse et profonde unité   6+3+3

also has a 'hémistiche simple', as if encompassing the 'hémistiche composée' which follows.

2. It is natural that these longer measures occur at 'stanza' ends. These are moments of relief and release, extended dying falls which are like a way out of the forests of meaning of the 'stanza's' interior. In the final 'stanza', this effect is amplified by the consecutive occurrence of two longer measures.

3. The odd man out is the first 'tercet', and not surprisingly, for traditional structural reasons. The absence of an extended measure at the end of this 'stanza' is to be explained by the interdependence of the tercets of a sonnet; the tercets are not structurally self-sufficient as the quatrains are, and as

162

the sestet as a whole is; each tercet needs the other for the completion of its rhyme scheme, for the transformation of the stanzaically *impair* into the parity of the whole unit. Furthermore, given the traditional *volta* or 'turn' of the sonnet, it is natural for the first tercet to begin with an introductory change of pace, a momentum, a confidence, which will impel it towards the resolution it so devoutly wishes.

It might be argued, then, that prose's phrasal resourcefulness is much greater than that of verse. Not only has prose a wider ranger of measure-lengths at its disposal, but it is much freer to arrange them as it wants. The first 'stanza', for example, is essentially a complex relation between 6 and 4. Of course, combinations of 6 and 4 will put the reader in mind of iambic pentameter, and it is true that 6 and 4 often occur together as adjacent measures:

> Nature is a temple: from time to time
> through symbols forest-thick, followed by eyes
> Like vibrant echoes which, from far away
> as vast as night, immense as light of day
> and others over-ripe—elusive, dense—

just as it is true that both 6 and 4 disappear at the same time (first 'tercet'). But, equally, 4 has interesting relationships with 5, and seems to be more predisposed to combine than 6 does: the more clearly 'composed' 8 at the end of the first 'stanza' has the same rhythmic constitution as the less clearly 'composed' 8 of the second 'tercet': /xx/x/x/; it is as if 4 had been assimilated into the verse in a way that 6 has not. And an octosyllabic configuration may also be heard, not just in the 4 + 4 at the end of the first 'stanza', but in the earlier 5 + 3 ('the living pillars, sibylline'), and in the 5 + 3 of the first 'tercet' ('as sweet as oboes…pasture-green'). It just depends on what second-level groupings the reading mind makes, and this option, to group or not, and the relative flexibility in partnering, is a further example of prose's paralinguistic invitations.

The other aspect of prose rhythm that we have identified as peculiar to the medium is what we have called 'the music of junctures'. When rhythms become phrasally based, we find that the points of contact between phrases correspondingly become places of particular interest, because this is where the music may change or discharge itself with differing degrees of intensity. In a predominantly iambic pattern, a stress at the beginning of the phrase will produce a syncopation (consecutive stresses buffered by a silent off-beat) and have one of the following consequences. It will either

(a) maintain the dominant metre after a reversed first foot; or (b) create a momentary rupture in the metre by introducing an alternative configuration.

In our rendering, we have three instances of inverted first feet, and four instances of trochaic modulation (if we count the opening clause as trochaic). But what I would like to concentrate on here are those instances in which a stressed first syllable announces an amphimacer (/×/) ('sibylline', 'pasture-green'), largely because these figures of metrical inturnedness resolve, in the final measure of the poem, into two amphibrachs (×/×) ('rejoicing', 'and senses') with their medial apices which resonate into fadingness. We may then become aware of other trisyllabic words, which will bear out what we may already suspect: that while the amphimacer expresses the self-assertiveness of physical phenomena, the amphibrach informs the more negotiable and fluid world of affect and diffuse sensation:

Amphimacer	*Amphibrach*
sibylline	bewildering (if treated as a trisyllable)
forest-thick	deep-reaching
pasture-green	elusive
over-ripe	rejoicing
benjamin	and senses

What effects measures which end with unstressed syllables can have we have already intimated: the text is aerated, expanded, gives pause to the mind which floats out of the text for a moment, on errands of its own, nowhere more so than in 'blend in a dark, deep-reaching unity', or 'as sweet as oboes'. Sometimes the expansion is something we are subject to ('domineering'). Junctures are the points at which the voice chooses its mode of release and its mode of attack (pace, loudness, etc.), defines the intonation contour of the phrase and the pausing attached to it. All this might suggest that, in prose, the linguistic music is more geared to activate paralinguistic music than it is in verse. This is a highly relative matter, and although there may be some truth in it, the more underlying principle, perhaps, is that prose localizes rhythmic awareness and rhythmic effects; this is not to imply that Bonnefoy is wrong, and that prose in fact cultivates the instant; it is to say that prose organizes temporality more randomly and multiply, more digitally than analogically. For example, it is clear that the sound /aɪ/ is dominant in the quatrains, often creating the effect of rhyme (first 'quatrain': 'time'/'sibylline'/'aisles'/'eyes'/'mind'; second 'quatrain':

'like'/'vibrant'/'night'/'light'/'reply'), while /I/ tends to replace it in the 'sestet' (first 'tercet': 'children's skins'/'elusive'/'domineering'; second 'tercet': 'incense'/'benjamin'/'with'/'rejoicing in exhilarated') (this again is a relative matter, and both sounds recur with greater or lesser frequency throughout). But despite the pattern of this distribution, we cannot call these sounds 'structuring', that is to say that, although we may see connections after the event, these sounds' recurrences do not, are not designed to, activate any processes of prediction and expectation. Prose, the prose poem, allows the world to come together in exhilarating experiences of *coincidence*, of surprised colloquy; in the manner of the surrealist *flâneur*, the writer and reader of prose encounter the 'merveilleux quotidien' [marvellous of the everyday] and 'hasard objectif' [objective chance] in its fluid meanderings; or, as Eliot puts it, in his 'Reflections on *Vers Libre*', 'Rhyme removed, much ethereal music leaps up from the word, music which has hitherto chirped unnoticed in the expanse of prose' (1953: 86). There are, of course, ways in which a text can bring sounds/words to our attention, but it is not within the *structure* of prose to do so, and so any connections we make lie in a no man's land between textual persuasion and personal caprice. If I pick up the string in /ɛns/ ('immense'/'dense'/'incense'/'senses'), do I hear them as unsorted *degrees* of likeness—in which case, the prevocalic 's' of 'incense' and 'senses' gives them a privileged intimacy in the group—or do I hear them 'conventionally', as punctuations of internal rhyme? And if I hear them as 'unsorted degrees of likeness', which is surely what the music peculiar to prose is all about, then this acousic fraternity will also include 'blend' and 'benjamin', and will congregate, if only subliminally, or at the very limits of acoustic recognition, in the 'temple' (/tɛmpəl/).

The prose version of 'Correspondances' shadows the verse ST in its wrought-up diction and the apparent activity of its effects. I would like to further pursue my speculations about the prosaic by offering a much 'flatter' version of another poem, 'Le Mort joyeux':

> Dans une terre grasse et pleine d'escargots
> Je veux creuser moi-même une fosse profonde,
> Où je puisse à loisir étaler mes vieux os
> Et dormir dans l'oubli comme un requin dans l'onde.
>
> Je hais les testaments et je hais les tombeaux;
> Plutôt que d'implorer une larme du monde,
> Vivant, j'aimerais mieux inviter les corbeaux
> A saigner tous les bouts de ma carcasse immonde.

O vers! noirs compagnons sans oreille et sans yeux,
Voyez venir à vous un mort libre et joyeux;
Philosophes viveurs, fils de la pourriture,

A travers ma ruine allez donc sans remords,
Et dites-moi s'il est encor quelque torture
Pour ce vieux corps sans âme et mort parmi les morts!

Spleen

Rage, rage against the dying of the light
(Dylan Thomas)

I'd like to dig myself a grave,/ good and deep,/ in a piece of loamy
land,/ full of snails,/ and there I'd lay my poor old bones to rest,/ nice
and leisurely,/ and be forgotten,/ like a shark on the sea-bed.// I hate
wills,/ and I'm none too keen on tombs either.// I've no mind,/ while
I've still got breath,/ to go begging folk to shed a tear or two;/ I'd
rather ask a pack of crows/ to peck a hole/ in every inch of my filthy
carcass.// Look sharp, black worms,/ my deaf and sightless friends,/
here comes a corpse/ who's willing and high-spirited.// You take life
as it comes,/ enjoy a feast,/ and need some rotting flesh/ to do your
breeding on.// So don't think twice,/ and give what's left of me/ a
proper going over.// Just let me know though,/ when I'm dead and
gone,/ if this old and soulless body/ has torments still to reckon with.

[Tabulation of measures: 8/3/7/3/10/5/5/7//3/9//3/5/11//8/4/10//4/6/
4/8//6/4/6/6//4/6/7//5/5/8/8]

This poem, entitled 'Spleen' when published in *Le Messager de
l'Assemblée* (9 April 1851), has attracted little critical attention. Adam
(1961: 360–1) looks upon it as a piece of attitudinizing in the macabre, a
poem with its eye on derisive shock-value, not to be confused with later
poems of genuine despair. Pichois (*OC*, I, 970) similarly finds in this poem
'le ton Jeune-France', and itemizes what he regards as its weaknesses:

Il serait facile d'en signaler, à côté de réussites, les faiblesses:

comment les vers, s'il n'ont pas d'yeux, peuvent-ils voir venir le mort? Sont-ce les vers qui sont dépourvus d'oreille (au singulier) et d'yeux (au pluriel), non pas les cadavres qu'ils ont dévorés? Même gaucherie dans les rimes de ce quatorzain: croisées dans les quatrains, elles hésitent entre la différence et la ressemblance, entre l'assonance et la rime à proprement parler (escargots, os; tombeaux, corbeaux).

[It would be easy to point out the weaknesses, alongside the felicities: how can the worms see the dead man coming, if they have no eyes? Is it the worms who are without ears (in the singular) and eyes (in the plural) and not the corpses they have devoured? Same awkwardness in the rhymes of this sonnet: alternating in the quatrains, they hesitate between difference and similarity, between assonance and rhyme in the true sense (escargots, os; tombeaux, corbeaux).]

But if parody is among Baudelaire's principal purposes, these criticisms may seem to miss the point. At all events, I have, following prose's own promptings, retreated from rhetorical invocation to conversational monologue, from poet to persona, from prematurely aged maturity to an older, less educated and somewhat diffident speaker. The epigraph is designed to throw this tonal shift into relief and to underline how the poem quietly rebels against high-sounding rebellion. Instead of offering sustained utterance, it creates a more open weave, both by multiplying slight variations in mood and attitude, and by making the temporality of the text much more diverse and unresolved.

I refer to the speaker as 'somewhat diffident', by which I mean that his posture towards his own wishes and motives has some uncertainty, and that he has to feel his way towards the note he wishes to strike. In fact, he tends to start under the note and is ever in danger of not quite reaching it. The first sentence, for example, follows Baudelaire's text quite closely: the search for peace, which threatens to sideline any other consideration, manifests itself in the stanza's rhythms which stabilize themselves in a trisyllabic equilibrium, before a final 4+2 precipitates the descent into self-effacement:

$$4+2+2+4$$
$$4+2+3+3$$
$$3+3+3+3$$
$$3+3+4+2$$

In my version, in rather similar fashion, the phrase-length, which to begin with is polarized between long and short, begins, as the sentence comes to a close, to find a mean, and the rhythm of the last measure—xx/xx//— shows us an anapaest intensifying itself to ionic as it emphatically and at last reaches its desired destination. This movement is supported by the /l/ of 'like' as it becomes the phoneme of rich restfulness: 'like' > 'loamy land' > 'full of snails' > 'lay' > 'leisurely'.

In casting my speaker as older and less educated, I have resorted to three devices: (i) coordinating intensification ('good and deep', 'nice and leisurely', 'dead and gone'); (ii) phrasal verbs, combined with a lack of embarrassment about clause-terminal prepositions and adverbs; (iii) a preference for bare monosyllables. But there are moments of knowing linguistic adaptation in this piece, when the speaker comes back on himself in revealing collocations. For example, having adopted the conciliatory, even slightly submissive, 'folk', he then interprets this term by collocating 'crows' with 'pack', so that we can hear 'pack of wolves' and more easily anthropomorphize the crows. Similarly, his choice of 'high-spirited' (translating 'joyeux') is archly mischievous: 'Look sharp black worms [...] here comes' etc. is a travesty of Pilate's 'Ecce homo' (John 19:5), and makes 'high-spirited' more a tart comment on divinity of origin than an affirmation of lightness of heart. Correspondingly, the paradoxical 'Look sharp [...] sightless friends' assumes more taunting hues (Pichois simply seems pedantic here). This 'sightless' bounces us forward to 'soulless' a connection which liberates the metaphorics of blindness, and underlines the Laforguian vision of blind reproductive drives fed by equally blind internecine ones. Even a compound like 'sea-bed' shows a certain pleasure in lexical aptness.

I do not wish to undertake a thoroughgoing analysis of the whole version, but the tabulation shows that the speaker's utterance favours 6s and 4s, that is, less varied and more balanced cadences, when he turns to address his friends, the worms. It also shows that the final sentence—5/5/8/8—is a paired structure whose initial stipulative tone gives way to the expansiveness of wearied resignation as the uncertain future opens up ahead of him.

As we read through these measures, however, we can only register structure as it unfolds, *ex nihilo* as it were. We have a very poor under-standing of rhythm as sequentiality, as an experience of hypothesizing uncertainty, and of the expressive nature of vocal adjustment, of reading as the construction of rhythmic relationships between consecutive phrases. For example, in 'I've no mind,/ while I've still got breath,/ to go begging folk to shed a tear or two', the bacchic (x//) of the initial measure puts some pressure on the reader to complete the second measure with a parallel pair of stressed syllables and accordingly to demote the stress on 'still': 'while I've still got breath' (×××//). And this tendency might extend itself into the next measure, so that 'to go begging' is informed by a contemptuous tone, necessitating a further juncture after 'folk', before the clause eases into even-tempered iambic: 'to go begging folk [×//×/]/to shed a tear or two [×/×/×/]'. I have supplied a scansion and phrasal segmentation of the passage, but as just intimated, this should not be treated as reliable or be allowed to interfere with all those individual variations and adaptations which prose so freely invites.

When we speak about the peculiar temporality of prose, it is not just rhythm apprehended sequentially that we mean. We also mean the way in which prose can relativize temporality. However many layers of time there may be in verse, however many temporal modalities and aspects may be in play, the very metricality of verse maintains a certain temporal homo-geneity in the reading process and tends to confine differing degrees of pausing within fairly narrow parameters. Without a metrical imperative in prose, the voice can not only pace utterance with much greater freedom (relatively speaking), but also exploit pausing more uninhibitedly. If I have scanned 'Look sharp black worms' as a pair of spondees, rather than as a pair of iambs, it is because I have the freedom to install nonce rhythmic deviations and the temporal flexibility to allow such deviations to 'operate'. I can insert as many silent off-beats between these stresses as I need, and I can widen the intonational spectrum to differentiate the 'notes' of stressing.

Similarly, pausing at junctures is not metrically defined, is without expectation of metrical *continuity*, and can therefore make *incises* and 'afterthoughts' much more powerful instruments of rhythmic periodization. To return to the first sentence, we might propose a pattern of pausing something like this (although there are plenty of other options), where # = a unit/syllable of pause:

> I'd like to dig myself a grave ### [let it sink in with listener, of what kind] good and deep ### [reflective, is that my only stipulation, no ...] in a piece of loamy land # full of snails #### ['snails' to confirm 'loamy', whose first syllable is dwelt on—next stage] and there I'd lay my poor old bones to rest ### [thinks of 'rest', thinks of vulnerability of old bones] nice and leisurely ## [intensifying afterthought, with protraction of /naɪ-ɪ-s/ and drawling of 'leisurely'—is that all, is there anything beyond rest, now suitably qualified, yes ...] and be forgotten # [the simile then comes quickly, with conviction] like a shark on the sea-bed.

So within the sentence-unit there are many different paces of thought and existence, creating complex temporal sequencing, more staccato perhaps, but also, in the longer segments, more legato,[3] and, above all, with more rubato.

And as before, the music which 'leaps up' from the page has no particular mandate, is not the inevitable concomitant of some overall acoustic agenda, but is the product of happy chance, the coincidence of what language involuntarily makes available and the reader's being geared to perceive it. I take an obvious instance: the /ɑ:/, which emerges from 'I'd rather ask', is picked up by 'carcass' and generates a link with the following sentence through 'sharp'. Perhaps the real question is whether this 'sharp' recalls 'shark' for us; if it does, then the shark image might insinuate that any peremptory resoluteness on the part of the speaker is but cover for, or instrument of, a more deeply ingrained desire for undisturbed inertia. Similarly, 'dead'/'death', the poem's principal preoccupation, might inject 'shed', 'breath', 'deaf', 'sea-bed' with a note of obsessive morbidity, or help to locate them more unequivocally in a world already beyond the grave. And into this orbit might gravitate words such as 'peck', or 'flesh', or 'friends'. Whereas in verse one might feel that this is all part of the design, part of the consistency and indispensability of acoustic activity across the poem, from phoneme through metre to rhyme, we must here feel that our observations are the dispensable products of a kind of unintended surplus, of distraction, or absent-minded attention to detail.

Equally, one might argue that the reassuring recurrence of iambic sequences in the text do not at all betoken a metrical aspiration in the prose, but rather characterize a voice which wishes to make its peace, wishes to settle into an existential security which is undemanding and self-perpetuating. If metricity, and a certain kind of metricity, is a vocal inflexion and not a linguistic given, then prose puts us, paradoxically, in a position to restore expressivity to metre.

This then is a vision of prose which corresponds with Mallarmé's reversal of the meaning of Baudelaire's thyrsus, as described by Johnson (1979: 175–80).[4] While for Baudelaire the straight line of the stick is prose, and the arabesquing flowers poetry, for Mallarmé it is the other way round:

> Le vers par flèches jeté moins avec succession que presque simultanément pour l'idée, réduit la durée à une division spirituelle propre au sujet: diffère de la phrase ou développement temporaire, dont la prose joue, le dissimulant, selon mille tours.
>
> A l'un, sa pieuse majuscule ou clé allitérative et la rime, pour régler: l'autre genre, d'un élan précipité et sensitif tournoie et se case,

au gré d'une ponctuation qui disposée sur papier blanc, déjà s'y signifie.

(1945: 654–5)

[The line of verse discharged like a volley of arrows less in succession than simultaneously for the mind, reduces duration to a spiritual division peculiar to the subject: it differs from the sentence or temporal development, which prose makes use of, concealing it, by innumerable turns.

The one has its pious capital letter or alliterative key and rhyme, to regulate it: the other genre, with a precipitous and responsive impulse, swirls about and finds its place, at the behest of a punctuation which laid out on the white paper, is already its own meaning.]

Prose, for Mallarmé, is a medium which is supple, which exploits its own temporality, now revealing now concealing it, but not apparently transforming it into a 'division spirituelle propre au sujet'. Punctuation is the presence of time inscribed on the white paper, the injection into the text of voice and the paralinguistic; punctuation is the typography of pause, but a typography not bounded by the fulfilment of measure, and therefore not measurable, but floating elastically in the reading consciousness. In this sense, prose enacts Barthesian *signifiance*, that process of coming and uncoming to meaning, that play of signifiers with changing values which will not resolve themselves into expression or representation; here the linguistic is constantly destabilized by its own unrealized possibilities and by paralinguistic interferences. Or in Kristeva's terms, prose is positioned in the passage from the geno-text, the prelinguistic but articulate language informed by ephemeral impulsional drives, to the pheno-text, the communicative, the coded and systemic.

We have been looking at the prose translation both as a prose poem in which the medium creates and exploits a formal tendentiousness in order to imply a certain aesthetic self-sufficiency, and as prose, a medium pure and simple, with its own ethos of reading. We hardly need reminding that translation is both the source of, and lends continuing sustenance to, the prose poem proper. Chapelan (1946: viii) sets the *terminus a quo* of French poetic prose in Jacques Amyot's translations of the *Œuvres de Plutarque* (1559), but more immediately mention might be made of Victor-Aimé Huber's 1756 translation of Gessner's *Idyllen*, Mme Bontemps's 1759 translation of Thomson's *Seasons*, and Pierre Le Tourneur's translations of Young's *Nights* (1769) and of *Ossian* (1777). From the prose poem's own history we might select Évariste Parny's *Chansons madécasses* (1787),

Judith Gautier's *Livre de jade* (1867, 'translated' from the Chinese), Pierre Louÿs's *Chansons de Bilitis* (1895, 'traduites du grec' [translated from the Greek]) or Segalen's *Stèles* (1912, Chinese texts as distant points of departure). In this history, phantom verse sources leave their teasing scintillations on the drabber livery of prose, as signs of a poet who could not be found. Barbey d'Aurevilly describes his *Niobé* (written 1834) to Guillaume Trebutien in the following terms:

> On dirait—si je ne me trompe—ce morceau-là traduit de quelque poète inconnu. Et de fait il y a dans le diable de *fouillis* qui est ma nature [...] couché quelque part, un poète inconnu et c'est des œuvres cachées de ce poète que ceci a été traduit dans la furie ou la Rêverie d'un moment. Voilà la meilleure explication à donner peut-être de cette *strange thing* qu'un Académicien ne saurait classer.
>
> (1966: 1612)[5]

> [You might think—if I am not mistaken—that this piece is a translation from some unknown poet. And in fact there is, buried somewhere in this devilish *muddle* which is my nature, an unknown poet and it is from the hidden works of this poet that this piece has been translated in the frenzy or Revery of a moment. There is, perhaps, no better way of defining this *strange thing*, which an Academician would not know how to classify.]

Thus it is that the prose poem is likely to activate a metatextual blind field, a sense that it is reaching toward another (verse) text which we think of as originary, as lost and to be reconstructed through the prose survival. This might lead us to suppose that, whatever critics may say about its autonomy, the prose poem is an open and unstable form.[6] We have already seen how this might be, from a rhythmic point of view. But, unfortunately, the prose poem's metatextual blind field cannot be reinhabited, simply because the prose is so much more a transposition than a translation that it is impossible to know what path to take on the 'journey back'. The prose poem might then prove peculiarly and disturbingly ambivalent: its metatextuality, unable to realize any other text, is constantly being drawn back into the textual; or rather, the reader floats between textual and metatextual perspectives.

The mode of thinking outlined above seems to be an attempt to bolster the prose poem, to make it easier for the reader to think beyond it, to lyricize it. The prose poem is a banalization of a verse original and needs to be enhanced by borrowed aura. But if our findings have any foundation, then prose does not need this kind of enrichment. Prose is not the failure of poetry. However, as we saw in Chapter 4, the translator's posture towards the ST can be liberated, rejuvenated, by the device of the detour, whether that detour be intralingual translation or transposition into another art or medium (as, here, prose). In other words, prose translation/poem should not perhaps encourage us to look upon it as the imperfect ('fallen') copy, which still bears the palimpsestic traces of a lyric origin, but rather as something which can relocate us in relation to a surmised (TW) or existent ST, something which bestows a freedom of re-imagining rather than an obligation to recover.

To conclude, then, I offer, briefly, a translation of 'Assommons les pauvres!' (see Appendix III for French text) into verse, and indeed into a sonnet, a choice made easy by the sudden change of pace and style between the seventh and eighth paragraphs ('"[…] qui sait la conquérir."// Immédiatement, je sautai sur mon mendiant'). As far as I know, however much he may have changed rhyme-sounds in his quatrains, Baudelaire never changed rhyme-schemes, as I have done; nor, as far as I know, did Baudelaire ever use the three rhymes of his sestet in consecutive strings, such as efg/efg, or, as in my version, efg/gfe. But I would like to think that Baudelaire's experiments with poetic form, and with the sonnet in particular, would have soon taken him in these directions, had he continued to write verse:

> I'd spent some time confined among my books,
> And chewed, re-chewed and swallowed all the dross
> Of so-called experts touting happiness,
> Persuading beggars to be slaves or crooks.
>
> I needed air. I couldn't rid my mind
> Of whispered notions of equality,
> How cruelty might help us to be kind—
> Just then a beggar poked his hat at me.
>
> I threw my fist and closed his eye,
> I tenderized him with a stick,
> Broke teeth: it was enough for him.
>
> He oathed revolt in every limb,
> His blows repaid me fast and thick—
> If we were quits, then what was I?

Hiddleston (1987: 39–40) has warned us of the dangers of treating Baudelaire as anything other than an arch ironist and mystifier in pieces such as this. Is there here a debunking of Proudhon's 'mutualisme'? Is this an incitement to riot and revolt? Is this an exposure of the fascistic brutalism which lies at the heart of every law-abiding citizen, and which assorts so well with his 'cudgel moralism' (Evans 1993: 65, 67–8)? Is this a world in which equality is the lowest common denominator, where all are equal because nobody is better than anyone else? How rich does the victim have to be before assault and battery becomes criminal? It seems impossible that the poem should not end with a question, impossible, too, that the 'we' of line 14 should be anything more than momentary and hypothetical, before the first person splits off again, leaving the third person to squander the moral.

If, as Baudelaire describes them to Jules Troubat, in a letter of 19 February 1866, the prose poems are 'encore *Les Fleurs du Mal,* mais avec beaucoup plus de liberté, et de détail, et de raillerie' [still *Les Fleurs du Mal,* but with much more licence, and detail, and raillery] (*Correspondance,* II, 615), I have moved in the opposite direction, stripping out the detail, moderating the raillery and using the constraints of the sonnet to maintain the impetus. In fact, at the 'turn' from octave to sestet, I have shifted from pentameter to tetrameter to accelerate the action and to leave the poet less prepared for, more vulnerable to, the question he is left holding. If there are gains made in the translation, they are, I think, principally twofold. First, the poem allows me to give more relief to the mastication metaphor. The second line of the first quatrain picks up and amplifies Baudelaire's 'J'avais donc digéré,—avalé, veux-je dire,—toutes les élucubrations [...]'; no amount of pondering the thoughts and maxims of the 'good life'-mongers will make them digestible. And in the parallel position, the second line of the first tercet, the poet describes his efforts to make his own cannibalistic message digestible ('et je le battis avec l'énergie obstinée des cuisiniers qui veulent attendrir un beefsteak'—my version omits the modal 'veulent'). But the tenderizing has the opposite effect: the meat is 'brought back', regurgitates itself, in a shower of blows. Secondly, I have chosen for the tercets the rhyme-scheme which allows the structure to enact the idea of the poet going into an action from which he emerges moving in the contrary direction. This tit-for-tat structure means, too, that each action taken by the poet, which in the apparently unrhymed first tercet seemed to enjoy a real freedom, is bound back into the pre-ordained and predictable in the second tercet. This scheme also helps to reinforce the systole-diastole rhythm of sado-masochism and the poet's inescapable egocentricity: the octave begins with 'I' and ends with 'me', while the sestet begins with 'I' and ends with 'I', but again in an agent > patient development.

Among the sonnet's disadvantages in relation to the ST, one might again mention two factors. First, the verse overlooks the irony of a situation in which the reciprocal beating has really nothing to do with with the 'successful' outcome of the poet's lesson; if the beggar accepts the poet's precept with alacrity, it is because he now has a share of the poet's purse. Secondly, the verse does not take up the prose's observation 'je me trouvais [...] hors de la portée de tout agent de police', an omission which perhaps has an ulterior motive: Evans (1993: 91–2) suggests that 'Assommons les pauvres!', like other of the prose poems, is interested to break the law, to lay down the law of lawlessness, and the sonnet is hardly the vehicle to endorse this position.

Prose translations have yet to find their true place on the translational map, and this unfortunate situation is no doubt partly a consequence of the mischief done to perception by the plain prose translation. It is partly a consequence, too, of prose's profoundly ambiguous position: we do not do justice to versions such as that of 'Correspondances', or to the prose poems of a Bertrand, or a Mallarmé, or a Rimbaud, if we do not place prose and verse on the same continuum, at opposite ends perhaps, but always in potential dialogue with each other. On the other hand, we are likely to misrepresent the kind of version that 'Spleen' is, that the prose poems of a Baudelaire or a Mac Orlan are, if we do not think of prose as a different medium, presupposing different habits and manoeuvres in the reading mind. But at least the same choices of stance are as much available to the prose translator as to the prose poet, and the very 'unreliability' of prose will act as a salutary reminder that translation itself is caught in the same contradictory position, hearkening to, referring to, remembering, an original and yet understanding its obligations to difference, differentiation, to the translation's own native specificity.

The Criticism of Translation

Translation, certainly in the pre-postmodernist era, was implicitly, and against its own evidence, tied to a Cratylic view: it posits an Adamic language (the ST) in which word and reality live intimately together, in which the word is endowed with a particular authority because it is peculiarly and beautifully able to say what it means. It is back towards this pre-Babel text (original text = original language), that the post-Babel TT must struggle, marked as it is by the curse of fallenness; translation is a state of punishment, in which we are compelled to reiterate our sense of loss. Even in Benjamin's reading of the situation, even if a putative (TW) creates more self-respect and freedom for the TT, translation is still trying to rectify its assumed deficiency. This Cratylic view of translation, and its relation to the ST has two immediate and closely related consequences:

1. It endows language used creatively with a status apparently not shared by translation, principally because of translation's metatextual nature, its being in some sense reported speech (saying what *someone else* means).

2. It ties the criticism of translation into tunnel vision, that tunnel vision which enjoins on the translator the Adamism of the ST, but at one remove, as an Adamism of the relationship SL word/TL word. But no one, not even a translator, has sufficient linguistic and cultural knowledge to judge what the parameters of equivalence are. Not only do we have to say that the position of, for example, 'eyelid' and 'paupière' are different within their respective language systems—'eyelid' is much less flexible, and 'eye' is frequently used in its place ('abaisser les paupières d'un mourant'; 'paupières gonflées'; 'ombre à paupières'); 'lid' can be used separately; etymologies point in different ethnic directions; apparently similar

collocations work in different ways ('bat an eyelid' is only used negatively and in the singular, and is not equivalent to 'battre des paupières')—but the divergence is further aggravated in the language systems created by national versifications (what these words can rhyme with, what their rhythmic potentialities mean in terms of possible positions in the line, and thus possible collocations, etc.).

Such issues as these are anyway undermined by the profound ambiguity of Adamic naming, which Eco, among others, has reminded us of:

> But Adam might have called the animals 'by their own names' in two senses. Either he gave them the names that, by some extra-linguistic right, were already *due* to them, or he gave them those names we still use on the basis of a convention initiated by Adam. In other words, the names that Adam gave the animals are either the names that each animal intrinsically *ought* to have been given, or simply the names that the nomothete arbitrarily and *ad placitum* decided to give them.
>
> (1995: 8)

If the translator, too, is a nomothete, which Adam is he/she? If he is the latter kind pretending to be the former, then he might just as well be the latter in good faith. The relation between text and metatext would then be one in which the metatextual becomes textual by naming (not translating) the ST. In other words, the translator does not draw meaning out of the ST and embody it in another language, but instead confers meaning on the ST by using another language. This is tantamount to saying both that the ST does not know what it means, and that the arbitrary is to be condoned as an 'authentic' act (it is easy enough to explain this in terms of some existentialist 'acte gratuit' [gratuitous act], or of Bergson's closely related claims that the more arbitrary the choice, the more deeply it is driven:

> Nous voulons savoir en vertu de quelle raison nous nous sommes décidés, et nous trouvons que nous nous sommes décidés sans raison, peut-être même contre toute raison. Mais c'est là précisément, dans certains cas, la meilleure des raisons. Car l'action accomplie n'exprime plus alors telle idée superficielle, presque extérieure à nous, distincte et facile à exprimer: elle répond à l'ensemble de nos sentiments, de nos pensées et de nos aspirations les plus intimes [...].
>
> (1984: 112.)

[We want to know in accordance with what reason we have made a decision, and we find that we have made a decision without reason, perhaps even *against* reason. But that, precisely, is, in certain cases, the best of reasons. For, then, the action performed does not express some superficial idea, almost outside us, distinct, easy to express: it is a response to the totality of our feelings, our thoughts and our most intimate aspirations.]

If we believe that Adamism, as applied to translation, is a dangerous working mode, the assumption that all texts, both STs and TTs, are afflicted with the curse of Babel may seem equally unfruitful and convince us once again of the futility of translating the untranslatable. One argument runs:

> Language, whether or not it is a built-in physical grammar with which man is endowed by his inheritance, is virtuous precisely because it can't 'communicate'; it can only indicate; [...]. It is precisely the fact that each man within the limits of his own society and culture speaks his own language that makes him human. When he is angry with his fellow he may say of him 'We don't speak the same language'. But it is a very good thing we don't. It is each individual's own language that is his *raison d'être*. And with no-one, of course, is this more so than with the poet. He does not communicate. He creates. His language is his own, and untranslatable.
>
> (Moore 1990: 16)

But there is much consolation in these words. Moore's vision of a national language as a compound of intersecting languages, none of which duplicates another, allows us to enter into a more personal possession of (our) language, allows us to develop our own language, refine it, make it more expressive of us as individuals; the imperfection of our language makes us strive harder to energize it; the imperfection of our language provides each user with greater margins of flexibility and invention. Without the approximate nature of language, where would the delights of linguistic suggestion, ambiguity, understatement be? Relationships are soldered by the reciprocal effort to create and maintain meaningful dialogue. And as far as translation is concerned, such a view warrants the proposal that translation has less to do with national languages than with idiolects, that the concept of TL should be removed and that all should revolve around the TT as, precisely, one half of a personal dialogue.

All of which leaves us not quite knowing what to do when it comes to the criticism of translation. A recent review by Graham Robb of two translations of Baudelaire points up the difficulty of establishing a stable critical position. To begin with, Robb comes to this conclusion:

> Although, in a blind reading test, no single translator stood out as the obvious best, Leakey's fluid free verse should be preferred for its faithfulness to the spirit of the original.
>
> (1998: 30)

That 'no single translator stood out as the obvious best' is perhaps the result of our inability to escape the 'curate's egg' approach to translations— we come to 'all-in-all', complex balance-sheet decisions, based on short-termist treatments of slices of text, rather than struggling to see the translation project whole. And we are left with the gaping critical black holes of 'faithfulness' and 'the spirit of the original' (how does this differ from 'the original' and where is it to be found?). We are still in that critical world where Baudelaire and his critic know best and translators are on a hiding to nothing. But there follows an odd transformation: after faulting liberties taken by Walter Martin—liberties the less forgivable because they have no explanation—Robb rebounds with this view:

> However, in the face of so many other approximations, one is grateful when the translator turns himself loose and the English version serves as a commentary on Baudelaire's modernity. [...] Every translation is a linguistic *coup d'état*.
>
> (1998: 31)

It is a little difficult to tell whether this is a vindication of freedom in the interests of modernization or whether it is the acceptance of freedom as a necessary *pis-aller*, given that all attempts at faithfulness end so dismally.

Robb is writing a review, and no doubt speed of treatment and conceptual ellipses are characteristic of the genre. But even where examination of translations is more thorough, as in Nicholas Linfield's assessment (1995) of four translations (by Roy Campbell (1952), Enid Peschel (1981), Richard Howard (1982) and himself (1995)) of Baudelaire's 'Les Bijoux', we still run across 'curate's egg' criticism and untheorized exhortations to good practice. Linfield has certain rule-of-thumb criteria, which remain critically unjustified and non-negotiable:

> The one absolute rule is consistency: regularity in the original must

179

be matched by regularity in the translation, and irregularity by irregularity.

(p. 37)

Unfortunately, Peschel transgresses this rule, which leads her into a hybrid of French and English: 'This is a flaw which damages most of her work.' As so often happens, translation criticism seems to be in the hands of a critical police rather than critical sociologists. That Peschel's practice stems directly from a declared 'project'—

> First and always, I tried to remain as close, as faithful as possible to the original poet's meanings and intentions. Always, I aimed to reproduce the original poet's words and tones... Wherever possible, I also sought to re-create the flow of the French word order.
>
> (quoted by Linfield, p. 41)

—constitutes no mitigation; no attempt is made to evaluate her work on its own terms. And what conclusions does Linfield draw? Well, the overall conclusion is a resonant evasion:

> My own experience as a translator and as a reader of translations constantly confirms my conviction that the relative adequacy or inadequacy of translations depends to a great extent on the quality of the reading and writing involved in the task.
>
> (p. 53)

Earlier Linfield has concluded:

> The principal conclusion that I hope has emerged from this detailed comparison is that many of the processes involved in good verse translation have nothing to do with translation as such.
>
> (p. 51)

So an evaluative comparison of translations which has little to do with translation as such? What then has it to do with? First, 'good reading: seeing what is there in the original'. Secondly—the part that *is* to do with translation—'trusting the original: retaining (as far as the target language will permit) the details of the original'. And finally, rendering the poem in English ('The verse translator must therefore possess the skills of a poet'). Once again, uninspected and untheorized principles and begged questions.

Our chief objections, then, to the critical strategies just encountered are: first, that translation is judged by product rather than by process, largely because translators insufficiently contextualize their own products. This criticism implies that translation is perfectible (without, however, being able to achieve perfection) and that the critic is the person who has, or can construct from the work of others, the *corrigé*. Failure to meet the standard nullifies what may have been interesting about the effort. The idea that translating might be a test-bed for translational theory and/or principles is not apparently to be entertained. The failure of product makes all questions about theory and principle otiose. Why could Linfield not entitle his article 'Four approaches to the translation of Baudelaire's "Les Bijoux"'? What is worrying is that product evaluation has an inconsistent attitude to motive: it feels free to disregard motive if the product falls short (Peschel), and yet also feels free to reconstruct motive when it needs to. Linfield's confident assessment of Campbell's account of the final line of the first stanza is: 'Campbell's singular is rhyme-induced ("him" to rhyme with "whim"), which means that in all four lines of his first stanza rhyme results in falsity' (p. 39). A little further up the same page, Linfield has told us that '"whim" too is rhyme-determined'. It does not occur to Linfield that Campbell's 'trivializing' translation may be a possible interpretation of the poem, or, better, a reflection of Campbell's reaction to the poem. Nor does it occur to Linfield that Baudelaire's verse-making may itself be trivializing, in its awkward facture:

> Me ravit en extase, et j'aime à la fureur
> Les choses où le son se mêle à la lumière.

Is not 'à la fureur', and its bathos, rhyme-induced? It is the last of a lexical sequence which is quickly squandering its semantic capital: 'cœur' > 'vainqueur' > 'moqueur' > 'fureur'. And why did Baudelaire pick up the /œR/ rhyme of the first stanza in the second, almost as if he had initially imagined a sonnet which turned out not to have the intensity he needed?

Secondly, there is a tendency in translation criticism of this kind to regard freedoms as moral cowardice or an admission of defeat. This view is closely connected with the belief that translation is a set of skills, like those itemized by Linfield, which a good translator can bring to bear on any text (the need to be a poet is the fly in this particular ointment). This all has the advantage of reminding us that scholarship is a significant factor in the assessment of the ST's 'textuality' (all the elements that make it the text it is). But translation is also, I believe, part of the spiritual autobiography of a relation with the ST. Translation is not only an account of a text, but an account of a response to a text, of cohabitation with a text. We read translations not only to understand the ST better, but also to come to know another reader, and to come to know about the process of translation.

My own persuasion is to develop translations as products out of a critical discourse about the text being translated, and about the translation as a project, as this book tries to do. The relationship between translation and criticism certainly needs to be better defined. Marilyn Gaddis Rose (1997) argues that translation should be used much more as an instrument of literary criticism than it is at the moment, to enrich our perception of the ST, and to make us more sensitive to the operation of literary texts generally (for the cultural version of this argument, see Venuti 1998: 88–105). As part of her case, she offers a comparative study of two German translations (by Stefan George and Walter Benjamin) of Baudelaire's 'Recueillement' (pp. 39–54), with the intention not of discovering which is the better, but what their differences tell us about the kinds of translator they are. Her conclusion is that George's translation is 'target-oriented, domesticated, interpretive, meaning-based', while Benjamin's is 'source-oriented, foreignized, language-based' (p. 49).[1] I would like to pursue further Gaddis Rose's even-handed and constructive practice, also in relation to Baudelaire's 'Recueillement'. But first, more clarification of the founding methodology is required.

It is not difficult to agree with Berman's initial diagnosis:

> Mais si critique veut dire analyse rigoureuse d'une traduction, de ses traits fondamentaux, du projet qui lui a donné naissance, de l'horizon dans lequel elle a surgi, de la position du traducteur; si critique veut dire, fondamentalement, *dégagement de la vérité d'une traduction*, alors il faut dire que la critique des traductions commence à peine à exister.
>
> (1995: 13–14)
>
> [But if criticism means rigorous analysis of a translation, of its underlying features, of the project which gave birth to it, of the perspective within which it emerged, of the position of the translator; if criticism means, basically, *the laying bare of the truth of a translation*, then it must be said that the criticism of translations has hardly begun to exist.]

The real problem is then to know in what exactly the truth of a translation might lie, and more especially the truth of a translation of poetry.

When Widdowson confronts the problem of poetry translation, he emphasizes three factors which are salutary caveats for those trying to formulate a criticism of translation:

(a) The translation of poetry is much concerned with the translation of a poem's effect on the reader. Poetic texts invite us to use them to activate our own meanings.

(b) Process, certainly from an educational point of view, is more important than product. (This should, I think, be expressed slightly differently. The crucial thing is that product and process should not be separated; it is more important for a critic of translation to try to reconstruct the processes by which a TT has found its shape than to compare it 'cold' with the original; this last is not the acid test.)

(c) '[...] it may be possible that lack of expertise in the language may not preclude expertise in translation' (1991: 160)—particularly if (a) is our principal preoccupation. The 'authority' of the translator is of no interest to the critic of translations. Knowledge itself can be constraining and may tend to display itself in a propensity for 'literalness'.

Where Widdowson seems to me to be at fault, or inconsistent with himself, is in his identification of the act of reading with the act of *interpretation*. This same connection seems to lie behind Berman's position: '*La critique d'une traduction est donc celle d'un texte qui, lui-même, résulte d'un travail d'ordre critique*' [*The criticism of a translation is thus the criticism of a text which is itself the result of work of a critical order*] (1995: 41). I have two objections to this assumption. The first is a procedural one. This approach seems to imply that, before one embarks on a translation, one must have done with interpreting the ST. One then translates one's interpretation into one's own language, accommodating its form as closely as possible to that of the original (piously assuming that there is some natural coincidence of form and content in the ST). More 'truthful' to translation would be, for me, not to know what the ST means, not to have already interpreted it as one embarks on the translation, but instead to use translation to discover what the ST might mean, or to use translation to map out the parameters of an ST's possible modes of meaning. Too often we content ourselves with the observation that 'anguish' is not a very good translation of 'remords', or that a change to a passive construction has diminished the sense of agency to be found in the original.

Secondly, and more critically, reading is not necessarily, or only, interpretation. Reading is the experience of the primary operation of language, which is not to produce meanings, but to produce, to use Widdowson's word, 'effect'. In reading of this kind, modalities oust meanings. Where interpretation turns text into meaning, reading turns text into texture, into attitude, into inflexions of time and space, into tensions between the acoustic and morphological, into the idiosyncrasies of our psycho-perceptual lives. The experience of language fully lived makes interpretation superfluous, or too impoverished and opportunistic an activity to be bothered with. Reading is the process of activating the text, in a multi-level encounter. And the TT is a way of re-activating the ST, albeit in its own activity, and probably in another key, or another voice.

It is not difficult to imagine interpretations as the necessary fall-back position of translational transference, because the experience of text, as we have described it, is clearly 'untranslatable'. But inasmuch as translation is a search for, an exploration of, a reconfiguration of, the experience of reading, it must be different, it must always be in a mode of approximation, of coming near or standing off in order to see. And it must be different, too, in that the TT, in pursuing the reading experience activated by the ST, activates its own. But this does not mean that the reader of the TT needs to read bifocally. The two experiences are fused into a whole; the TT is an expansion of the ST. Reading, like interpretation, requires training (the modalities of tense and adjectival position, the nature of acousticity and rhythm, the 'characters' of parts of speech, etc.). But once the reader is trained, this kind of reading becomes second nature. Interpretation remains singularly unreliable and psycho-physiologically unassimilated.

When Berman regrets:

> Cette tendance à vouloir 'juger' une traduction, *et à ne vouloir faire que cela*, renvoie fondamentalement à deux traits fondamentaux de tout texte traduit, l'un étant que ce texte 'second' est censé correspondre au texte 'premier', est censé être véridique, vrai, l'autre étant ce que je propose d'appeler la *défectivité*, néologisme qui cherche à rassembler toutes les formes possibles de défaut, de défaillance, d'erreur dont est affectée *toute* traduction.
>
> (1995: 41)

> [This tendency to want to 'judge' a translation, *and only that*, relates back to two underlying characteristics of every translated text, one being that this 'second' text is supposed to correspond to the 'first', is supposed to be authentic, truthful, the other being what I propose to call its *defectivity*, a neologism designed as a gather-all for the

various kinds of infelicity, weakness, error with which all translations are inevitably afflicted.]

he is regretting, too, habits of criticism that tell us nothing about the process of translation, that base themselves on no theorization of translation, and that institute no methodology peculiar to the assessment of translation. These are things that the proper inclusion of the reading experience would put right; and the inclusion of the reading experience would, at a stroke, nullify the apparent contradiction which lies at the heart of the dominant critical practice as Berman describes it: namely, how one can demand fidelity from a practice which is inevitably defective. Reading experience finds the truth of a translation not in the fidelity of the TT to an interpretation of the ST, but in its fidelity to the text as a choreography of effects. The necessary 'defectiveness' of translation makes this latter fidelity possible because in reading those effects, and making the text 'effective' in another language, and in making the new text 'effective', truth comes to lie in a negotiated settlement, satisfactory to all interested parties.

Armed with these thoughts and resolutions, let us then return to our consideration of Baudelaire's 'Recueillement':

1. Sois sage, ô ma Douleur, et tiens-toi plus tranquille. 2+4+3+3
2. Tu réclamais le Soir; il descend; le voici: 4+2+3+3
3. Une atmosphère obscure enveloppe la ville,   4+2+3+3
4. Aux uns portant la paix, aux autres le souci.   2+4+2+4

5. Pendant que des mortels la multitude vile,   (2+4)+4+2
6. Sous le fouet du Plaisir, ce bourreau sans merci,   3+3+3+3
7. Va cueillir des remords dans la fête servile,   3+3+3+3
8. Ma Douleur, donne-moi la main; viens par ici,

                    3+5+4/3+3+2+4

9. Loin d'eux. Vois se pencher les défuntes Années,   2+4+3+3
10. Sur les balcons du ciel, en robes surannées;   4+2+2+4
11. Surgir du fond des eaux le Regret souriant;   2+4+3+3

12. Le Soleil moribond s'endormir sous une arche,   3+3+3+3
13. Et, comme un long linceul traînant à l'Orient,   4+2+2+4
14. Entends, ma chère, entends la douce Nuit qui marche.

                    4+2+4+2

Valéry, in his essay 'Situation de Baudelaire', expresses the view that, of the 14 lines of 'Recueillement', 'je m'étonnerai toujours d'en compter cinq ou six qui sont d'une incontestable faiblesse. Mais,' he goes on, 'les premiers et les derniers vers de cette poésie sont d'une telle magie que le milieu ne fait pas sentir son ineptie' [it will always surprise me to count five or six which are undeniably weak. But the first and last lines of this poem are so magical that the ineptness of the middle is not obtrusive] (1957: 610). While Pichois (*OC*, I, 1109) identifies these weak lines as 5–7, Chesters, who investigates the charge (1988: 135–8), opts for looser margins: 3/4–7/8. Chesters's case for the defence rests on (i) Baudelaire's aesthetic of gradation, whereby the ensemble, or more specifically, the good lines, justify the bad—bad lines act as a *repoussoir* for the good; and (ii) on the proposition that 'the bad lines mime the distaste the poet feels towards a group of people who deserve clichés' (p. 138). Riffaterre (1971: 182–8) defends the troublesome lines on the grounds that they are stylistically active. And Jean Prévost (1953: 333–6) imagines Baudelaire submitting his poem to the rigorous scrutiny of a Nisard or a Lanson and their pointing out to him the manifold awkwardnesses, pleonasms and repetitions. In response to these charges, Baudelaire 'transmetricizes' (Genette 1982: 254–7) his poem, reducing it by a third, to the dimensions of an octosyllabic sonnet:

> Ma Douleur, tiens-toi plus tranquille.
> Tu voulais le Soir; le voici:
> L'air obscur verse sur la ville
> Plus de paix ou plus de souci.
>
> Cependant que la foule vile
> Que fouette un plaisir sans merci
> S'écœure à la fête servile,
> Prends-moi la main; viens par ici.
>
> Aux balcons du ciel, mainte année
> Se penche en robe surannée;
> Émerge un regret souriant;
>
> Le Soleil s'endort contre une arche;
> Un linceul traîne à l'Orient:
> Entends la douce Nuit qui marche.

This controversy brings to light a preoccupation with lexical semantics and register which overlooks a number of other ways in which words exist in, impinge on, consciousness. Inevitably our notions about what constitutes a pleonasm, or a cliché, or a *cheville*, are preconceived; we could not use the terms if they were not. But we should recognize that in using these terms, we are denying the offending words the chance to re-argue their case, on other grounds.

I want now to proceed to a reading of 'Recueillement' which gathers together some moments of encounter with the text, perceptions of structural and expressive modality which characterize my own experience of the poem. I have not pursued these to any conclusions, believing it is neither desirable nor possible to do so, but equally believing that these are *achieved* and 'informed' moments of experiential significance. The 'moments of encounter' are these:

1. The first line as a discharge of acousticity and latent intention
2. The imperative personal glide
3. Rhymes: gendering, and dynamic of structure, and richness
4. Articulation of e
5. Crossing the bar
6. The punctuation of line 12
7. Abstractions and allegories and articles

The first line as discharge of acousticity and latent intention

The first line:

swasaʒomadulœR//etjẽtwaplytRãkil

offers us a sequence of lexemes in which all initial consonants are voiceless, with the exception of /[ʒo]madulœR/. The second hemistich is dominated by /d/'s voiceless counterpart /t/. The poem's project, we might thus think, is to unvoice sorrow. The first line also poses the crucial question: What kind of space is the second hemistich?

The 'Douleur' of the first hemistich wishes to become the 'douce' of the second hemistich of line 14. 'Douleur', then, must be unvoiced in order that its substitute, 'douce Nuit', can be *heard*. 'Douleur' must be transformed, second-hemistiched. 'Douce' (/dus/), for its part, takes over the unvoiced /s/ of line 1, but more particularly assimilates, in reverse form, 'sous' (/su/).

We find /su/ not only in 'sous' ('sous le fouet du Plaisir', 'sous une arche'), but also in 'souci' (4) and 'souriant' (11). One might expect there to be some meaningful collision with /syR/ ('sur les balcons' (10), 'surannées' (10), 'Surgir' (11)). But there is instead a peculiar collusion: 'Surgir', for example, is movement upward, but from underneath. But as we consider 'douce Nuit', knowing how closely related in function and articulation are the vowel /y/ and the glide /ɥ/, we can see that /u/ and /y/ were bound to converge.

The imperative personal glide

If /ɥ/ is an important glide, so is /w/, which relates to the vowel /u/. The pattern of /w/s across the poem is:

1.	/swa/			//	/twa/
2.			/swaR///		/vwasi/
6.		/fwɛ/			
8.			/mwa///(?)		
9.	/lwɛ̃/		/vwa/	//	

The glide first appears as an imperative, and continues to act imperatively, or to be informed by imperativity, even when it does not explicitly have that grammatical status: we feel the imperative permeating 'le voici' or 'fouet', for example. Otherwise, it relates closely to imperative constructions or constructions with imperative force, e.g. 'Tu *réclamais* le Soir'. The dominant vocalic combination with /w/ is /a/, and on two occasions the preceding consonant is /v/: hence the centrality of 'voix'. The imperative with which the poem ends is 'Entends' (/ɑ̃tɑ̃/), the /ɑ̃/ repeated insistently after its preparation by 'souriant', 's'endormir', 'traînant' and 'Orient'. We must, it seems, speak to hear, and hear what we speak.

Rhymes: gendering, and dynamic of structure, and richness

As one moves through the *a* rhymes—'tranquille'/'ville'/'vile'/'servile'—one moves from *rime suffisante* (/il/) to *rime riche* (/vil/). These *feminine* rhyme-words seem to belong, but in disproportionate ratio, to the two worlds of the poem, that of reclusive and recollective quietude, and that of masochistic and gregarious pleasure-addiction. The *masculine b* rhymes—'voici'/'souci'/'merci'/'ici'—are all *suffisantes,* and seem to speak of proximity ('voici', 'ici') achieved after separation by negative states: carewornness and harassment by the aggressive metropolis. What is also important in this rhyme-sequence is the achievement of a doubling of the rhyme-vowel (/isi/). This doubling is echoed much later on in 'Entends', itself doubled, at a point when /i/ becomes an important keynote ('Surgir', 'souriant', 'moribond', 's'endormir', 'Orient', 'Nuit qui marche').

After the quatrains, the rhyme is as if momentarily immobilized in the excess of leonine repetitiousness: 'Années'/'surannées'. The *dead* weight of the years drags the verse to halt, before 'Surgir' gives it a kick-start, so that it can resume its journey to its destination, but still with a three-element leonine rhyme ('souriant'/'Orient'—/Riã/) and a three-element rich rhyme ('arche'/'marche'—/aR∫/).

Articulation of e

All instances of words ending in an articulated e mute occur in second hemistichs ('enveloppe' (3), 'autres' (4), 'multitude' (5), 'fête' (7), 'défuntes' (9), 'robes' (10), 'douce' (14)), except for 'donne' (8), which occurs either in the first hemistich if the line is read as a standard *tétramètre* (3+3+2+4), or in the medial measure, if the line is read as a *trimètre* (3+5+4). We shall have more to say in a moment about the general expressive characteristics of the second hemistich in relation to those of the first. But we might note now the predominant expressive effects of the articulated e:

(a) It is an element of lexical liaison and thus may seem to pre-ordain certain collocations.
(b) It can act imitatively: 'enveloppe' and 'douce', for example, are both qualities of the night, emanations which are also suffusions, thanks to e's dispersive note.
(c) The articulated e lengthens the preceding vowel, particularly where that vowel is accentuated. This facilitates tonal input (pathos, irony, regret, longing) into the pronunciation of the word.

Crossing the bar

To find a place in the second hemistich seems to be an increasing preoccupation within the poem. One other acoustic transformation which seems to indicate this desire to 'cross the bar' is the shift from /ɔR/ to /aR/. Initially, /ɔR/ is a first-hemistich, generally unaccentuated element ('portant' (4), 'mortels' (5), 'remords' (accentuated) (7), 'moribond' (12)). As we move into the second tercet, however, it crosses the caesura into the second hemistich ('s'endormir' (12), 'Orient' (13)), and at the same time modulates into the /aR/ of the final rhyme. This vowel modulation entails the following shifts:

(/ɔR/) low-mid back > low front (/aR/)
half-open > open
rounded > unrounded, spreading
unaccentuated (exc. 'remords') > accentuated, rhyme

Punctuation at line 12

Why is line 12 punctuated with a comma rather than a semi-colon? The progression of clauses operates like this:

1. ll. 9–10: 'vois' + infin. + obj. + adv.
2. l. 11: ('vois' +) infin. + adv. + obj.
3. l. 12: ('vois' +) obj. + infin. + adv.
4. ll. 13–14: interpolated simile + 'entends' (bis) + obj. + relative clause

How do we account for the comma at the end of line 12, which conflates the two final clauses (3 and 4) and effectively separates 3 from 1 and 2? Clauses 3 and 4 also share a type of noun (concrete, natural phenomenon) which contrasts with the more abstract variety of 1 and 2; and they share a dynamic, too: while 'se pencher' and 'Surgir' suggest actions of shorter duration, 's'endormir' and 'qui marche' are more gradual and continuous. But then how do we account for the discontinuity of construction between 3 and 4, the replacement of an infinitive by a relative clause? As an answer to this question, we might suggest the following:

(i) The relative here is both restrictive and non-restrictive, where the infinitive is restrictive.
(ii) The relative increases the degree of active agency.
(iii) The relative increases the degree of perceptual proximity or immediacy.

Abstractions and allegories and articles

1.	ma Douleur//	
2.	le Soir //	
4.	la paix //	le souci
6.	du Plaisir//	
7.	des remords//	
8. Ma Douleur	//	
9.	//	les défuntes Années
11.	//	le Regret souriant

12. Le Soleil moribond	//	
13.	//	[l'Orient (?)]
14.	//	la douce Nuit

David Saunders (1970:769–70) suggests that Baudelaire's use of capitals to denote personified abstractions is inconsistent. The evidence he adduces does much to confirm his view, but it would be dangerous to assume that it is always so. Variants show us that in 1862, in *Le Boulevard* and *Almanach parisien*, 'Douleur' appeared without its capital, and there can be no doubt that the poet's personal appropriation of 'Douleur', with its possessive adjective, is a radical move, as Saunders points out (p. 777). Allegory is an assertion of communal values, presupposes a shared and durable knowledge, presupposes the demonstrable. Baudelaire's monopolization of this knowledge is both, possibly, an act of self-derisive irony and an index of a widening within, as the micro swallows the macro and uses its inclusiveness to dilate the domestic. What is clear is that the lower case abstractions—'paix', 'souci', 'remords'—belong to an alien and non-discriminating world, a world presided over by capitalized 'Plaisir', the superordinate, the antagonist of 'Douleur', highly personified, a relentless taskmaster, visible to the poet, obeyed but unseen by the masses.

The table of occurrences might lead us, however, to revise what we have just said. If 'la douce Nuit' is the alternative to 'Le Soleil moribond', and 'le Regret souriant' to 'remords', are not the 'défuntes Années' an answer to 'Plaisir', whose whip is the urgency of instant gratification, the embodiment of the pressure of the present? 'Douleur' unwittingly calls down an evening which will release 'Plaisir', a wished-for anaesthetic perhaps, and has to be led away by the poet; 'Douleur' is imprisoned in the left side of the alexandrine's world, in the first hemistich. How can it migrate to the right side? Well, as our observations have already implied, it must transform its /dul/ into /dus/ by combining with 'souci', itself the provider not only of /s/ but also of /i/, the /i/ of 'Nuit' and proximity ('ici'). 'Souci's' right-half position indicates that, however much it may belong to an undramatized or unmythicized collection of qualities belonging to the urban population generally, it must be assimilated by the poet, even if unobtrusively, if he is to sooth his 'Douleur' into a right-sided mentality.

This is a poem dominated by the definite article. In allegory/personification, the definite article vouches for a status, a reliability. In connections of possession and belonging, the definite article will promote a sense of the liturgical and formulaic, the definiteness of one element endorses the definiteness of the other, e.g. 'la multitude vile des mortels', 'le fouet du Plaisir', 'les balcons du ciel', 'le fond des eaux'. In instances where nouns have attributive adjectives—'la fête servile', 'les défuntes Années', 'le Regret souriant', 'Le Soleil moribond', 'la douce Nuit'—the definite article transforms the freely chosen epithet into a culturally dictated one, begins to imply that an 'épithète de circonstance' [circumstantial epithet] is in fact an 'épithète de nature' [natural epithet].

The specificity of the definite specifies the poet: it not only assumes an inescapable knowledge in him, but provides the web in which he is caught, the design by which he is orientated.

Values here are diametrically opposed: the unavoidable Devil and the certainties of a spiritual anchorage.

What are we to make of indefinite and zero articles in these circumstances? These, too, have contradictory values. If we leave aside 'un long linceul', the indefinite article conventionally associated with the structure of simile, we might gather the following connotations:

- 'une atmosphère obscure'—here the indefinite article aids the consoling power of something without hidden intention or guile
- 'en robes surannées'—the zero article increases our sense of the multiform, multiplying and freely arranged
- 'sous une arche'—here the indefinite frees semantic potential, but leaves the image, if mysterious, unforbidding[2]
- 'des remords'—here everything turns round, because the indefinite drives home a lack of moral discrimination, the petty disorderedness of the moral world, the randomness of its operation in the minds of the people. If elsewhere the indefinite article bespeaks a freedom and a peculiar kind of candour, here it allies itself with the anarchic and the carelessly haphazard.

I would like now to move on to matters more properly rhythmic, and, to begin with, two underlying convictions. The first is that the rhythmic configurations within hemistichs of the alexandrine, and the relationship between hemistichs, is as much a modal matter as a cognitive one. I am happy to believe that metre/rhythm is a bringing to consciousness, is a process of perceptual organization; and equally that the relationship between hemistichs is frequently one of intellectual structuring: parallelism, complementarity, antithesis. But this should not lead us to forget that rhythmic configurations and hemistichial relationships are modal, attitudinal, inflexions of feeling, psychic postures towards language. My second accompanying conviction is that the functions and modalities with which particular combinations of measure are invested varies from poem to poem, and may indeed vary within a poem, while remaining structurally significant; the same applies to the relationship between hemistichs.

Speaking generally, we may say that the alexandrine has developed, over the three centuries of its ascendancy, from a conjunction of two hexasyllables to an integral dodecasyllable, from a 'vers composé' to a 'vers simple'. The sense that the caesura was a clearly marked juncture, accompanied by a perceptible break or pause ('repos'), persisted into the nineteenth century, and its converse, that the major syntactical break was where the caesura must be, justified theorists in entertaining the notion of a mobile caesura. But even the classical dramatists had recognized the inappropriacy of the idea of a 'rest': the two halves of the alexandrine had become so intimately feathered together that the caesura was now a feature of the sixth syllable itself—obligatory accent, point of structural focus, pitch variation, semantic intensity—and not an event which took place *after* the sixth syllable. In dealing with the regular alexandrine, particularly of the nineteenth century, we are much better advised to think of it not as a combination of hemistichs of equal value, but as a sequence of half lines which have sought to complement their similarities with significant differentia.

Taking into account the natural circumflex shape of the alexandrine's intonation curve—I am not of course suggesting that this shape is not frequently varied by questions, enjambement, staccato utterance, and so on—and the differing structural functions of the caesura and line-ending, we might offer the following typology of first and second hemistichs, as I have done elsewhere (Scott 1998: 71):

	First hemistich	*Second hemistich*
1.	rising intonation	falling intonation
2.	main clause	subordinate and circumstantial
3.	with impetus, élan	withdrawn, entropic
4.	public, aloud	private, sotto voce
5.	dynamic singleness	cumulative complexity (semantic loading of rhyme)
6.	towards syllable 6, which confirms or undermines the metrical integrity of the whole line	towards syllable 12, which confirms or undermines only the line-ending

7. towards an intensified form   towards a different mode
    of the same kind of meaning   of meaning (rhyme, which
                                      transcends the line)

8. caesura not necessarily a   line-ending usually a
    significant syntactic break   significant syntactic break

In our preliminary skirmish with 'Recueillement', we have noticed that articulated e's naturally gravitate towards the second hemistich, where their yielding quality turns them towards memory, or perhaps, given a new weight by verse, they suggest an associative or semantic richness. We have seen in our treatment of /ɔR/ how there is something of a pull from top left to bottom right, but more particularly, we have suggested that /ɔR/ is reaching for the /aR/ first adumbrated in 'Soir'; and this resolution, in rhyme, would be a variation on my point 7. We have considered the disposition of the abstract nouns and explored the existential predicament of 'Douleur', marooned in the first hemistich. We might even propose that the glide/semi-consonant /w/ increasingly declares itself a first-hemistich inhabitant, an inhabitant of a time and place ultimately foreign to the poet's designs for the transformation, rather than mere appeasement, of his 'Douleur'; it is for this reason that it is jettisoned at the caesura in line 9. And my point 6 might have some bearing on lines 8 and 9, for if the metrical integrity of the line, as a regular alexandrine, is lost thanks to the syntactical breaching of the caesura, the *rejet* which disrupts the first hemistich of line 9 is not created by any enjambement at the end of line 8, but is an impulsive or impatient move initiated by the first hemistich itself.

But all this is merely to suggest the further investigation of a possible field of enquiry. As far as the combinations of measures themselves are concerned, I would like to comment briefly on the instances of 3+3 and those of 4+2.

It may seem odd that the majority of the 3+3 configurations fall in the second hemistich, but this observation should be qualified by two others. First, it is noticeable that of the 11 instances of 3+3, six appear paired, the trisyllabic measure recurring across the whole line:

1. Sous le fouet du Plaisir, ce bourreau sans merci
2. Va cueillir des remords dans la fête servile
3. Le Soleil moribond s'endormir sous une arche

About 1 and 2 one might propose that, over these two lines, it is in the poet's interest to establish a narrative continuity, in which expressive nuance would undermine lofty disdain and sententious impassivity. Baudelaire has expended his bile in 'la multitude vile' (4+2), and by the time we arrive at the 'fête servile', for all the potential paradoxality of the lexical combination, 'servile' has become no more than an automatic 'épithète de nature'. About 3, we shall have more to say in a minute.

My second qualifying observation is this: these paired 3+3's aside, the other 5 appear in second hemistichs, in stanzas 1 (3) and 3 (2). The stanza 3 instances both concern the actors in the poem's twilit drama, the objects of 'vois': 'les défuntes Années' and 'le Regret souriant'. It is not surprising that these elements should belong to the world of the sotto voce and entropic. Nor, then, is it surprising that the third element in the list, 'Le Soleil moribond', though it appears in first hemistich, should have the same rhythmic structure; indeed, it is not surprising that the entropic nature of the second hemistich, now invading the infinitive form too ('s'endormir sous une arche') should reach back into the hemistich we associate with impetus and élan.

The second-hemistich 3+3's in the first quatrain are movements of reassurance and pacification. The importunity implied in the first hemistichs of lines 1 and 2 is quietened in their second hemistichs, where lexical items—'plus tranquille', 'descend'—are imitated by, or imitate, a falling intonation. The predicate in line 3, 'enveloppe la ville' completes the evidence for the defence at the same time as it images a gesture of embrace.

If 3+3 can be said to predominate in the second stanza, then the second tercet is 4+2's ground. This combination of measures strikes me as an act of parturition. The tetrasyllable acts a preparatory moment of 'recueillement' which is released in a begetting. We can imagine, as mentioned, that this process sometimes produces a release of accumulated bile (line 5); but mostly, it is a movement of achievement, and this naturally attaches it to the first hemistich and the push towards the apex of the caesura; little wonder then that line 5's 4+2 occurs in the second hemistich. These remarks leave us with the last line to account for. In some senses the first hemistich is similarly an act of parturition: after the 'recueillement' of an earnest but recessed imperative of entreaty, the second 'entends' *creates* the perception rather than exhorting it; hearing lifts itself into activity, becomes outward-directed. At the same time, this 4+2 is a pre-echo of the second 4+2, the moment of 'recueillement' which wills the second hemistich into audibility, into audible discernibility. And since the second hemistich *is* the place of 'recueillement', what is here conjured up *is* 'recueillement'. But if there is a sense in which the second hemistich's 4+2 is a 2 to the 4 of the first hemistich's 4+2, it is also a 4+2 in its own right. But because it occurs in the second hemistich, what is conjured up is not an achievement, a stable state, but a process, a leakage, a thwarting mortality. More stability would have been provided by an infinitive ('entends marcher la douce Nuit'); by opting for the relative, Baudelaire gets sensory proximity, but correspondingly, increased temporal flow. The pursuit of 'recueillement' in this poem sets up a strong top-left to bottom-right movement; unfortunately, we arrive in 'recueillement' only to find that a small hole in the fabric of reclusion will compel us to act again, before too long. It does not surprise me that 'La Vie antérieure' also ends with a 4+2 hemistich:

> Le secret douloureux qui me faisait languir.

This, then, is what I am calling a reading of 'Recueillement', my reading, rather than an interpretation. I have tried to trace the ways in which this poem has operated in my consciousness, the features which my own response has selected as salient (perhaps without my quite knowing why). I have, I think, said more about the way this poem means than about its meanings; I have tried to describe what this poem is as a linguistic experience, as a play of modalities activated by verse-structure and by grammatical and syntactical categories, as a reading in progress, rather than as a message. Simply and crudely put, I have been concerned to convey a sense of the *growth* of meaning rather than of the *recuperation* of meaning. And this, I think, is also what our readings of translations should be about: to watch the growth of *an* ST meaning in the TT and not, definitely not, to retrieve *the* ST's meaning from the TT.

It is equally critical, then, that when I come to read a translation of 'Recueillement', I should come without knowing exactly what 'Recueillement' means and what are the good words and what are the bad words for conveying that meaning. I come, having read the text and having related its potential for meaning to a set of specific experiences of form, structure and acousticity. 'Recueillement' is thus for the translator a raw material still in a state of rawness, undetermined and therefore significantly undetermining. I have read 'Recueillement' and felt its semantic directions and its semantic irresolutions, and I have read the critics, whether Galand (1969), or Fongaro (1973), or Geninasca (1980) or Adatte (1986), not to endorse or adjust a 'reading', but to enlarge reading, to activate other capacities of response, to assimilate other modalities and intra-textual cross-references. And when I come then to, say, Roy Campbell's translation of 'Recueillement', I am continuing this operation, this process of extending the text, of uncovering its possible modes of activity and semantic range:

Meditation

1.	Be good, my Sorrow: hush now: settle down.	5/2/3
2.	You sighed for dusk, and now it comes: look there!	4/4/2
3.	A denser atmosphere obscures the town,	6/4
4.	To some restoring peace, to others care.	6/4
5.	While the lewd multitude, like hungry beasts,	6/4
6.	By pleasure scourged (no thug so fierce as he!)	4/6
7.	Go forth to seek remorse among their feasts—	6/4
8.	Come, take my hand; escape from them with me.	4/6
9.	From balconies of sky, around us yet,	6/4
10.	Lean the dead years in fashions that have ceased.	4/6
11.	Out of the depth of waters smiles Regret.	7/3
12.	The sun sinks moribund beneath an arch,	6/4
13.	And like a long shroud rustling from the East,	5/5
14.	Hark, Love, the gentle Night is on the march.	2/4/4

As previously, I will limit my comments on this translation to features which particularly struck me.

1. 'You sighed for dusk'. One might argue that 'sighed' loses all the potential petulance or tyranny of the child, that is in 'réclamais'. One might argue that 'rustling' is neither what a shroud does, nor what 'traînant' says. To argue these things is to argue either that Campbell did not think enough about his choices, or that he could not metrically fit 'asked', 'insisted', 'wanted', 'demanded', or 'trailing', 'dragging', etc. These suppositions are evidently absurd, and alert us to the drawbacks of paradigmatic criticism (single-word substitution), as opposed not so much to a syntagmatic criticism as to a 'textemic' one. In Baudelaire we spoke of the importance of the voiced /d/ and the voicelss /t/. Here Campbell has made much play with /d/. But its voiceless counterpart is now /s/ (and perhaps /tʃ/ and /ʃ/), and Sorrow needs not so much to be unvoiced as to recover the repose of its voicelessness. The final sequence is a beautiful threefold movement from voiced to unvoiced: 'gentle', 'Night', 'march'. 'Sighed', more than 'asked', throws itself, through /aɪ/, forward to 'sky', 'smiles' and, more especially, 'Night'. 'Rustling' picks up another important vowel, /ʌ/, which starts out by inviting somnolence ('hush', 'dusk', 'comes', 'some'), is hijacked and violated by 'multitude', 'hungry', 'thug' and 'among', before

returning to 'us', 'sun', 'moribund', 'rustling' and 'Love'. In fact, as we look and listen, we might begin to believe that 'us' is phonetically or graphemically the heart of this family, ousted momentarily by the second-stanza occurrences.

2. The predominant caesural juncture in these lines is after the sixth syllable (six times). Between lines 5 and 10, 6/4 alternates with 4/6; this is the poem's central moment of uncertainty—the vile crowd pursuing pleasure (and remorse), the speaker and Sorrow seeking to escape to a dead past. The closing four lines then trace a movement from polarisation (7/3), by gradation, to balance (5/5), but in a syntactically suspensive line which heralds a trimetric structure, itself an exhortation, 'Hark, Love', followed by a balanced resolution (now down to 4/4). This trimetric structure also acts as a resolution to the more troubled and less controlled trimetric structures of the poem's first two lines.

3. Line 8. This wonderfully simple, predominantly monosyllabic line, given a powerful acoustic cohesiveness by /m/, is a movement not only away from the city's debauchery, but also from the rather archaic language of moral allegory and censure (even the modern 'thug' is set in a quaint syntax), as indeed it is in the ST. It is a line which one can read either with a reversed first foot (as is more probable), or as iambic throughout. It is not the first time we have met a disturbance in the first foot (line 5 opens with an ionic (××//)). But line 8 heralds the increasing metrical variety of line-openings in the tercets:

> line 10: /×//×/×/×/
> line 11: /××/×/×/×/
> line 12: ×///×/×/×/ (?)
> line 13: ×/×///×××/ (?)
> line 14: //×/×/×/×/

These variations seem to indicate the greater involvement of the voice, the paradoxically more complex music of the coming of peace, a music further complicated by the way it plays against the pattern of caesural juncture and syllabic balance.

4. Line 10. I stop on this line simply because 'fashions that have ceased' sounds like a rather poor shot at 'robes surannées'. About this I would say two things. The alternating rhymes in Baudelaire's quatrains are made more difficult to disentangle from each other by a shared, fixating /i/.

198

Indeed, the desire of the poet to isolate himself with his 'Douleur', as evening falls and Pleasure dons its glad-rags, is only realized in the *rejet* of line 9, 'Loin d'eux'. But the poet's oscillation between self and crowd, pain and pleasure, embodied in the alternating rhyme, is counterpointed by other patterns: semantically, the rhymes of the first quatrain create couplets of complicity—'tranquille' ('Douleur')/'le voici' ('Soir') v. 'la ville'/'le souci'—while in the second quatrain, the final rhyme ('par ici') is an attempt to escape the pressure of the other three ('vile'/ 'sans merci'/'servile'). Campbell maintains the alternating pattern of rhymes through his octave, but changes his rhyme-sounds in the second quatrain. He indicates the acoustic kinship between the rhymes only in the assonant /iː/ of the second quatrain. However, he does extend his /iːst/ rhyme into the tercets, now shorn of a plurality which distracts and disperses perception. Instead, in the tercets, we have the lost time of a past participle conjoined with a cardinal point which is certainly the source of encroaching darkness, but also the promise of future awakenings. Secondly, the line begins with an /iː/ as it ends with one, and, graphemically at least, the -ea- also appears in 'dead years' (/dɛdjɪəz/). One might then propose some kinship between /iː/ (-ea-) and /ɛ/: 'dead' generates 'depth', which is part of 'Regret'; 'beneath' and 'East' summon 'gentle'.

If now we turn to Lowell's version—

Meditation

1.	Calm down, my Sorrow, we must move with care.		5/5
2.	You called for evening; it descends; it's here.		5/3/2
3.	the town is coffined in its atmosphere,		5/5
4.	bringing relief to some, to others care.		6/4
5.	Now while the common multitude strips bare,		8/2
6.	feels pleasure's cat o'nine tails on its back,		7/3
7.	and fights off anguish at the great bazaar,		5/5
8.	give me your hand, my Sorrow. Let's stand back;		7/3
9.	back from these people! Look, the dead years dressed		5/5
10.	in old clothes crowd the balconies of the sky.		3/5/3
11.	Regret emerges smiling from the sea,		7/3
12.	the sick sun slumbers underneath an arch,		5/5

| 13. and like a shroud strung out from east to west, | 4/6 |
| 14. listen, my Dearest, hear the sweet night march! | 5/5 |

—it is to undertake a brief comparative analysis, not in order to show in what ways one is better than the other, but rather to explore the ways in which comparison may begin to reveal to us what the translational parameters of a given ST might be.

1. Evidently we might speak of rhythms here. Both poets use iambic pentameter, but in relation to caesural juncture, Lowell clearly favours 5/5, which is a strong presence in the first quatrain and second tercet, but is hanging on by its fingernails in lines 5–11. This as good as reverses the situation we found in Campbell. Here the simile at line 13 is not a final consolidation of suspensive balance, but a wobble, just to alert attention, a phatic gesture almost. And yet in similar fashion to Campbell, Lowell seems to use a reversed first foot at the beginning of line 8 to initiate a sequence of metrical variations in the lines following.

2. It may seem odd to find an exclamation mark at the end of a poem whose final lines are devoted to the establishment of a soothing quietude. The confidence of the 5/5, or the repetition of the exhortation, might explain it. Or it might signal the release of an accumulated pressure, the consummation devoutly wished for. Be that as it may, punctuation remains an underestimated resource. Campbell, like Baudelaire, has no final exclamation, but, interestingly, he uses colons in the first two lines of the poem, rather than commas or semi-colons. We have already enquired into the nature of the colon, in the previous chapter. The colon seems to reach down, as it were, from the outer voice to the inner. We are beyond the realm of socially shared linguistic operations, free floating across clauses whose connections have lost their innocence, have become charged; the relationship concealed by the colon is, as Gracq expresses it, 'plus dynamique et comme électrisé' [more dynamic and as if electrified] (1980: 258).[3]

3. Part of the reason for Campbell's subtilizing the relationship in these opening lines may lie in his decision to reduce the number of personified abstractions to Sorrow, Regret, Love and night, where Sorrow and Love are the same person. This conflation of figures perhaps necessitates a more ambiguous tone, a more nuanced and knowing exchange, understood more by the participants than by us. In Lowell's version, Sorrow is the only surviving personification it seems, although it is impossible to be sure about

sentence-initial Regret. These moves remind us that part of translation's margin of flexibility lies in degrees of figurativeness and didacticism. Personification tends to de-metaphorize anthropomorphizing images. Without its capital, the sun has to renegotiate its relationship with 'moribund' or 'sick'.

4. Lowell maintains the interrelatedness of the octave's alternating rhymes through the close acoustic kinship of /ɛə/ and /Iə/, but relies on the shared grapheme 'a' to hold his rhymes together in the second quatrain, aided by word-initial /b/ (presumably 'bare' rhymes with 'bazaar' in Lowell's pronunciation, or almost). Most curiously, in the tercets, he rhymes 'sky' with 'sea'; or, rather, they are *compelled* to rhyme by the other line-endings. The sea is indeed supposed to mirror the sky: the dead years call forth regret. But even as this pair 'rhymes', a huge phonetic chasm opens up between them. Will the peaceful death of the sun be echoed here on earth? Is regret, however smiling, indissolubly attached to the 'gouffre amer' and incapable of 'élévation'? ('Élévation', in fact, with its image of the swimmer in the ether, is an important intertext for Lowell's translation in a way that it is not for Baudelaire's ST). This collision of sea and sky is made the more piquant by Lowell's studied cultivation of homonyms ('care', 'back'); the principle of the homonym ('sounds the same, means different') cannot be reversed by 'sky' and 'sea'. This is to suggest that the changeability in Lowell's rhyming modes allows him to create his own drama of rhyme, his own rhyme semantics. The incompleteness of Lowell's rhymes is put to good expressive use: it gives us the sense that certain illusions cannot be sustained, that rhyme, that instrument of affirmation or confirmation, that reassurance that the order of received knowledge still stands, has for too long papered over dissonances that it can no longer hide. Rhyme, in Lowell's version, is like a fabric which is being torn and hastily stitched up again. To ask translators either to rhyme regularly or not at all is to deny them the opportunity to use rhyme creatively, as a weapon of personal intervention in the text.

5. As in Campbell's version, and almost inevitably, given the principal actor, /s/ is Lowell's voiceless keynote, and as in Campbell's last line, and not surprisingly, Lowell finishes with a sequence of three words in which the voiced moves to the voiceless: 'sweet night march'. But where /d/ continues to play a central role in Campbell's translation, Lowell has chosen a second voiceless consonant, /k/, as his accompaniment. The first stanza opens with 'Calm' and ends with 'care', and it is the 'c' grapheme, in its word-initial mode, which animates this quatrain ('Calm', 'care',

'called', 'coffined', 'care'). The second quatrain introduces the more aggressive, angular 'k' grapheme, in its word-terminal role, where 'c' comes to collide with it ('back' (bis)); 'c', in this stanza, has a pejorative colouring ('common', 'cat o'nine tails'). 'Back' is the link to the first tercet, where the significance of the relationship becomes more indeterminate ('clothes', 'crowd', 'balconies'; 'Look', 'sky'). 'Sick' introduces us to the second tercet, where the 'k' of 'like' is the only other /k/, but where the grapheme 'c', now combined with 'h' to produce /tʃ/, is a critical element in the final rhyme ('arch'/'march'). The de-/k/ing of 'c' is like the removal from consciousness of a troublesome thought—in fact, it is the discovery of the new partnership with 'h' which is the cause of the de-/k/ing of 'c'. It would be absurd to say that Lowell's 'Meditation' is about the activity and ultimate evaporation of 'c' (/k/); but a poem produces within its structure many different destinies, all playing themselves out alongside each other and in their interwovenness generating the poem's coming to meaning(s). Poems are multivocal choruses in which all elements have a certain degree of autonomy, if only because the psycho-perceptual mechanisms of readers have such a variety of focuses. To ask a poem to be interpretable is to ask it to forgo its polyphonic *signifiance* (in the sense given that word by Barthes and Kristeva).

As a final element in this process of open-ended and speculative assessment, I would like to make a small number of observations based on the concordancing of the translations of F.W. Leakey (1994) and Richard Howard (1982). These are corpora of very different dimensions: Leakey has translated a selection of 46 poems, while Howard offers a complete complement of 157 poems. Leakey's vocabulary, including titles, consists of some[4] 2,758 words, whilst Howard's, also including titles, is some 5,944. Given that the Leakey corpus is less than one third that of the Howard corpus, this may cause no surprise. The important thing is that concordancing allows us to evaluate the significance of size of vocabulary, whether the translation wishes to turn within the relatively confined circle of recurrent existential and psycho-perceptual fields of reference, or whether the extension of the vocabulary of single occurrences opens up vents in language, which allow glimpses of a liberating otherness or diversity, the promise of self-replenishment, and so on. In Leakey's account of 'Recueillement', 'Douleur' is translated by 'Pain':

Evening Meditation

Pain, cease your clamour; rest awhile; be still.

The evening that you craved at last has come.
The city sinks beneath its shadowy pall,
To some brings peace, to others care and stress,
While the vile multitude, upon its hectic round,
Under the scourge of pleasure, lays up future remorse.

My Pain, come closer; let me hold your hand,
Draw you this way, far, far from them. See now
The bygone Years lean out, from balconies in the sky,
In their quaint, charming dresses; see
Smiling Regret rise up from watery depths; see there
The dying Sun droop low, beneath an arch;
And, trailing from the East her long, funereal shroud,
Hear Night, with gentle steps, pace softly on and on.[5]

There are only two instances where Leakey uses words with the 'sorrow' lemma, and only one of these ('La Vie antérieure') corresponds to a 'douleur' lemma; in 'Elévation', Leakey's 'sorrows' translates 'chagrins' or 'ennuis', or both. The 'douleur' lemma, on the other hand, appears 34 times in the Baudelairean corpus (Cargo 1965: 95). Does Leakey, then, actively avoid the 'douleur' = 'sorrow' equivalence? In 'A une passante' ('douleur majestueuse'), for example, Leakey does not translate, apparently deeming the reference to 'mourning' sufficient. In 'Le Jeu', Leakey renders it again by 'pain', in 'Le Cygne' by 'grief' (bis), in 'Le Rêve d'un curieux' by 'anguish'; in 'Le Crépuscule du soir', it is engrossed with other ills in 'suffered' (1.8) and conflated ('les douleurs des malades', l. 31) into 'illnesses'. In 'Semper eadem', it is not translated. In 'L'Ennemi', it appears as 'suffering', in 'Un voyage à Cythère' as both 'sufferings' and 'anguish', in 'L'Horloge' as 'anguish', in 'Le Crépuscule du matin' as 'pangs' (of childbirth). Our purpose in collecting this evidence is not so much to judge each instance as a translational choice within a particular context, as to try to detect tendencies, proclivities, in Leakey's translating self. We know that 'douleur' has a wide semantic range—from direct physical suffering (as Leakey's 'illnesses' or 'pangs') through moral suffering to the sufferings which accompany various kinds of loss. The degree of suffering covers an equally broad spectrum. But we might propose that Leakey's inclination is to intensify the pain in 'douleur': 'pain', in his selection, also translates 'torture' ('Le Rêve d'un curieux'), just as 'Anguish' translates 'Angoisse' ('Quand le ciel bas et lourd...'); and 'grief' is perhaps more vivid than 'sorrow', has a more specific object, is more turbulent. But if we are to speak of an inclination—

and one, it seems, strong enough to run the risk, in 'Recueillement' at least, of collapsing into bathos, thanks to the proximity of colloquial expressions such as 'He's a pain in the neck' or 'Stop being a pain'—what reasons might we suggest for it? Is Leakey registering a refusal to subscribe to nineteenth-century sentimentalizations of pain? Is he resisting the view that some might have, namely that 'douleur' is a Baudelairean keyword and that translators should treat it with the necessary respect and render it as consistently as possible? Does Leakey feel that the Baudelairean text is in danger of being lyricized out of its hard-hitting and confrontational character, just as earlier translations tended to sensationalize, not to say satanize, the text? Of course we cannot answer these questions, but the very fact that we have asked them at least demonstrates that we are trying to constitute the translator, that we are attempting to identify the propensities which textually impel him.

We might feel, looking at Leakey's translation of the punctuation at the end of line 12 (he has converted Baudelaire's comma to a semi-colon) and his removal of the colon at the end of line 2, that his translation is syntactically normalizing, that Baudelaire's typographically insinuated sub-texts have been silently erased. But this would be a remarkably erroneous impression. If one looked at Leakey's use of suspension points one would not find anything to comment on; there are 8 instances to be set against the 10 to be found in Baudelaire, although they coincide in only three cases. Leakey looks to suspension points to curtain off something whose considerable consequences or implications can be only too clearly seen, as in 'Au lecteur':

> an involuntary tear
> Flooding his eye as he dreams of scaffolds…All too well
> You, my dear reader, *know* this delicate monster:

Much more interesting, however, is the punctuation with which this quatrain ends—Leakey may have dispensed with colons in 'Recueillement', but the concordancer reveals 67 instances in the selection as a whole. Quite clearly this is an important expressive resource in Leakey's translational language; Baudelaire's use, on the other hand (26 instances in Leakey's selection, 10 of which occur in 'Le Voyage'),[6] is highly conventional: in the majority of instances it introduces speech, and elsewhere clarifications or itemizations. These latter functions are also performed by Leakey's colons. But additionally they act as thresholds of radiation, or the window within which other windows are stored:

Nature: a living temple live with murmuring sound,
Its pillars eloquent, their glances meaningful
To Man [...]

('Correspondances')

Or they push the consecutive towards the simultaneous and problematize the relationship between actions, as we have already seen. In his translation of 'Don Juan aux Enfers', one might indeed argue that his reordering of Baudelaire's syntax forces him to replace Baudelaire's coordinating and sequencing 'Et' with a more temporally suspended and baffling colon:

The sky was black and lowering, and as they glided on,
A howl of execration rose up from every side:
Baring their breasts, writhing in shame, in their accusing herd,
The women that the Don had wronged were massed to watch
him pass.

And sometimes the complexity of the punctuation produces an experience for the reader at once stark and confused, in which planes of perception and space have shuffled themselves like cards. This is certainly one of the effects of the colon-within-a-colon to be found in Leakey's rendering of 'Quand le ciel bas et lourd...':

—And then the funeral march, within my mind,
Begins: hearses; no drums, no music: vanquished Hope
In tears—while the despotic victor, Anguish, clamps
His black flag onto my defeated skull.

One of the other elements in this potent mix of psychological levels, perceptual hallucination diversified but undifferentiated, is the dash, and Leakey's selection provides us with 58 examples. Baudelaire, for his part, has 37 in the same selection, 26 of which occur at the beginnings of lines; and of these 26, 14 introduce the poem's final statement. Dashes in Baudelaire, where they are not performing a parenthesizing function, have a phatic, as much as expressive, role to play. They are signs to the reader to prepare for the pay-off, as the poet checks himself, to ponder the road he has travelled, before delivering himself of a lapidary, and often exclamatory, peroration. In Leakey's work, they are equally brief moments of self-collection; but they beget afterthought rather than resounding summary. They give the impression of utterance improvising itself, stumbling across the real implication, or the lateral *aperçu*:

205

> Stupidity and error, sin and avarice,
> These fill our minds, erode us inwardly—
> Until, that is, we feel the comforts of remorse, [...]
> ('To the Reader')

On occasion, these dashes also represent the crossing of an expressive line, where a reformulation occurs, but in a different key ('Uplifted, Soaring', 'The Carrion'). Sometimes they announce the shift into something essentialized, telegraphic ('Don Juan in Hell', 'To a Fair Passer-By'). Sometimes they are jolts in the mind, triggers that release memory and association:

> you recall
> The true river Simois in your own native Troy—
> This image from your story, in my fertile mind
> A further intimate memory stirs as I traverse
> The new, wide Carrousel.
> ('The Swan')

Sometimes they are moments of self-correction, or self-disabusement, when with a bitter irony the poet nullifies a hope or an intention:

> Now to forgive her—if I can!
> ('The Murderer's Wine')

> "Love, glory, happiness
> Ahead!"—and on the rocks, alas! we sadly come to grief.
> ('Travellers')

There can be no doubt, I think, that many of Leakey's characteristic modes of thought, of response, of connection, are embedded in these conjunctival forms of punctuation: the colon and dash provide him with just the kinds of articulations that he needs, to express the temperamental and tautly strung self he finds in Baudelaire's poems.

The final feature of Leakey's translation of 'Recueillement' which I would like to explore through concordancing occurs in the poem's final line—'Hear Night, with gentle steps, pace softly on and on'—namely the adverb 'on'. This adverb wills the expansion of space and time, rather in the fashion of Baudelaire's 'surnaturalisme':

> Le surnaturel comprend la couleur générale et l'accent, c'est-à-dire

206

intensité, sonorité, limpidité, vibrativité, profondeur et
retentissement dans l'espace et dans le temps.

(OC, I, 658)

[The supernatural comprises general colour and accent, that is to
say intensity, sonority, clarity, vibrativity, depth and resonance in
space and time.]

The concordancer listed 74 occurrences of 'on' in Leakey's translations.
Besides prepositional uses, I found 'on' adverbially combining with several
transitive verbs (e.g. 'passes', 'lures', 'drawing') and though these may be
important contributors to the sense of extension, they are less significant,
and indeed less numerous, than the intransitive combinations ('glided'
(bis), 'lingers', 'lives', 'shines', 'flowed', 'wandered', 'sleeps', 'shining',
'wail', 'grows', 'pace', 'echoing', 'waited', 'bound') which project the
activity of the agent out, without confinement, and endow it with a curious
autonomy. What makes the 'on' of these examples so poignant is that the
perpetuation it offers is, potentially, as much the perpetuation of a
monotony, of an unmodulated reality, the 'on and on' of spleen, or the
magnet which draws one further out of one's depth, as the freedom
spiritually to fare forward, to devour distances in heightened
consciousness, to have one's sense of existence amplified, or to proceed
with therapeutic gradualness and solicitude (the opposite of the jagged and
staccato experience of the metropolis). And as we look through the
examples, we shall discover instances where 'on' is a supplement supplied
by Leakey, e.g.:

Nous accompagnaient lentement

As through the silent night we wandered on
('The Heart's Confessional')

La toile était levée et j'attendais encore

The curtain now had risen at last, and still I waited on…
('A Curious Man's Dream')

'On' would appear, if unobtrusively, to have for Leakey, too, something
magnetic about it.

One of the reasons one might adduce for preferring 'Sorrow' to 'Pain'
as a rendering of 'Douleur' in 'Recueillement' is the title of the poem itself.
One is looking for that feeling which has a contemplative capacity, that has

a gently suffusive activity. 'Sorrow' wins over 'Pain' because its two syllables modulate it, nuance it, shifting it from unrounded to rounded; in comparison, 'Pain' is single, univocal, undifferentiated. Sorrow is peculiarly infectious, radiant, while anguish, for example, feels more inturned and self-engrossed. Sorrow ennobles ('douleur majestueuse'); pain simply afflicts. Howard chooses 'Sorrow' for his translation of this poem:

Meditation

Behave, my Sorrow! let's have no more scenes.
Evening's what you wanted—Evening's here:
a gradual darkness overtakes the town,
bringing peace to some, to others pain.

Now, while humanity racks up remorse
in low distractions under Pleasure's lash,
grovelling for a ruthless master—come
away, my Sorrow, leave them! Give me your hand...

See how the dear departed dowdy years
crowd the balconies of heaven, leaning down,
while smiling out of the sea appears Regret;

the Sun will die in its sleep beneath a bridge,
and trailing westward like a winding-sheet—
listen, my dear—how softly Night arrives.

I do not want with Howard's text to further pursue the 'anguish', 'pain', 'sorrow', 'care' family, but to turn instead to a rather smaller issue. Howard translates 'fouet' (1.6) by 'lash', where Leakey has 'scourge'. 'Lash', as a noun, is the blow rather than the instrument that delivers it; it is a blow we think of as sharp, cutting, and resonant. The instrument which gives lashes is supple and fairly light. 'Scourge', where it is not an all but automatic translation of 'fléau' (as in 'Causerie'), maintains its biblical overtones; it is a whipping which has moral intentions, which is the administering of punishment or retribution. 'Scourge' is not the blow but the instrument, which is capable of dealing blows heavier than lashes. Both 'lash' and 'scourge' can be used as verbs. Any conclusions drawn about the habits of our translators in this instance would have to remain highly speculative, since quantitative evidence is extremely limited. But we can at least see the way in which English alternatives operate around a single French element 'fouet'/'fouetter'. In the versions we have before us, it is as if Leakey has responded to the 'fouet…bourreau sans merci' combination—for, clearly, 'scourge' evokes not only 'official' punishment, but also relentless determination—while Howard has thought more of the connection with 'Plaisir', pleasure in the giving and receiving of pain, pain as exquisitely sharp and capriciously administered. What is then perhaps surprising is that each of the translators should have chosen in the opposite direction, for the line which most closely echoes the one before us, from 'Le Voyage':

> Et le peuple amoureux du fouet abrutissant.

Leakey renders this as:

> We have seen torturers delight, martyrs in agony;
> Feast-days perfumed and drenched in blood; despots, maddened
> > by power,
> Coercing subjects humbled but yet grateful for the whip

and Howard gives:

> victims in tears, the hangman glorified;
> the banquet seasoned and festooned with blood:
> the poison of power clogs the despot's veins,
> and the people kiss the knout that scourges them

where 'knout' is a heavy Russian punishment whip. But these 'inconsistencies' are not surprising given the contexts in which they occur. Leakey seems to emphasize physical sensation, the coloured, the epidermic and the uncontrolled ('torturers', 'martyrs', 'delight', 'agony', 'perfumed', 'drenched', 'maddened'), while Howard's images are more restrained and abstract, more concerned with political structure, more imbued with heaviness. The biblical credentials of 'scourge', the connections with divine punishment (motivated or not by jealousy and retributive sadism) are clearly important in promoting a certain view of the moral preoccupations of *Les Fleurs du Mal*, and not only in those poems which are explicitly biblical, e.g. 'Le Reniement de saint Pierre':

> Tu fouettais tous ces vils marchands à tour de bras

> You scourged those money-lenders within the temple walls
> > (Leakey)

209

you whipped the moneylenders out of that place—

(Howard)

So far, it might seem that Leakey is marginally (proportionately) more inclined to underline the punitive moral forces at work in Baudelaire's world, where the dispensers of retribution are no better than their victims, where punishment serves both design and whim, indistinguishably. But this conclusion might be mistaken. 'Scourge' in its diverse forms occurs in Howard's work as a translation not only of 'fouet' and 'fléau' ('Causerie'), but also of 'effrayant' ('Hymne à la Beauté'), 'porte le châtiment' ('Les Hiboux'), 'frappe à traits redoublés' ('Le Soleil'), 'flagellés' ('Femmes damnées: Delphine et Hippolyte'), and 'tortures' ('La Prière d'un païen').

Howard's version of 'Recueillement' might lead us to suppose that, as for Leakey, punctuation is for him a crucial resource of expressivity, the space in which his voice, though silent, is remarkably active, full of tone, and pace, and pressures to utter of various kinds. The proposition that punctuation can be *peculiarly* the site of the translator's voice is in need of urgent investigation. At all events, the concordancer gives 412 instances of the dash, and 150 of the colon. Its finding of 24 occurrences of *points de suspension* seemed unreliable, and my own count produced a figure of 91. (It should also be said that Howard is quite as exclamatory a poet as Baudelaire: 427 exclamation marks!) Even in 'Meditation', one can begin to feel the significance of the dash as an index of self-interruptive impatience, changes of direction; and in lines 13–14, what might look like dashes used in a parenthesizing pair, turn out to be more ambiguous than that. It is true that we can read over 'listen, my dear'; the 'how' ceases to part of a verb + 'how' construction ('see how', l.9 > 'listen how'), and becomes instead an exclamatory adverb (but there is no exclamation mark to confirm that, and Howard is a natural exclaimer). In this scenario, 'Douleur' has been only just remembered; the poet is totally absorbed in his solitary anticipation of the coming night. But if we read the syntax as 'listen how', then the last lines act more as suicidal, or murderous, embrace: 'winding sheet' triggers 'listen, my dear'; the dash, here, does not mark a sudden deviation of thought, but rather a more purposeful connection. And then the dash between 'dear' and 'how' acts again as a welding together, both of first and second persons, and of contrary impulses (taut anticipation and dissolving self-surrender). But we have already explored some of the dimensions of the dash in our treatment of Leakey; Howard gives us the excuse to take a closer look at suspension points.

In Howard's particular usage, suspension points indicate the text's withdrawal into itself, into a private space with its own unseen extensions or implications. In 'Meditation', this manoeuvre relates particularly to the sonnet-form, closing off the octave and wiping the verbal slate clean, so that the sestet may inscribe itself with added authority. The same move occurs in Howard's renderings of 'Le Parfum' ('Un fantôme'):

> l.8:   plucks subtle flowers of memory...

'A une dame créole':

> l.8: and when she smiles, assurance lights her glance...

and 'Une nuit que j'étais près d'une affreuse Juive':

> l.8: whose memory wakens me to love once more...

Even here, where one might suppose that the *points de suspension* enact a process of distracted revery, which they do, we still have a sense of a couple leaving the stage in order to return transformed. In 'A une dame créole', for instance, a third person leaves the stage, in order to return as a second person. And the revival of the poet's desire, in his memory of the absent 'triste beauté' ('Une nuit que j'étais près...'), is not then to be con-summated, out of sight, with the 'affreuse Juive', but in a purely hypothetical encounter, which spans a period between lost opportunities in the past ('Car j'eusse...') and a mobile time ('quelque soir') in the future ('Si.../Tu pouvais...'), and which is dependent on a newly compassionate mistress.

These moments of erasure prior to a clarification, may not occur, in the sonnet at least, at a convenient structural juncture. In 'Le Rêve d'un curieux', Baudelaire himself supplies suspension points at the end of line 10, which Howard duly 'translates'; while in 'Obsession', Howard replaces Baudelaire's exclamation mark at the end of line 11 with suspension points:

> I long for darkness, silence, *nothing there...*

In 'Travelers' ('Le Voyage'), erasure has another face, that of impulses unable to sustain themselves, linguistic journeys which lose belief in their power to summon reality and peter out:

> Yet we are his in the end. One hope remains:
> to venture forth, with 'Onward!' as our cry...

211

we shall embark upon the Sea of Shades
with all the elation of a boy's first cruise...

The connection between voyaging and linguistic self-perpetuation, or the immortalization of others, is, of course, the opening gambit of 'Je te donne ces vers afin que si mon nom':

Suppose my name were favored by the winds,
my voyage prospered, and the future read
all that I wrote, and marvelled...Love, they're yours!
I give you poems to make your memory

and the felicity of Howard's translation here lies in the way in which the suspension points allow the poem to establish its equivocating position: either the poet does then manage to go on, having cleared the creative ground for himself, to depict his mistress unforgettably:

my jet-eyed statue, angel with brazen brows!

or his ambition runs into the sand as she exceeds linguistic control and eludes him by her very changeability. Here both kinds of erasure operate at once, as they do in Howard's account of 'L'Ennemi' where, significantly, suspension points replace Baudelaire's question mark at the end of the first tercet:

I dream of new flowers, but who can tell
if this eroded swamp of mine affords
the mystic nourishment on which they thrive...

In other instances, suspension points do not so much erase as invoke, or provoke, rather as they might in a newspaper caption. Howard's account of 'Sed non satiata' ends:

become
in your bed's inferno...Persephone!

Here, suspension points install suspense, the pregnant pause of the complacent magician, of innuendo and the sly wink, or of portentousness, of outleaping one's own invention:

O squalid dignity...Sublime disgrace!
('You'd sleep with anyone...')

212

Perhaps the most satisfying examples in this category occur in Howard's rendering of 'Les Ténèbres' ('Un fantôme'). To begin with the poet finds himself disempowered, like a painter condemned to paint on blackness:

> as if a scoffing God had forced
> my hand to fresco...silhouettes!

Reference to the French text tells us that the *points de suspension* are in a sense a punctuational transliteration of 'hélas!' But there is still the pleasure in revelation, however bitter and disbelieving. And then into this darkness comes a dark figure:

> but then a shape looms, shining,
> and as it moves it modifies:
> a lovely...something—is there not

> all the East in its easy way?

What here is revealed by the colon is an inability to reveal, the offer of an answer that proves premature. In the ST, the poet achieves recognition through the agency of the visitor (capitalized) herself, with the colon as if delayed (in comparison with Howard's) to ensure its arriving at just the right moment:

> Je reconnais ma belle visiteuse: 4//6, 4+2+4
> C'est Elle! noire et pourtant lumineuse.   4//6, 3'+1+3+3

And we can see how important rhythmic disposition is. Baudelaire's second tercet slips into a consistent 4//6 division, where previously there had been 6//4 interspersions, and the final line invites a tetrametric reading (with a *coupe lyrique* after the first measure) rather than the more usual trimetric one. This allows the 'lumineuse' to radiate out of the hemistich in greater fullness, while the 'noire' still gets its full value as an isolated accentuated syllable, putting the conventional caesura in place, after 'Elle' had seemed to be a disruptive anticipation of it. Howard, for his part, attributes more power of divination to the poet, so that discovery is already achieved (and endorsed by an exclamation mark) before 'she' arrives. But her presence is in no way diminished, thanks to the clustering of stress and the postponement of the burst of light to the last word, as in the ST:

> I know my visitor! *She* comes, x/x/xx//
> black—yet how that blackness glows!   /—x/x/x/

213

As we see, the dash has a caesural value, even if radically displaced.

This enquiry into the potential use of concordancing in the criticism of translation has set out from a very narrow quantitative base, and I have not drawn upon many of concordancing's available functions, particularly those that lie in the area of textual comparison. But it has not been my purpose to undertake a thorough comparative study. I have only been anxious to show how helpful, how essential, concordancing is to the study of translation, and most particularly to the construction of the translator as writer, and to an identification of what Berman (1995: 74–5) calls 'la position traductive' [the translational position]. Additionally, concordancing can help the critic to map the different territories occupied by words belonging to the same semantic field, and to test notions of equivalence.

Judgements of the quality of translation will too often, as we have seen, be based on the quality of the lexical choices made. I say 'quality of choice' on the supposition that no choice can be self-evidently absolutely right; and, by the same token, no choice can be absolutely wrong. Choices which are absolutely wrong are mistakes and cease, by that fact, to have any interest as choices. I also assume that the quality of a translation does not depend on the number of its mistakes. It may well be that a translation ultimately disqualifies itself by dint of being too frequently erroneous, but this remains a quantitative question and of relatively little relevance to qualitative issues. True, the point at which a wrong choice, or poor quality choice, becomes an error is critical, precisely because it is the point at which considerations of quality close off. Equally crucial is the point at which poor quality choice and error meet (justifiable) freedom.

Let us then recapitulate. In the first instance, we should be more interested to assess the quality of choice (which we cannot do without some knowledge of motivations) rather than the choice itself (which we can do on the basis of outcomes). But we must be careful, in our reconstruction of motivations, in our attempt to understand choices themselves as the 'systematic' implementation of a translational project and the production of an autonomous text whose raw material is an ST, not to fall into the trap of supposing that we all choose from the same position and in the same way. And we must make allowance for the aleatory, for what we might think of as irrational choice, or as non-choice, or as the unavoidable result of other choices. And within this category, we must distinguish between what we identify as the flotsam of the process, details which are non-marked and of no particular significance, and those moments of arbitrariness, or apparent whimsicality, which are the very measure of the translator's sensibility, are, as it were, where sensibility is delivered to us naked. And these latter instances, in their turn, may be difficult to distinguish from 'expressive rationality' (Hargreaves-Heap, Hollis, *et al.* 1992: 21–4) whereby the subject tries to make sense of himself through creative choice, through choice which is necessarily open-ended, because, precisely, it is a making sense, because it is concerned with establishing the value of the ends pursued. And is this not the appropriate way to represent translation?

It would be wonderful to be able to formulate a theory, or theories, of choice for translation, as economists, sociologists and philosophers do for their disciplines (see Hargreaves-Heap, Hollis, *et al.* 1992), but the variables seem too numerous, and the dependency links—which choices are superordinate, which subordinate, and what the proper chain of priority is in the sequence of choices—too fragile. Among the variables, we might mention the number of translations of a particular work available at any particular time, which will affect what the reader is prepared to take for granted, what degree of exploratory novelty he is prepared to tolerate:

> From the 1960s onward 'straight' versions of his [Baudelaire's] poems begin to give place to freer and more radical approaches. His creative and personal identity and the cultural meaning of his work are taken more and more as given—a consensus is assumed to exist which can serve as a point of departure: the poem to be translated becomes a found object to be distorted at will or to serve as the armature for a new work; or it is a text to be treated ironically, and redirected by internal references to Baudelaire's life or other writings
>
> (Clark and Sykes 1997: xlviii)

The dependency links are fragile in one respect simply because the poetics of translation is itself historically evolving, the elements of translation are constantly subject to reconfiguration, to changes of focus (gender, post-colonialism, intertextuality) and changes of function. And unfortunately change occurs so unevenly across cultures that an age is never in a position to formulate stable evaluative criteria for itself. This is perhaps why we are so likely to end up with the lowest common denominator—word-for-word or phrase-by-phrase assessment.

But even if we cannot develop a *theory of choice*, it is in the interests of translation criticism that we should continue to *theorize choice*, (a) because we must avoid untheorized, lowest-common-denominator, micro-level approaches, and (b) because translation, as we have already had plenty of cause to observe, displays choice and seeks to be that ambiguous thing: a text fully in possession of its textuality while constantly flirting with, tempting, other kinds of textuality. We do not in any event need the dogma or illusory panacea of a theory in the essentialist tradition (Arrojo 1998); but we do need theorizable procedures.

In this chapter, we have attempted to imagine some of the lines of investigation entailed in the pursuit of the translational project and the translator. Above all, we have tried to distinguish between reading and interpretation, and to understand some of the motives for choice at the textual level. In the final chapter, I wish to essay a translation, in free verse, of the final poem of *Les Fleurs du Mal*, 'Le Voyage', assimilating into it some collateral reading and moments of my own writing triggered by the text itself. Part of the criticism of translation must also be to identify, and to incorporate into the process of evaluation, that twin supplement: the supplement, the accretion, which grows with the ST's traversal of time and space, and which is a vital element of its life in the TT; and the supplement of the translator's writing which may be on occasion separable and explicit, but is more often an implicit part of the complex jigsaw of choice we have just spoken about.

By way of epilogue to this chapter, I offer my own translation of 'Recueillement', without further comment:

> Sorrow, simmer down
> > stop pestering me
> If it's evening you wanted
> > then look about, it's here
> A murky atmosphere
> > swallows the city up
> Brings peace to some
> > to some a world of cares
>
> The loathsome masses
> > under the licking lash
> Of our unpitying
> > headsman, pleasure
> Are off to harvest conscience
> > in abject revelry
> Sorrow, give me your hand
> > come this way
>
> far from them all
> > See years long past
> > > lean down

216

in dresses long outmoded
                        from sky-borne

                                        balconies
                                        See

from the waters' depths
                        Regret rise

                                        smiling

and the sun in its declining hours
                        stretch out

                                        to sleep

under an arch

                                        while
                                        like a winding sheet
                                        slowly unravelling
                                        from the East—
                                        listen, dearest—
                                        you can hear
                                        Night
                                        tiptoe in
                                        on stockinged
                                        feet.

Translation and Intercutting

Anyone contemplating a translation of Baudelaire's 'Le Voyage' (see Appendix IV for full French text), with the intention of drawing on the resources of montage, in a free-verse framework, will inevitably be tempted by the formal suggestions of works like Mallarmé's *Un coup de dés,* or Apollinaire's 'Du coton dans les oreilles' (*Calligrammes*) or Butor's *Mobile.* For after all, translation, and more especially still, free-verse translation with montaging, is as much a process of linguistic engineering and editing, as of writing. As we have already seen, the process of choice, almost hypertrophied in translation, subtly changes the mode of writing. While the ST writer has made choices which become a progressive concealment of the alternatives, the choices and the alternatives of the translator remain peculiarly visible. Translation is, like the Centre Pompidou, an inside-out architecture. The translator's special task is indissolubly to marry creative linguistic engineering and writing, choosing words and forms and being chosen by them. But for all its concern with lexical and syntactic choice, translation criticism is profoundly insensitive to structural and formal choices; these latter tend to reduce themselves to either/or choices among basic alternatives: regular or free? rhymed or unrhymed? If I have a quarrel with F.W. Leakey's translations of Baudelaire it is this: that where his translation produces heterostrophic or stichic accounts of Baudelaire's homostrophic poems or sonnets, these formal variations are neither explained nor theorized.

Montage only aggravates this 'embarras du choix' to disabling proportions. Montage provides an opportunity for the translator of 'Le Voyage' to compile a florilegium of favourite travel snippets and to do justice to the poem's many intertexts (Homer, Shakespeare, Du Camp, Borel, O'Neddy, de Quincey, Nerval, Tennyson, Gautier, Poe, etc.).

Many of the sources have the added lure of memorability, and may pick up or anticipate other Baudelairean threads, as does Nerval's meditation on the child and 'la vie antérieure':

> C'est une impression douloureuse, à mesure qu'on va plus loin, de perdre, ville à ville et pays à pays, tout ce bel univers qu'on s'est créé jeune, par les lectures, par les tableaux et par les rêves. Le monde *qui se compose ainsi dans la tête des enfants* est si riche et si beau qu'on ne sait s'il est le résultat exagéré d'idées apprises ou si c'est un ressouvenir d'une existence antérieure et la géographie magique d'une planète inconnue.
>
> (*Voyage en Orient*, quoted by Pichois, *OC*, I, 1098)
>
> [It is a painful impression, as we travel further and further, to lose, city by city and country by country, all that wonderful universe which, as children, by reading and by dreaming and by looking at pictures, we constructed for ourselves. The world *which puts itself together like this in the minds of children* is so rich and so beautiful that one no longer knows if it is the exaggerated result of learnt ideas or a resurgent memory of a former existence and the magic geography of an unknown planet.]

or, more text-specifically, Tennyson's 'The Lotos-Eaters':

> In the afternoon they came unto a land
> In which it seemèd always afternoon.
>
> (ll. 3–4)

Beside the montaging of sources and extracts from an anthology of associated travel-writing, one might insert lines from Baudelaire's own poems or an appropriate sample of obiter dicta. For 'Le Voyage', one might, for example, return to Baudelaire's avowed intention to use the poem as a means of discrediting the idea of Progress. Announcing 'Le Voyage' to Charles Asselineau, in a letter of 20 February 1859, Baudelaire wrote:

> J'ai fait un long poème dédié à Max Du Camp, qui est à faire frémir la nature, et surtout les amateurs du progrès.
>
> (*Correspondance*, I, 553)
>
> [I've written a long poem dedicated to Max Du Camp, fit to make nature and those in love with the idea of progress shiver in their shoes.]

219

And among the pages of *Fusées* and *Mon Coeur mis à nu*, one might find passages on the same topic, which are either explanatory,[1] expressive,[2] or open on to the concerns of other writers, on to Wilde's Individualism, for example:

> Il ne peut y avoir de progrès (vrai, c'est-à-dire moral) que dans l'individu et par l'individu lui-même.
>
> (*OC*, I, 681)
>
> [There can be no progress (true, that is to say moral, progress) other than in and through the individual himself.]

But one quickly understands that the text would suffocate under such an accretion, that multiple textual interventions would disperse the native energy of, live vampirically off, the mother-poem. Besides, all of these possibilities, apart from the travel anthology, only serve to push the text back into itself. Quite simply, such quotations would be too literal, too confining, too much a retracing of steps, along a path that scholarship had already taken. Translation, as part of its mission to disseminate the ST, must travel *away* from the ST, *but in the company of the ST*; and the ST's sources must also become part of this travelling away, like the works for which the ST might, in its turn, be a source.

If one's task as a translator is to expand the texts one is translating, this need not entail physical enlargement and may take many forms: the translation fills out, or complements, the poet's voice with that of the translator; the translation may attempt to incorporate into itself the time and space, with all their added voices, which have 'elapsed' between the ST and TT; the translation may attempt actively to change the ways in which the ST has hitherto been approached—it is not for the TT merely to confirm some current view of the ST.

Inasmuch, therefore, as I have been able to pursue a policy in this matter, I have limited the number of such textual incorporations; I have tried to ensure that they can be integrated seamlessly into the main text; I have chosen texts which might be seen as ancestors and progeny of Baudelaire's poem; I have chosen texts which extend the range of the ST, either in terms of images depicted, issues raised, or symbolic patterns revealed. I have given space to my own verse, but strictly regulated the dose and tried to keep its voice light and unobtrusive; on the other hand, I have given text of my own the first and last word, to enact that being-in-the-text that translation is, to make Baudelaire's text an incident within my own discourse with myself, as a reader of Baudelaire, and as a translator.

Translation and Intercutting

The Voyage

I

soundings
    legs braced
strung to the dead eye
calling the fathoms
    Fathomless

For the child
poring over prints and maps
        the world expands to feed
        a growing appetite
By lamplight we cannot make out
        the edges of the world
        the Marquesas
        Gilbert and Ellice
        St Kitts and Nevis
        (looking to leeward)
        Oceanides in an
        old album
What memory's seen might just
        but only just
cover a postage stamp.

We leave quite suddenly
        scudding on a stiff breeze
        sprawled in the sheets
one morning
        all fired up
resentful, rancorous, embittered
surrendering to the rhythm of the waves
(when you go sweeping the air with your ample skirt
walk, and your wide skirts swirl with every step
when you step out, your broad skirt sweeps the breeze)
we lull all our uncharted dreams
        on to the well-mapped spaces
        of the open seas

Some are glad to leave a discredited homeland; while others flee a blighted infancy; and others still, readers of the night sky of a woman's eyes, suddenly drowning, must break the spell of their heavy-scented, and despotic, Circes.

Long draughts of space and light and flaming skies are what they take to ward off beasthood. The ice that bites their skin, the sun that burns, erase, little by painful little, the vivid imprints of the witches' lips.

What reason have I for being here, in Venice? None, if the nostalgia for foreign parts, so familiar to travellers, had not taken possession of me, one evening, on the steps of Tortoni's. When you go down with this illness, your friends grow deadly dull, your mistresses bore you to tears, and all women, even other men's wives, are unattractive: Cerito's lame, Alboni out of tune; two stanzas of Musset is already too much; [...] To dispel this particular form of spleen, the only remedy is a passport for Spain, or Italy, or Africa, or the East.

But the only true travellers are those
    who leave   caprice
    for leaving's   of
      sake   promptings
      hearts   the
          unballasted, as   following
               airy   balloons
                  as
   and who,
         without quite
           knowing
              why
      never
        tire of saying
                    'Andiamo'
   those whose   of clouds
      whims   shape
        have the
  who dream
       just as the gunner
          newly conscripted
       dreams of cannon
       of

boundless   pleasures
     changed and changing
     pleasures we
         have yet
             to name

II

We bounce
        like balls
good God
like tops
        gyrate and even
        in our sleep
the lure of what's unknown
digs us in the ribs,
        sets us to
        toss and turn
        planets whipped
        to motion
by some malicious angel

A puzzling state,
        in which
the goal may shift
        from one day
        to the next
It has no bearings
        so can be
wherever the fancy takes you
        and in which
with hope eternal
scampering
        this way and that
        like lunatics
we look for rest.

Our hearts are frigates
combing the seas to find
        Icaria

On deck a voice
                    rings out: 'Eyes skinned!'
Another,
                    from aloft
excited, crazed
shouts: 'Love!…
                    Glory!…
                    Happiness!…'
Shit! it's a reef.

The same broadside I lost my leg,
Old Pew lost his
                    deadlights
I could hear his stick go
                    tap-tap-tapping
into the distance.

Each paltry island conjured by
                    each 'Land ahoy!'
is the Eldorado Fortune promised us
Our greedy Fancy fills its gut with feast
and gets its morning-after wrecking.

What's to be done with them,
the addicts of fabled landfalls
the drunken inventors of Americas?
Throw them in irons? Or
                    overboard?
Each vanished mirage
                    leaves a bitterer taste.

Such is the grizzled tramp
                    feet in the mud
but nose in the wind
                    dreaming of Elysian fields
his glazed eyes
                    spotting the lights of Capua
each time a candle flickers
                    in a dingy shack.

The worn-out sponge, who scuffles through our slums

sees whiskey, paradise and liberty
wherever oil-lamps shine in furnished rooms—
we see Blue Grottoes, Caesar and Capri.

III

Bearded, with tawny faces, as they sat on the quay, looking listlessly at
nothing with their travelled eyes, I questioned them:

Amazing travellers!
What edifying tales
Lie waiting to be dredged
from eyes as deep as seas.
Open the jewel-boxes
of your hoarded memories
Show us the gemstones
made of sky and stars.

We don't need steam or sail
to get us there
To cheat the boredom
of our banged-up lives
Just blow into our minds
stretched tight as canvas
Those things remembered
and horizon-framed

Come, tell us
what you've seen.

IV

We've seen stars and waves, and sand, too, acres of it; and although
we've had a bellyful of nasty surprises, and unexpected disasters,
for most of the time we sat around, as we are now, twiddling our
thumbs… *in the doldrums, in the zone of calms, le cafard, le marasme,*
broyant du noir, browned off, so many words for something so much the
same. Language twists and turns to get away.

225

"The radiance of sunlight
                    on violet seas
The splendour of cities
                    in the lengthening rays
                    (Do you want more?)
Fired our hearts
                    with a nagging need
To dive in the sky's
                    enticing reflection.

Shall we go on?
                    Is this the kind of stuff?

The richest cities, the
                    sweeping rural prospects
Could somehow never equal
                    the mysterious allure
Of those the clouds
                    might chance to make.
And desire never gave us any peace."

A bit too romantic?
                    Are we tourists or Flying Dutchmen?

Pleasure only fuels desire, that age-old tree
Whose mulch is pleasure,
Whose branches, as its bark grows thick and harder
Strain up towards the sun

Will you always go on growing then, great rooted tree,
More rooted than the cypress—Yet
We've careful sketches, friends, for hungry albums,
Where 'exotic' merits beauty's own cachet.

We've honoured idols in the shape of elephants
Seen diamond-constellated thrones,
And ornate palaces whose fairy pomp would fill
Your bankers' heads with plans for bankruptcy.

Garments which intoxicate the eye,
Women with painted teeth and nails,

Learned charmers with their snakes entwined.

Dressed
in rippling pearl,
her 'fesses'
my rolling breakers,
her silk distressed,
her look the undertaker's

Dressed
in organdie and calico,
stiffened pressed
and braceleted,
her eyes a treasure chest,
her silk elated

V

And then, what next?

VI

(Infantile minds!)

Let's not forget
   the point that's cardinal
Wherever you look
   without especially looking
In each single station
   of human life
There's the wearisome sight
   of congenital sin

Woman
Vile-bodied, swollen-headed,
Stupid, enslaved;
Lovesick, enraptured

As she looks in her mirror
                with no hint of a smile
                or trace of disgust. And Man,
Tyrannical, gluttonous,
Tirelessly sniffing out skirt
Intractable, grasping
Slave of the slave, and waste-water
Swilled through the sewer.

The ragman dosses on the ledge,
The goose hangs by her song,
The butcher's knife has lost its edge
Somewhere on the common.

The public hangman
                relishing his work
                the sobbing martyr
The blood-dressed celebration dinner
The despot made touchy
                by the poison of power
The street mob made brute
                by a taste for the lash.

Religions, all
the spitting image
                of our own
leapfrogging their way
                to heaven;
and sanctity,
                like a sensitive soul
                wallowing deep in his feather-bed,
pursuing
with hair-shirt and sharpened nails
its short-lived ecstasies.

Humanity, stuffed
to the teeth with talk,
drunk on the dream
                of its own genius
as demented now as it always was,
raving to God in the throes of its dying

'My master, my brother, I damn you to hell'.

And those with the last remnants
                     of sense
bold lovers of folly
fugitives from the herd corralled
                     in destiny's pens
looking for solace
                     in opium's
                     expanding
                     universe—

well, that, world-wide,
                     is the daily résumé.

VII

It's bitter, the knowledge
                     to be had from travelling
The world, monotonous and small
                     today and yesterday
Tomorrow and every day
                     shows us to ourselves,
An oasis of horror
                     in a desert of listlessness

Should we leave? Or stay?
                     If you *can* stay, stay.
But go if you must.
                     While we can't see one for dust
The other lies doggo,

          'He walked out on the whole crowd'
          Leaves me flushed and stirred,
          Like 'Then she undid her dress'
          Or 'Take that you bastard';
          Surely I can, if he did?
          And that helps me stay
          Sober and industrious.

        both trying to deceive
Time, whose beady eyes
        will never miss a trick

There are those, alas,
        who're always on the run
The Wandering Jew
        for instance, Christ's apostles,
But railway carriage, ship,
        will never be enough
To slip the clutches of
        this felon retiarius

Others slit his throat
        while still tucked
        in their cradles

And when at last
He pins us down
His foot set firmly on our spines
We'll go on shouting 'On, let's go!'
As though we still believed it
Just as, in years gone by,
We set our course for China
Our eyes fixed on the open sea
Our hair dishevelled by the wind.
So we'll embark on the Dark Sea
With the buoyant spirit
Of a first-time passenger
Voices, can you hear them
Singing,
Baleful but enticing,
'Come this way for a taste
Of perfumed lotos;
There is sweet music here that softer falls
Than petals from blown roses on the grass,
Music that gentlier on the spirit lies
Than tired eyelids upon tired eyes.
Here's where we pick those fruit
Your heart has always hankered for,
Goldenkernelled, goldencored,
Sunset-ripened [...] on the tree,

230

Apples of the Hesperides.
Come and bask in the light
Uncanny torpor
Of an endless afternoon.'
We guess at the ghosts
By their familiar tones:
Our Pylades stretch out their arms to us;
And she, whose legs we used to kiss, invites:
'If you wish your heart refreshed, then swim
To your Electra'.

VIII

Quid mihi est　　　　　　*if you, death, are*
ut honores mei　　　　　　*the endless*
sculpantur　　　　　　　　*corridor*
in silice si solum　　　　　*of the last,*
mihi superest　　　　　　　*then we have not*
sepulcrum　　　　　　　　　*begun,*
　　　　　　　　　　　　　or have slipped
　　　　　　　　　　　　　the straits into
　　　　　　　　　　　　　another sea

Old sea-dog
　　　　　　Captain Death
　　　　　　　　　　　　it's time
to weigh anchor
This country's tricks
are all played out,
　　　　　　Captain Death.
Put on more canvas
Sea and sky may be
　　　　　　black as pitch
but our hearts
　　　　　　are alight
　　　　　　with appetite

Your poison's just the grog we need
to keep our spirits up

231

So driven by this furnace in our brains
we'll head for the world's end
        and *Vasco's pale smile*
for another Valparaiso or
        a Devil's Island
        yet to be discovered
            who cares
to the furthermost
Terra Incognita
just to get a taste
        of something
           new.

Here the voice
dipped
out of earshot;
and its wake
left churned and splintered
spars, taff-rails
and capstan bars.
I wintered
in the still, uneasy
sound.

This translation allows us, requires us, to make some concluding observations about free verse as a translational medium. There are perhaps two things which are centrally important. First, and most obviously, free verse is not formless, but rather a capacity to find form, and to find form variously and in self-differentiating ways, but where the differentiations occur on a continuum which leaves differentiation controversial. In other words, free verse is a coming to form which never quite, unequivocally, comes to form. It allows the translator to work in the very medium of the problematic, of that which does not quite declare itself, while providing wonderfully flexible parameters for formal exploration of the ST.

'Le Voyage' is a poem in 'movements', but within these movements there are changes of pace and tone and rhetorical posture, which I have tried to capture in perceptible variations of free-verse mode and the concomitant rhythmic handling. In the last sequence of part VII, for instance, I have tried to create a free verse reminiscent of the irregular choric songs of Tennyson's 'The Hesperides' and 'The Lotos-Eaters', published together in the *Poems* of 1832. It is as much this rhythmic connection between the two poems, as their appearing adjacently in Tennyson's collection, which persuaded me to conflate lotos and the golden apples in the 'fruits miraculeux'. Similarly I have let the free-verse rendering of the fifth and sixth stanzas gravitate towards the calligrammatic, to reflect a passage buoyed up by a lack of ulterior motive, of harboured grudge; these travellers can pursue pleasures which are generative and metamorphosing, which are not branded by a name. Again, in the opening of part II, up to the quotation from *Treasure Island*, I have tried to produce a verse in which the second margin nags at the first, knocking it off course, harassing it, distracting it, preventing it from settling, hurrying it along at an uncomfortable pace. But there are moments, too, of more measured and 'traditional' discourse, as in the closing stanzas of part IV. Here, I needed to increase the sense of self-satisfaction, of the worldly-wise exercising a taste for resonant philosophizing. The sequence of lines on Woman and Man in part VI is again something a little different, a sustained diatribe with hardly any hint of relenting (other than where the second margin makes a brief appearance). In both these instances, the line-initial capitals convey a certain self-consciousness, a certain portentousness, a certain sense of audience, a reaching for the lapidary, an enjoyment (and indulgence) of linguistic and vocal control. The lines with lower-case initial letters, on the other hand, tell us of voices centred in their own saying, not reciting what they have already thought, voices of more direct address, rather than voices addressed to the wings, or the auditorium, voices with the resourcefulness of natives of the text, rather than the domineering voice of the arriving colonist. The lower-case initial is, as we have already seen, more related to the being of that other kind of 'stanza', to be found at the 'bottom end' of the continuum called free verse, namely the prose stanza. If prose is here, it is not 'plain' prose but a prose always looking for a way into periodicity, looking to pull itself into a rhythmically animated state of concentration. In the first two examples in part I, for instance, I have started each on fairly expansive movements, only then, by phrasing and punctuation, to encourage them to wheel round on themselves, in more troubled forms of dynamism. And the presence of a prose emerging from the text itself obviously facilitates the assimilation of prose passages from elsewhere, as though, indeed, the text were inviting those passages.

The second observation is simply this: free verse prevents the habits and assumptions of through-reading. The consequences of a statement like this are multiple and, I think, far-reaching. The through-reading of lines, that is to say, reading a poetic text stabilized by principles of isosyllabism and isometrism, so that the reader can *confidently* and continuously realize metrical expectations, leads naturally into its converse, namely that metrical regularity *can* only be realized by through-reading. This locks the perception of metre and a certain kind of reading (sustained, intoned, minimizing syntactical eventfulness, promoting 'naturally' unstressed words to stress, and demoting the 'naturally' stressed to unstressed, as the metrical need arises) very intimately together. Free verse, at least of the kind I am essaying here, tries to drive these two factors, reading and textual metricality apart, so that their relationship has constantly to be recreated. Metrical awareness is no longer guiding; the rhythmic cohesion of the line has to be found, and offers no guarantees that adjacent lines will conform to the same rhythmic configuration. This will naturally have two further effects. First, free verse must, and does, build significant juncturing into its unfolding. In fact, juncturing is an integral part of the motion of free verse. Of course it can be overdone. The voice easily tires of a stop-start mechanism, and textual fragmentation leads to a fatiguing inflation of too many semantic elements. Secondly, the increase of juncture keeps the voice inventive, both rhythmically and expressively. Each new piece of text may repeat, establish as a leitmotiv, a certain rhythmic figure; but it may equally entail an adjustment of rhythmic perception: the duple may shift to the triple, the rising to the falling, or, quite simply, the rhythmic presence may go flat. The reader has to make his own rhythmic running. As Impressionist/Neo-Impressionist painting aims to transfer the task of optical mixture from the painter's palette to the spectator's eye, so free verse looks to pass metrico-rhythmic construction from the text itself (achieved through a certain level of regularity) to the reader, intent on making the text optimally readable and expressive. But just as, in looking at Seurat's *Un dimanche à la Grande Jatte* (1884), we are as much aware of a reconciling underpainted ground as of the optically dizzying *pointillisme* of the surface, so in free verse a ground of stressed/weak alternation may facilitate the reader's shifts from iambic to trochaic, from iambic to amphimacer or choriamb, etc.

Two further points should be made. Juncturing may ease collocation and thus extend the number and kinds of collocation available to the poet. It is a topic difficult to speak of with assurance, because it depends so much on what an individual voice feels that it can comfortably handle. But, where, for example, I find the phrase 'in opium's expanding universe' cumbersome on the tongue, the free verse alternative—

in opium's	x/xx
expanding	x/x
universe	/xx

—creates the space, the renewal of attack, which makes it much more amenable to the voice. And part of this amenability is to do with my ability to see a rhythmic relationship between the lines: 'in opium's' second paeon is like a conflation of the amphibrach of 'expanding' and the dactyl of 'universe'—'opium' possesses its 'expanding universe' in a rhythmic, as well as a grammatical, sense. In the through-read version, it is difficult to negotiate the run of three unstressed syllables: x/xxx/x/xx. Similarly, 'Lovesick, enraptured, as she looks in her mirror' also produces, if through-read, a stumbling sequence of three weak syllables. But junctured as it is in the final version:

/xx/x
xx/xx/x

it breaks the sequence of weak syllables and allows us instead to read a choriamb + 'feminine' syllable (adonic foot), followed by two anapaests + 'feminine' syllable, which sits more fluently on the tongue. This particular resource, one crucial justification of free verse, has, to my knowledge, never been properly commented on.

Secondly, free verse allows the multiplication of margins. It always seems odd to me when free verse does not avail itself of this option, which enables texts to operate at different levels of consciousness, which engineers tonal modulation, and which may institute different kinds of semantic hierarchy or, indeed, different degrees of textual credibility. We shall have more to say about margins in a moment. Additionally, and relatedly, we should mention that although the option on lower-case line-initial letters (in place of capitals) is not limited to free verse, free verse has made it peculiarly its own. We have already referred to this topic in Chapters 2 and 7; and we have already made further brief comments above, in relation to the present translation.

If translation, then, needs more effectively to involve its readers, to persuade them from an inertia of acceptance to participation in the 'optical mixture' of the text, then free verse is a valuable asset. If the reader is to enter into an at once more tentative and constructive relationship with the text, then the text must itself be more evidently eventful, more challenging, more equivocating. Equally, if it is true that free verse extends collocational possibilities, by increased juncturing and the concomitant easing of rhythmic continuity, then free verse naturally serves translation, and is, more clearly than regular verse, a medium in which choice never finally hardens into the apparently pre-ordained, or masks its continuing possibility, either at a formal or at a lexical level.

My version of Baudelaire's text is designed to play periodically with the idea of translation. This preoccupation first appears early in part I, in the three translations—by Scarfe (1964: 120), Howard (1982: 56), and McGowan (1993: 107)—of the fifth line of 'Le Beau Navire' ('Quand tu vas balayant l'air de ta jupe large'). These three lines are intended to represent the thyrsus, itself an image of translation; they are sufficiently unlike each other to constitute meaningful variations on a theme, where the theme is the absent line of the ST (or possibly of a (TW)). Baudelaire's description of the thyrsus, in his prose poem of the same name, serves to perpetuate the sexual prejudice long built into the perception of the TT's relation to the ST; but it also releases other possibilities:

> —Le bâton, c'est votre volonté, droite, ferme, et inébranlable; les fleurs, c'est la promenade de votre fantaisie autour de votre volonté; c'est l'élément féminin exécutant autour du mâle ses prestigieuses pirouettes. Ligne droite et ligne arabesque, intention et expression, roideur de la volonté, sinuosité du verbe, unité du but, variété des moyens, amalgame tout-puissant et indivisible du génie, quel analyste aura le détestable courage de vous diviser et de vous séparer?
>
> (*OC*, I, 336)
>
> [The stick is your will, straight, firm and unshakeable; the flowers are your fantasy twining round your will—the feminine element performing its dazzling pirouettes around the male. Straight line and arabesque, intention and expression, inflexibility of the will and sinuousness of language, singleness of purpose and variety of means, the all-powerful and indivisible amalgam of genius, what analyst will ever have the appalling audacity to divide and separate you?]

The modern translator might wish the relationship between the 'bâton' and the flowers a little less indivisible, since translation itself is more properly parturition and separation than a uterine return. And one would like to think that it is the purpose of the TT to soften and diversify the will of the ST, and not to fall prey to the mirage of recuperable intention. But images of the TT as arabesque, linguistic sinuousness, fantasy, as something which has a variety of means at its disposal to reach a shared goal, are very germane to the approach adopted here.

The translation of the opening of Gautier's *L'Orient: Voyages et voyageurs* (written in 1842) in part I introduces the theme of bibliophobia, that state in which books themselves are unable to awaken desire or trigger revery. This splenetic experience of the exhaustion of the book is part of Mallarmé's impulse to run off to sea in 'Brise marine':

> La chair est triste, hélas! et j'ai lu tous les livres.

The motives to travel here run directly counter to those of the Baudelairean child; while, for the child, the world grows larger 'à la clarté des lampes', for the Mallarméan poet, 'la clarté déserte de ma lampe/Sur le vide papier que la blancheur défend' is blinding rather than animating, and paralyses the verbal imagination (but see Pearson 1996: 48–9, for the poem's hints of compensation).

Where the trio of translations of 'Quand tu vas balayant l'air de ta jupe large' is designed to produce in the reader's mind the sense of lines freeing themselves from their source and beginning to make their own way in the world, the quotation of a stanza from Lowell's translation of 'Le Voyage', in fact a translation of the final stanza of part II, is intended as a delayed double-take. At first, the tramp and the sponge appear to be two different characters, from different points on the social scale—shacks become furnished rooms, candles become lamps, and the extent of knowledgeable reference increases. But the shift in Lowell's text from third-person singular to first-person plural places us in a Baudelairean position where 'tout pour [nous] devient allégorie'. The figures begin to gravitate together, to indicate a shared behavioural, if not linguistic, matrix. While the lines from 'Le Beau Navire', therefore, suggest that the ST is a pretext, a competence generating performances which are bound to supersede it, is a *terminus a quo*, whose lines radiate out into an ever more complex future, the Lowell stanza projects the ST either as a 'contemporary' text, alongside the translations, another embodiment of the missing (TW), or as a prior text in which the (TW) has survived and from which it needs to be resurrected. In both instances, the ST becomes the instrument of its own passage; this is not to say that the ST becomes extinct, but rather that it is the distributory nexus of its own flow.

Ernest Dowson's 'The Fortunate Islands' (*Decorations*, 1899), from which the extract at the beginning of part III is taken, is a kind of abbreviated prose adaptation of 'Le Voyage', which also seems to lie behind a verse fragment in the Flower Notebook (one of Dowson's manuscript notebooks):

> In vain we cross the seas change lands,
> In search of that we know not.
> (Flower 1967: 188)

Longaker (1962: 251–2) suggests that Dowson's experiments with the prose poem may owe something to the *Poèmes en prose* (1898) of his Paris friend, the vicomte Gabriel de Lautrec, to whom Dowson dedicated 'Amor Profanus' (*Verses*, 1896).[3] Just as prose is one pole of the continuum of free verse, so prose translation is one pole of the continuum of verse translation; and not only that, but because prose is the point at which verse tips into another medium, so it is the point at which translation tips into transposition. This we have already explored in Chapter 7.

Abbreviation is the starting point for the two stanzas at the end of part IV. The tercet which precedes them—'Garments which intoxicate the eye', etc.—has within it two of those elements which naturally converge in Baudelaire's imagination : clothing, rhythmic walking and the snake-charmer. This tercet, in fact, begins to sound like a slightly impoverished version of 'Avec ses vêtements ondoyants et nacrés', and it is this poem which I wanted to render in more telegraphic mode in 'Dressed'. I particularly wanted to capture the paradoxes and reversals in the feminine which Baudelaire is fond of pursuing (the harmonious and supple turns into the hard and unyielding, the conflicting and sexual turns into the consoling and maternal); and so have produced two stanzas which are designed to complement one another dialectically, each one having two final lines which run against the current of the first four; in short, mine are 4-line + 2-line sonnets, where there is some dialogue of rhyme across the break, rather than octave + sestet, where there is usually no such dialogue.

Finally, in part VIII, there is a brief reference to the closing line of Mallarmé's 'Au seul souci de voyager':

Au seul souci de voyager
Outre une Inde splendide et trouble
—Ce salut soit le messager
Du temps, cap que ta poupe double

Comme sur quelque vergue bas
Plongeante avec la caravelle
Écumait toujours en ébats
Un oiseau d'annonce nouvelle

Qui criait monotonement
Sans que la barre ne varie
Un inutile gisement
Nuit, désespoir et pierrerie

Par son chant reflété jusqu'au
Sourire du pâle Vasco.

The song of the bird 'd'annonce nouvelle' reflects a useless bearing ('Nuit, désespoir et pierrerie') on to Vasco's smile. This poem, Mallarmé's last sonnet, which celebrates the quatercentenary of Vasco's rounding of the Cape of Good Hope, now a rounding of the cape of Time, embarks upon a free-ranging voyage of Mallarméan syntax whose destination turns out to be Vasco, himself engaged on a never-ending voyage which refuses a bearing (hence 'inutile'), and in particular a bearing which is also a treasure island, a deposit of 'pierrerie'. But the refusal of treasure is the refusal of a knowledge (see below) which brings despair. Vasco smiles perhaps because he will continue to ride the oceans of possibility; but in his pallor we may read the awareness that the oceans of possibility are a state of eternal stand-off. For Robb (1996: 100–6), the poem has a rather more positive outcome: it is: 'A sign in search of its referent, finding instead its place in a coherent, self-contained system. Or, in less mercantile terms: the "obstiné chercheur d'un mystère qu'il sait ne pas exister" [stubborn seeker of a mystery which he knows does not exist], smiling with desperate lucidity at his pseudo-victory' (p. 106). Robb's argument for the poem's self-containment derives from its final syllable having the same sound as its first, /o/, a sound relayed by the 'ois*eau*'. The distance between self-containment and stand-off may be considered no distance at all. But perhaps a shaft of light from elsewhere does penetrate this hermetically sealed darkness: the phonemes may be the same, but the graphemes are different. 'Au' speaks of objective, of direct address, of focus; when this notion is passed through the water of 'ois*eau*', its range and aspiration widen: it becomes the 'o', or 'ô', of poetic apostrophe, of invocation opening out on to renewable fictions. At all events, I have adopted in my own verse a similar tactic: my version begins with 'soundings'[4] and ends with 'sound', begins with investigation and measurement, and ends with both the safety of haven and the persisting resonance of the poem. The poem returns to its point of departure, still haunted by where it has been, the same diversified, 'still' yet 'uneasy'.

Also included in the text are 'translations' which are direct quotations from the 'original' work of English authors (I recognize that the distinction between translations and original work, given the infiltrations of many-headed Intertextuality, cannot be sustained; Dowson's 'The Fortunate Islands' is typically problematic). Most discreetly concealed perhaps is the Lawrence of *Sea and Sardinia* (1923) in the *'Andiamo'* towards the end of part I. Lawrence's text begins with an assertion, resolute, manly:

239

Comes over one an absolute necessity to move. And what is more, to move in some particular direction. A double necessity then: to get on the move, and to know whither.

(1944: 7)

But this fine decisiveness is quickly revealed as self-delusion: Lawrence knows neither why he needs to leave nor what his destination should be, and the Sardinia he ultimately chooses is a cultural zero, a gap on the map. He has to work his way into resolution from a position of total uncertainty:

Why, then, must one go? Why not stay? Ah, what a mistress, this Etna! with her strange winds prowling round her like Circe's panthers, some black, some white. [...] Perhaps it is she one must flee from. [...] Where does one go? There is Girgenti by the south. There is Tunis at hand. [...] Where then? Spain or Sardinia. [...] Sardinia is like nowhere. Sardinia which has no history, no date, no race, no offering. [...] Let us go, then. Away from [...] these maddening, exasperating, impossible Sicilians, who never knew what truth was and have long lost all notion of what a human being is. A sort of sulphureous demons. *Andiamo!*

(1944: 8–9)

Lawrence's phantomatic Sardinia polarizes naturalistic reality and symbolic 'figures in a landscape' in a way that allows him to explore his own existential polarization between the always slightly disgusted, rather fussy tourist and the mythomaniac traveller.

My inclusion of quotation from Stevenson's *Treasure Island* (1883) has a twofold motive. I wanted to approach Baudelaire's 'Les Aveugles' from the seaward side. Pew's death is curiously poignant: horrifying creature though he is, he is abandoned like a maroon by his shipmates, and his last moments are recounted with a sharp sense of the world's indifference and with an effort to lay him comfortably to rest:

and the four hoofs trampled and spurned him and passed by. He fell on his side, then gently collapsed upon his face, and moved no more.

(1996: 45)

And, as Silver points out, criminality never saved Pew from starvation (p. 100). The reference to an earlier page ('I could hear...' etc., p. 32) is there to promote the idea of a text marooned by its own narrative and narrator. This text, *Treasure Island,* the spur to so much childhood dreaming, is deserted by its narrator. How did Jim use his part of Flint's treasure? Why does it require the urgings of Squire Trelawney, Dr Livesey 'and the rest of these gentlemen' to persuade Hawkins to tell the story in the first place? Why, in short, would not 'oxen and wain-ropes' be enough to take him back to that 'accursed island'? There is, in the metaphor of treasure, the suggestion that the island and the questing journey have been squeezed dry of the knowledge they can give. What Hawkins learned we shall never know, but what is left to be learned—'the bar silver and the arms'—are not worth the candle, and the nightmare is in the inescapable and taunting invitation ('the sharp voice of Captain Flint still ringing in my ears: "Pieces of eight! pieces of eight!"'). The only lesson that Hawkins does learn perhaps, is that the knowledge to be derived from questing can never be more than the particular individual's ability to put it to use: 'All of us had an ample share of the treasure, and used it wisely or foolishly, according to our nature [*sic*]' (1996: 295). Or is this an act of self-gagging? 'Le Voyage' may also leave us with a sense of the poet abandoning his invention, seeking refuge away from an audience, in silence, not wishing to be responsible for the ill-effects of his own literature.

Our last view of Silver, a man of 'further wanderings', may momentarily remind us of Tennyson's Dantean Ulysses, until Hawkins surmises that he may find 'his old Negress, and perhaps still lives in comfort with her and Captain Flint'. Certainly there is no reason to suppose that Baudelaire was not familiar with Tennyson's poem (published in *Poems,* 1842); he had the measure of Tennyson's 'mélancolie molle, harmonieuse, distinguée' [soft, harmonious and refined melancholy] (*OC,* II, 336) when he published his 'Notes nouvelles sur Edgar Poe' in 1857. At any rate, there are lines in 'Ulysses' which sound persuasively prescient:

> Yet all experience is an arch wherethrough
> Gleams that untravelled world, whose margin fades
> For ever and for ever when I move.
> [...]
> 'Tis not too late to seek a newer world.
>
> (ll. 19–21, 57)

and which remind us that Homer lies as much behind the Lotus-Eaters (*Odyssey,* Book IX) as behind other figures in the poem (Circe, the cattle of Helios?). But about the presence of Tennyson and my insertion of lines from 'The Hesperides' and 'The Lotos-Eaters' we have already spoken.

The lines from Larkin's 'The Poetry of Departures' (*The Less Deceived*, 1955), within the second stanza of part VII, undermine the idea of the journey as existential transformation ('This audacious, purifying,/ Elemental move') with the insinuation that it is no more than a macho (if thrilling) gesture, or an artificial and 'deliberate step backwards/To create an object'. There are many who, having put on their coats, have argued that they do not need, after all, to go out. But in the end, in this bout of social and psychological one-upmanship, who is kidding whom? This group of lines will perhaps raise further questions about the final section of 'Le Voyage'. Is Baudelaire here derisively imitating the voice of the irrepressible traveller and indefatigable quester after new experience, Maxime Du Camp, the poem's dedicatee and ardent believer in technological progress (but see Burton's discussion of the dedication, 1988, pp. 64–7)? 'Audacity' begins to look like an easy-come and laddish commodity.

The Latin inscription at the beginning of part VIII ('What is it to me that my honours are sculpted in stone, if the grave alone is left to me') is taken from a tomb in the Cathedral of Cordoba. It continues: 'Rogate ergo pro me Cajetano Carrascal indigno presbitero ac immerito Tesaurio et canonico hujus almae ecclesiae. Obiit pridie idus septembris Anni MDCCCI' [Therefore pray for me, Cajetano Carrascal, unworthy priest and undeserving treasurer and canon of this bountiful church. Died the day before the ides of September of the year 1801]. My own lines are a riposte, designed to scotch the view that death is terminal privation and levelling, and to allow another death, co-explorer and bestower of opportunity, to emerge.

What little remains to be said about my own contributions can be included in the remarks about structure which follow. At this point, I would merely comment briefly on the additions made to the prose version of the first stanza of part IV. In insisting on the traveller's linguistic awareness, I did not merely wish to authorize the further interpolations which punctuate the description following, to remind us that the value of travel lies in its linguistic recuperability, that the appetite for travel is the appetite for yarn-spinning, that different kinds of travel, different places, generate different kinds of telling, different lexicons and registers. I wished to remind us, too, that it is not only armchair travellers who are hungry for the tales of those returning, but the home language as well. It is possible to travel both *in* language—etymologies, for instance, are journeys across time and continents, accounts of inter-racial exchange, verbal trade, pidginization, misunderstanding, adaptation and appropriation—and *by* language: Baudelaire's *'new'* is the neologism which promises new experience. Science fiction was bound to experiment with new languages. Histories of literature tell us that French verse of the early nineteenth century, tied to an increasingly etiolated neoclassical language constantly reinflated by a rhetoric itself ridden to the staggers, was saved from a premature death only by an input from abroad. We have elsewhere had occasion to mention the importance attributed to the orientalist translations of Ernest Fouinet by Hugo in his notes to *Les Orientales*,[5] and this particular collection emphasizes not only that translation is one of the kinds of travelling the home language needs and should be thirsty for,[6] but that neologisms of form are as important as neologisms of lexicon. Lexically, 'Le Voyage' is a remarkably quiet text, and relies heavily on known mythological and literary paraphernalia. No doubt Baudelaire wanted thereby to argue that no linguistic treasure was to be had, that the known language had already exhausted what was still to be discovered. But one can try, even with free verse, to imitate the formal variability of *Les Orientales*, and 'orientalize' Baudelaire's text, in spite of itself. In this way, the sad acknowledgement of an inability to rejuvenate human experience can be countervailed by a desire to find one's way into new forms of expression. Even if Baudelaire's travellers cannot discover novelty, at least we as translators and readers of translation, as travellers in Baudelaire's 'exotic' text, can.

In disposing text on the page, I have confined my use of the third margin to part VIII: 'it's time', 'who cares', '*new*'. This is the space on the page which the text, up to this point, has not ventured into; in that sense, it is a space at the very edge of the known world, in which certain impulses and modalities reach limits of distillation. All the phrases/words which occupy this furthest boundary are stripped down to their essentials, and their inescapability is proportional to their bareness; in fact, I count '*new*' as being part of the same desperate pursuit of the smallest degree of visible being that one finds in the substantival adjectives of:

> Car je cherche le vide, et le noir, et le nu!
>
> ('Obsession')

Time applies an accelerating pressure ('it's time') to act, which focuses desire down to a single point ('*new*'), while the very pressure persuades the subject to abandon discrimination along with patience ('who cares'). My own coda withdraws to the first margin: left, as it were, holding this poem, and still listening, I take to the safe waters of the sound in anticipation of the inhospitable assaults of winter. This movement of recoil reflects doubts about all utterance at the third margin. Baudelaire is far from being a Decadent at any price, and his remarks at this limit are unreliable testimony. We have already encountered a view of progress which, if individualistic, is moral; we know that Baudelaire belongs to a line of writers, including Chateaubriand, Nerval and Proust, for whom memory, including a prenatal memory, establishes an epiphanic presence to self, made of all the sediment of the past; we know that the child sees everything 'en *nouveauté* [as *novelty*], but we know, too, that genius is 'l'*enfance retrouvée* à volonté, l'enfance douée maintenant, pour s'exprimer, d'organes virils et de l'esprit analytique qui lui permet d'ordonner la somme de matériaux involontairement amassée' [childhood recovered at will, childhood now endowed, to express itself, with mature organs and the analytical spirit which allows it to give order to the sum of experiences involuntarily accumulated] (*OC*, II, 690), and so on. This ending is certainly not the last word. The exasperations aggravated by the poem's findings need to expend themselves in the transgression of certain boundaries.

The second margin has several functions, the least important of which, perhaps, is to act as a crude visual reminder of the medial caesura in Baudelaire's alexandrine, the division of the line into two hemistichs. This is certainly a function it has in in the closing stanzas of part II, in part III, in the first two stanzas of part IV, and in the opening stanzas of parts VI and VII. But even here, as in other instances, the second margin can convey an indrawing of expression, a restraining of intensity. It is the point, too, at which expression can sometimes relax and the mind retreat into its own imaginings, turning away from the text into a more private subjectivity:

> The splendour of cities
> > in the lengthening rays

> Each vanished mirage
> > leaves a bitterer taste

We have also seen its importance as an agent of interruption and harassment in part II. But most particularly of all, it is the cusp between the first and the third margins, between the too little and the the too much, the site where is played out the conflictual drama of the travellers themselves, the armchair stay-at-homes and the febrile globetrotters. In the world of the child of part I, the second margin is momentarily imagined as the pivot of both world and text, where all forces, lamplight and world's end, can be held in equilibrium; the few lines with the medial axis travel far and wide round a still centre and take us in the end, with

Oceanides in an
old album,

into the cadence of Eliot's 'Gerontion': 'Thoughts of a dry brain in a dry season', the organism coming to rest after vicissitudes whose design is impossible to read.[7]

But this balanced state cannot be maintained. The second margin's trisyllabic figures, beginning with the 'old album' (//×) and 'all fired up' (/×/), find their consummation in part VIII where the amphimacer (/×/) seems to take possession: 'Captain Death' (bis), 'black as pitch'. The amphimacer, the measure in which, like a vice, two stresses bear in on a medial weak syllable, has already been heard in part II: 'toss and turn', 'planets whipped', 'so can be'. Is the reversal of the amphimacer by the amphibrach (×/×) 'of something' sufficient to restore our belief in a way out, is the phrase sufficiently sure of itself? At all events, we cannot trust the anapaest (××/) which we also find in this final part: 'are alight'. The anapaest, up to this point, has been the lilt that utterance slips into, the more mechanical the world becomes:

There's the wearisome sight
of congenital sin

The despot made touchy
by the poison of power
The street mob made brute
by a taste for the lash.

But our hearts
are alight

My translation intends that, as the reader enters the material of the second margin, he/she enters, too, the area of gamble, of risk; sometimes this second margin will deliver us momentarily into reassurance or relaxation, but on sufferance; at other times it will plunge us into loss, into the irreversible.

The first margin, for its part, is the ever-reconstituted point of departure, a point, where, with the capital letter, speech affirms its right to speak, affirms its command of its own utterance, its authority. But there are many points, too, where, with a lower-case initial letter, speech is already on the run, heading towards destinations it cannot prevent, whether *im*pelled or *com*pelled is hard to say. All in all, free verse is a constant process of self-modalization. The translator of the ST makes the text into patterns and perspectives which are often vertiginous combinations of give and take. The freedom of the reader of the TT, as of the translator, still has to come to terms with a text, manipulable to a degree, re-expressible, but yet urging the plotting of a certain course, answering the imperious tiller of its helmsman.

Conclusion

The abiding upshot of the foregoing chapters can perhaps be best expressed as the conviction that we should translate not the meaning of the ST, but the ST as read by the translator (where reading is not to be confused with interpretation). This is to suppose that the translator seeks to comprehend the ST, not so much in a semantic sense as in the sense of being alert to its moods and directions, to the ways in which it *makes* its meanings. Many may object to this particular vision of translation on the grounds that it is not feasible; translation is possible only because we interpret the ST, because meaning is the negotiator between two texts which otherwise would remain locked in abiding hostility or non-communicativeness. This mediational role of meaning is, however, easy to overvalue, because what you put into a translation is what, primarily, the reader is likely to get out of it. If we feel that verse translations have not begotten a public better at reading verse, then the mediation of meaning may well be the reason. There is nothing worse than that the reader should think that rhyme and metre in the TT is simply compliant with, or going through the motions of, similar mechanisms in the ST. And free verse will equally find itself deprecated, as a solution which uses meaning as an excuse for baulking at formal difficulty.

Reading, as I suggested in Chapter 8, is *this side* of interpretation and looks upon interpretation as an impoverishing, if natural, superfluity. Reading is the site of the *making* of meaning; it is a state of suspended motility, in which the mind operates as what Mallarmé called a 'centre de suspens vibratoire' [centre of vibratory suspense] (1945: 386). The purpose of my using different modes of free verse in my translation of 'Le Voyage' was not the better to communicate the poem's interpreted lexical meaning, but to track the changing modalities and tones and expressive

247

postures and psychic rhythms which are the sources of meaning, which are the drives behind meaning, in my reading of Baudelaire's text. The result of such a strategy might be discrepancies between the ST and the TT, failures to correspond; in order to understand these discrepancies, to treat them with the proper critical sensitivity, no, critical *fruitfulness*, we must mentally replace the translator's reading of the ST. If we assume that the translator is interpreting the ST, then alarm about the discrepancies might have some justification; we regard the process of interpretation as something that can be publicly shared, at least by Fish's 'interpretive community' (1980: 13–14). The translator's reading is, then, something which we could not hope to reconstruct without his aid; it is too idiosyncratic a process. But, precisely, the important thing is not to imagine what exactly that reading is, but rather to imagine that it exists, that it has taken place. In this way, we will come to the TT already to a degree reconciled with it, ready to read the TT as an account of a relationship with a text, which may take the ideological loading out of notions such as foreignization and domestication, because they are so inevitably part and parcel of each other.

But this picture of translation needs a further complicating factor to be added to it: reading an ST, particularly of Baudelaire's vintage, is, in fact, reading with hindsight, where hindsight takes into account all that intervenes between the ST and the translator, and indeed all that precedes the ST. It is still too easy to assume that the ST is a founding text. It is still too easy to forget that the reading mind operates in an uncontrollably a-chronological and anachronistic way: a passage in the Bible reminds us of Baudelaire; Villon is reminiscent of Baudelaire; we find echoes of Baudelaire in the poetry of Ronsard. Reading is an amplifying experience, and so is translation: the ST is amplified by all the voices past and future which, for the translator, come to congregate round it.

And this notion of hindsight has implications for the ST in another sense. The voice of the TT can no longer originate in the ST (without *public* anachronism). The process of recuperation is one whereby reading is as much implantation as reception. We read the verse of others in order to hear ourselves speak. This is what, for me, disqualifies pragmatics approaches to the translation of poetry, such as advanced by Hatim and Mason (1997), with their belief that all texts have the same underlying communicative intention, and that this communicative intention is what translation imitates; translation is:

> an act of communication which attempts to relay, across cultural and linguistic boundaries, another act of communication (which

may have been intended for different purposes and different readers/hearers).

(p. 1)

I cannot concur with this proposition. And, indeed, when confronted by poetry, Hatim and Mason's pragmatics model seems to go very soft:

> There may be all kinds of constraints which make the translation of poetry a special case, with its own concerns and problems, but the fact remains that there are [sic] a text producer and a text receiver, standing in some kind of relationship to each other.

(p. 2)

This observation is too shamefaced to inspire much credence, and once the case is conceded for poetry, I suspect that all other kinds of writing will deserve both special scrutiny and special treatment. Hatim and Mason's assumption that the ST is an act of communication which the TT translates into another act of communication (however great the degree of equivalence or divergence) is to assume that the translator reads the ST as the recipient of a message. But what if reading and translation are processes of self-discovery? What if we read and translate in order to situate the ST in our own psycho-physiological response to it? I read Baudelaire in order to transpose him to my psychic, emotional and vocal range. This is not to confine the ST, but to be liberated by it, liberated not into Baudelaire so much perhaps as into territories of myself that Baudelaire makes available to me.

Hindsight, in both these senses, seems to be best served by free verse, by a medium with an open and expandable structure, which is capable, nonetheless, of generating very specific versions of itself, and which has within it all the resources necessary for the creation of disciplined forms of writing. Free verse favours a poetry at once assimilative and self-expressive, and in this sense can both retrieve the past and project a future. Free verse also allows the persona/self dichotomy to be pursued in prosodic circumstances as amenable to the protean as they are to the 'uncounterfeiting, uncounterfeitable' (Pound 1954: 9). And free verse's very dynamic, the visibility of psycho-physiological and paralinguistic presence which it carries in its eventful lineation, its shifting margins, its restive variations in phrasal length, all tell us that translation in this medium is to do with the existential as much as it is to do with the linguistic. I have tried to suggest intermittently that free verse compels the writer to assume ideological responsibility for his writing in a way that regular verse does

249

not, since regular forms will, if anything, have their ideologies already mapped into them.

This affirmation of the existential has consequences for attitudes to choice in translation, and suggests a comparison with photography. The inevitable discrepancy between a photograph and reality, between target text and source text, creates a situation of *comparison*. We can compare a photograph with its source in reality, but it would be inappropriate to say that reality is better or worse than the photograph, or indeed is more authentic (a photograph is an authentic object); they are, quite simply, ontologically different. Similarly, ST and TT are different kinds of writing, made comparable by the very process of translation. If we want to describe what this difference is, we might do worse than start from Ripoll and Roux's distinction between landscape painting and landscape photography: 'Contrairement au peintre paysagiste qui part d'une toile blanche et par touches de couleur remplit son cadre, le photographe agit de manière soustractive, en opérant un certain nombre de choix' [Unlike the landscape painter who starts with a blank canvas and fills out the frame with touches of colour, the photographer acts subtractively, by making a certain number of choices] (1995: 12). The choices include: a point of view on a given scene; *cadrage*, that is to say, what contextual elements are pushed into the blind field and how much the frame implies the blind field; depth of field/focal length. Expressed in translational terms, these choices concern the stylistic and cultural range of the TT, its specific emphases, whether it attempts to enclose itself in fairly narrow parameters and thus locate itself historically with some exactitude, or whether it allows itself sufficient flexibility to cover, inclusively, a whole span of decades and geographical distances. All these decisions, all these choices, contribute to the translator's constitution of a translational style, a style designed to get the most out of the ST, *to use it to the best translational advantage,* as far as that particular translator is concerned. Just as a landscape photographer will weigh possible lighting conditions and wait for those to obtain which will best 'translate', for him, the photographic character of the landscape, put the landscape to the best photographic use, make the landscape the most efficient instrument for the production of *his* photograph, so the translator will choose the optimal verbal conditions to make the ST, for him, the most efficient material for translation, to put the ST to the best translational use.

We must perhaps, then, go as far as reversing our criteria. No more do we ask the TT to do justice to the ST, but rather the other way round. And the translator's skill is to produce a TT which creates the impression that the ST has positioned itself to the best advantage to produce the TT. Since translation exhibits itself as a series of choices, then translational choice should be theorized, and perhaps theorized with the foregoing arguments in view. One suspects that the dearth of any such theorizations relates not so much to the inherent difficulties posed by the formulation of such a theory, but to the negative colouring which choice has in translation. If one starts from the premiss that translation is a *pis-aller*, then choices are about further loss, about inhibiting constraint, about making the best of an unlevel playing-field. But if we think our way into an affirmative version of choice, choice as *real* preference, choice as performance, choice as a way of defining or generating oneself, choice as the pursuit of certain linguistic values or perceptual positions, then translation itself begins to look very different as a kind of writing. At this point, the landscape photographer begins to operate like the landscape painter, additively rather than subtractively. Do we use translation to get to our own creativity, or do we use our creativity to get to the source text's best translational advantage? Either way, and both ways, translation, and the choices that go with it, begin to sound, as they surely should, like issues which engage the whole translator rather than the translator as mere linguistic facility.

It might seem that during the course of the foregoing chapters I have gradually released myself from any obligation to the so-called 'ignorant' reader, the reader unfamiliar with a poet because unfamiliar with his/her national language. This supposition is, to a degree, justified, for the following reasons:

1. As already observed, the translator of Baudelaire is in a rather privileged position. The history of translations of Baudelaire is already so rich, the ignorant reader already so well served by available 'plain prose' translations and otherwise faithful versions, that the new translator coming to this particular *œuvre* can afford to create his own kind of translational space(s) and more easily explore experimental fringes. Were the poet to be Yvanhoé Rambosson rather than Baudelaire, no doubt the story would be different. But whichever poet is the translator's subject, whatever the pedagogic needs, a foreignizing translation remains a fascinating proposition, of much linguistic consequence, and a challenge and training for the reading mind.

2. My central preoccupation *is* translation as the servant of self-expression rather than of pedagogy. I have wanted to explore the relationship not only between the existential and linguistic, but also between the translating self and the translating persona and between the different possible relationships with the ST: submissive, co-authorial, conflictual. Since it is

impossible not to 'interfere' with the ST in the creation of the TT, should one not capitalize on, display, amplify, that particular condition? Can the translator know what obligations he has to the ST, if he does not know what his obligations to the reader are? And can he know what his obligations to the reader are, if he does not know what obligations the reader has, or is prepared to shoulder? What *is* the contract between a translator and a reader of translations?

3. An informing conviction of this book is that translating foreign texts for readers not familiar with the language of those texts is only a part of translation's domain and should not be regarded as translation's founding justification, certainly not today at least. Translation is an integral part of creative writing, as the work of poets enough will testify. Translation is the way in which readers of a particular author can exchange their responses to him/her. Translation has a pedagogic value not only in the analysis of texts, but in comparative linguistics and comparative poetics (including the range of expressive possibilities within different forms). Translation is a process peculiarly generative of experimental writing: experimentation with self as much as with known forms and styles, or as with unknown forms, styles and modes of graphic (and electronic) presentation.

But despite these considerations, the ignorant reader should not feel disregarded. Inasmuch as no translation can offer itself as a 'reliable' image of the ST—although every translation is, in a sense, reliable as a translation—so each translation must implicitly incite its reader to read (or imagine) other renderings, to read the translation critically, not necessarily against another available translation, but in relation to choice, to a choice exhibited as choice, and thus to lexical neighbours and syntactic alternatives. The important thing is not to tell ignorant (and thus docile) readers how it is (as though one could), but to do justice to their intelligence and imagination by alerting them to the parameters within which one works, the bias that one's version has, the desirability both of thinking in alternative ways, and of reading widely enough to remove the translator from any position of privilege. This empowerment, or liberation, of the reader of translations calls for a new setting for translations, a setting in which they and their readers can be treated with more patience.

Appendix I

The Cracked Bell
(after Geoffrey Wagner 1971: 71)

Bitter-sweet
To sit, on winter nights,
By a smoking, dancing fire,
And listen to recollections
Faintly, slowly
Rising in the chimes
Ringing through the mist.

Happy the bell with a lusty throat
Which, aged though it is, is hale and well,
Calling the faithful to their devotions,
Spright-limbed, robust, like an old soldier,
On guard in camp,
Bellowing his 'Who goes there?'

But my soul is cracked, and when, careworn,
It tries to fill the chill night with its pealing,
Too often its enfeebled voice

Sounds like the thick, last gurgling
Of a wounded man,
Forgotten
Beside a spreading pool
Of blood, overheaped

With dead,
Dying, still,
Doing all he can
To breathe.

The Cracked Bell

(after Richard Howard 1987: 74)

If sweet, then bitter too, on winter nights
By the smoking, fitful fire, to hear
Those long lost memories coming up for air
In the rippling tunes of mist-enshrouded chimes.

Happy is the pealing, full-lunged bell
Whose years are cheated by its lively health,
As it proclaims its bold religious faith
Like some old trooper's ringing 'Who goes there?'

My soul is cracked and when, beset by cares,
It tries to animate the numbing dark,
Too often its enfeebled voice evokes

A wounded, corpse-encumbered soldier's croaks,
As, lying by a pool of blood, forgotten,
He mouths, unmoving, his last gasps for breath.

The Cracked Bell

(after Joanna Richardson 1975: 135)

Bitter it is and sweet, on winter nights,
To listen by the fitful fire,
To sluggish memories stirring back to life
In mist-wrapped church-bells' distant chimes.

Happy the bell that, sound in wind and limb,
And ageing though it is, has all its wits,
And rattles out its christian summons,
As can the veteran guard his ringing challenge.

But my soul's cracked and when, downcast,
It wants to fill the cold night with complaining,
It often happens that its croaking voice

Sounds like the death throes of a wounded man,
Lying by a pool of blood, forgotten, buried
Under dead, and, though quite still, still struggling.

The Cracked Bell
(after James McGowan 1993: 145)

How sweet it is, on winter nights, and bitter,
Beside the sputtering fire's smoking coals,
To hear dim recollections resurrected
In pealing bell-tones muffled by the mist.

Blessed is the lusty-throated bell
Alert and sound of wind, despite its age,
Loud in the declaration of its faith,
Like the veteran trooper's forthright 'Who goes there?'.

My soul is flawed, and, when low-spirited,
It looks to populate the chill night air with song,
Its weakened voice too often imitates

The last thick gurgling of a wounded man,
Lying beside a pool of blood, under a heap of dead,
Dying forgotten, straining, motionless.

Appendix II

Nevermore

Souvenir, souvenir, que me veux-tu? L'automne
Faisait voler la grive à travers l'air atone,
Et le soleil dardait un rayon monotone
Sur le bois jaunissant où la bise détonne.

Nous étions seul à seule et marchions en rêvant,
Elle et moi, les cheveux et la pensée au vent.
Soudain, tournant vers moi son regard émouvant:
"Quel fut ton plus beau jour?" fit sa voix d'or vivant,

Sa voix douce et sonore, au frais timbre angélique.
Un sourire discret lui donna la réplique,
Et je baisai sa main blanche, dévotement.

—Ah! les premières fleurs, qu'elles sont parfumées!
Et qu'il bruit avec un murmure charmant
Le premier *oui* qui sort de lèvres bien-aimées!

Paul Verlaine

Nevermore

Memory, why torment me? Autumn skimmed
A struggling thrush through the dull air. The sun
Darted a colourless wand of light upon
The yellowing wood which thunders in the wind.

We were alone, and as we walked we dreamed,
Our hair and thoughts both flying in the breeze.
And then she turned to me her touching eyes:
'What was your loveliest day?'—her golden sound,

Her sweet voice, deep, with a fresh angelic ring.
A tactful smile was all I need reply,
And kissing her white hand—religiously.

—Oh, the first flowers—what a scent they have!
And what a charm breathes in the murmuring
Of the first *yes* that comes from lips you love!

trans. Alistair Elliot

Le Balcon

Mère des souvenirs, maîtresse des maîtresses,
O toi, tous mes plaisirs! ô toi, tous mes devoirs!
Tu te rappelleras la beauté des caresses,
La douceur du foyer et le charme des soirs,
Mère des souvenirs, maîtresse des maîtresses!

Les soirs illuminés par l'ardeur du charbon,
Et les soirs au balcon, voilés de vapeurs roses.
Que ton sein m'était doux! que ton cœur m'était bon!
Nous avons dit souvent d'impérissables choses
Les soirs illuminés par l'ardeur du charbon.

Que les soleils sont beaux dans les chaudes soirées!
Que l'espace est profond! que le cœur est puissant!
En me penchant vers toi, reine des adorées,
Je croyais respirer le parfum de ton sang.
Que les soleils sont beaux dans les chaudes soirées!

La nuit s'épaississait ainsi qu'une cloison,
Et mes yeux dans le noir devinaient tes prunelles,
Et je buvais ton souffle, ô douceur! ô poison!
Et tes pieds s'endormaient dans mes mains fraternelles.
La nuit s'épaississait ainsi qu'une cloison.

Je sais l'art d'évoquer les minutes heureuses,
Et revis mon passé blotti dans tes genoux.
Car à quoi bon chercher tes beautés langoureuses
Ailleurs qu'en ton cher corps et qu'en ton cœur si doux?
Je sais l'art d'évoquer les minutes heureuses!

Ces serments, ces parfums, ces baisers infinis,
Renaîtront-ils d'un gouffre interdit à nos sondes,
Comme montent au ciel les soleils rajeunis
Après s'être lavés au fond des mers profondes?
—O serments! ô parfums! ô baisers infinis!

Charles Baudelaire

Appendix III

Assommons les pauvres!

Pendant quinze jours je m'étais confiné dans ma chambre, et je m'étais entouré des livres à la mode dans ce temps-là (il y a seize ou dix-sept ans); je veux parler des livres où il est traité de l'art de rendre les peuples heureux, sages et riches, en vingt-quatre heures. J'avais donc digéré,—avalé, veux-je dire,—toutes les élucubrations de tous ces entrepreneurs de bonheur public,—de ceux qui conseillent à tous les pauvres de se faire esclaves, et de ceux qui leur persuadent qu'ils sont tous des rois détrônés.—On ne trouvera pas surprenant que je fusse alors dans un état d'esprit avoisinant le vertige ou la stupidité.

Il m'avait semblé seulement que je sentais, confiné au fond de mon intellect, le germe obscur d'une idée supérieure à toutes les formules de bonne femme dont j'avais récemment parcouru le dictionnaire. Mais ce n'était que l'idée d'une idée, quelque chose d'infiniment vague.

Et je sortis avec une grande soif. Car le goût passionné des mauvaises lectures engendre un besoin proportionnel du grand air et des rafraîchissants.

Comme j'allais entrer dans un cabaret, un mendiant me tendit son chapeau, avec un de ces regards inoubliables qui culbuteraient les trônes, si l'esprit remuait la matière, et si l'œil d'un magnétiseur faisait mûrir les raisins.

En même temps, j'entendis une voix qui chuchotait à mon oreille, une voix que je reconnus bien; c'était celle d'un bon Ange, ou bien d'un bon Démon, qui m'accompagne partout. Puisque Socrate avait son bon Démon, pourquoi n'aurais-je pas mon bon Ange, et pourquoi n'aurais-je pas l'honneur, comme Socrate, d'obtenir mon brevet de folie, signé du subtil Lélut et du bien avisé Baillarger?

Il existe cette différence entre le Démon de Socrate et le mien, que celui de Socrate ne se manifestait à lui que pour défendre, avertir, empêcher, et que le mien daigne conseiller, suggérer, persuader. Ce pauvre Socrate n'avait qu'un Démon prohibiteur; le mien est un grand affirmateur, le mien est un Démon d'action, un Démon de combat.

Or, sa voix me chuchotait ceci: "Celui-là seul est l'égal d'un autre, qui le prouve, et celui-là seul est digne de la liberté, qui sait la conquérir."

Immédiatement, je sautai sur mon mendiant. D'un seul coup de poing, je lui bouchai un œil, qui devint, en une seconde, gros comme une balle. Je cassai un de mes ongles à lui briser deux dents, et comme je ne me sentais pas assez fort, étant né délicat et m'étant peu exercé à la boxe, pour assommer rapidement ce vieillard, je le saisis d'une main par le collet de son habit, de l'autre, je l'empoignai à la gorge, et je me mis à lui secouer vigoureusement la tête contre un mur. Je dois avouer que j'avais préalablement inspecté les environs d'un coup d'œil, et que j'avais vérifié que dans cette banlieue déserte je me trouvais, pour un assex long temps, hors de la portée de tout agent de police.

Ayant ensuite, par un coup de pied lancé dans le dos, assez énergique pour briser les omoplates, terrassé ce sexagénaire affaibli, je me saisis d'une grosse branche d'arbre qui traînait à terre, et je le battis avec l'énergie obstinée des cuisiniers qui veulent attendrir un beefteack.

Tout à coup,—ô miracle! ô jouissance du philosophe qui vérifie l'excellence de sa théorie!—je vis cette antique carcasse se retourner, se redresser avec une énergie que je n'aurais jamais soupçonnée dans une machine si singulièrement détraquée, et, avec un regard de haine qui me parut de *bon augure*, le malandrin décrépit se jeta sur moi, me pocha les deux yeux, me cassa quatre dents, et avec la même branche d'arbre me battit dru comme plâtre.—Par mon énergique médication, je lui avais donc rendu l'orgueil et la vie.

Alors, je lui fis force signes pour lui faire comprendre que je considérais la discussion comme finie, et me relevant avec la satisfaction d'un sophiste du Portique, je lui dis: "Monsieur, *vous êtes mon égal!* veuillez me faire l'honneur de partager avec moi ma bourse; et souvenez-vous, si vous êtes réellement philanthrope, qu'il faut appliquer à tous vos confrères, quand ils vous demanderont l'aumône, la théorie que j'ai eu la *douleur* d'essayer sur votre dos."

Il m'a bien juré qu'il avait compris ma théorie, et qu'il obéirait à mes conseils.

Charles Baudelaire

Appendix IV

Le Voyage

A Maxime Du Camp.

I

Pour l'enfant, amoureux de cartes et d'estampes,
L'univers est égal à son vaste appétit.
Ah! que le monde est grand à la clarté des lampes!
Aux yeux du souvenir que le monde est petit!

Un matin nous partons, le cerveau plein de flamme,
Le cœur gros de rancune et de désirs amers,
Et nous allons, suivant le rythme de la lame,
Berçant notre infini sur le fini des mers:

Les uns, joyeux de fuir une patrie infâme;
D'autres, l'horreur de leurs berceaux, et quelques-
uns,
Astrologues noyés dans les yeux d'une femme,
La Circé tyrannique aux dangereux parfums.

Pour n'être pas changés en bêtes, ils s'enivrent
D'espace et de lumière et de cieux embrasés;
La glace qui les mord, les soleils qui les cuivrent,
Effacent lentement la marque des baisers.

Mais les vrais voyageurs sont ceux-là qui partent
Pour partir; cœurs légers, semblables aux ballons,
De leur fatalité jamais ils ne s'écartent,
Et, sans savoir pourquoi, disent toujours: Allons!

Ceux-là dont les désirs ont la forme des nues,
Et qui rêvent, ainsi qu'un conscrit le canon,
De vastes voluptés, changeantes, inconnues,
Et dont l'esprit humain n'a jamais su le nom!

II

Nous imitons, horreur! la toupie et la boule
Dans leur valse et leurs bonds; même dans nos sommeils
La Curiosité nous tourmente et nous roule,
Comme un Ange cruel qui fouette des soleils.

Singulière fortune où le but se déplace,
Et, n'étant nulle part, peut être n'importe où!
Où l'Homme, dont jamais l'espérance n'est lasse,
Pour trouver le repos court toujours comme un fou!

Notre âme est un trois-mâts cherchant son Icarie;
Une voix retentit sur le pont: "Ouvre l'œil!"
Une voix de la hune, ardente et folle, crie:
"Amour...gloire...bonheur!" Enfer! c'est un écueil!

Chaque îlot signalé par l'homme de vigie
Est un Eldorado promis par le Destin;
L'Imagination qui dresse son orgie
Ne trouve qu'un récif aux clartés du matin.

O le pauvre amoureux des pays chimériques!
Faut-il le mettre aux fers, le jeter à la mer,
Ce matelot ivrogne, inventeur d'Amériques
Dont le mirage rend le gouffre plus amer?

Tel le vieux vagabond, piétinant dans la boue,
Rêve, le nez en l'air, de brillants paradis;
Son œil ensorcelé découvre une Capoue
Partout où la chandelle illumine un taudis.

III

Étonnants voyageurs! quelles nobles histoires
Nous lisons dans vos yeux profonds comme les mers!
Montrez-nous les écrins de vos riches mémoires,
Ces bijoux merveilleux, faits d'astres et d'éthers.

Nous voulons voyager sans vapeur et sans voile!
Faites, pour égayer l'ennui de nos prisons,
Passer sur nos esprits, tendus comme une toile,
Vos souvenirs avec leurs cadres d'horizons.

Dites, qu'avez-vous vu?

IV

"Nous avons vu des astres
Et des flots; nous avons vu des sables aussi;
Et, malgré bien des chocs et d'imprévus désastres,
Nous nous sommes souvent ennuyés, comme ici.

"La gloire du soleil sur la mer violette,
La gloire des cités dans le soleil couchant,
Allumaient dans nos cœurs une ardeur inquiète
De plonger dans un ciel au reflet alléchant.

"Les plus riches cités, les plus grands paysages,
Jamais ne contenaient l'attrait mystérieux
De ceux que le hasard fait avec les nuages.
Et toujours le désir nous rendait soucieux!

"—La jouissance ajoute au désir de la force.
Désir, vieil arbre à qui le plaisir sert d'engrais,
Cependant que grossit et durcit ton écorce,
Tes branches veulent voir le soleil de plus près!

"Grandiras-tu toujours, grand arbre plus vivace
Que le cyprès?—Pourtant nous avons, avec soin,
Cueilli quelques croquis pour votre album vorace,
Frères qui trouvez beau tout ce qui vient de loin!

"Nous avons salué des idoles à trompe;
Des trônes constellés de joyaux lumineux;
Des palais ouvragés dont la féerique pompe
Serait pour vos banquiers un rêve ruineux;

"Des costumes qui sont pour les yeux une ivresse;
Des femmes dont les dents et les ongles sont teints,
Et des jongleurs savants que le serpent caresse."

V

Et puis, et puis encore?

VI

        "O cerveaux enfantins!

"Pour ne pas oublier la chose capitale,
Nous avons vu partout, et sans l'avoir cherché,
Du haut jusques en bas de l'échelle fatale,
Le spectacle ennuyeux de l'immortel péché:

"La femme, esclave vile, orgueilleuse et stupide,
Sans rire s'adorant et s'aimant sans dégoût;
L'homme, tyran goulu, paillard, dur et cupide,
Esclave de l'esclave et ruisseau dans l'égout;

"Le bourreau qui jouit, le martyr qui sanglote;
La fête qu'assaisonne et parfume le sang;
Le poison du pouvoir énervant le despote,
Et le peuple amoureux du fouet abrutissant;

"Plusieurs religions semblables à la nôtre,
Toutes escaladant le ciel; la Sainteté,
Comme en un lit de plume un délicat se vautre,
Dans les clous et le crin cherchant la volupté;

"L'Humanité bavarde, ivre de son génie,
Et, folle maintenant comme elle était jadis,

Criant à Dieu, dans sa furibonde agonie:
"O mon semblable, ô mon maître, je te maudis!"

"Et les moins sots, hardis amants de la Démence,
Fuyant le grand troupeau parqué par le Destin,
Et se réfugiant dans l'opium immense!
—Tel est du globe entier l'éternel bulletin."

VII

Amer savoir, celui qu'on tire du voyage!
Le monde, monotone et petit, aujourd'hui,
Hier, demain, toujours, nous fait voir notre image:
Une oasis d'horreur dans un désert d'ennui!

Faut-il partir? rester? Si tu peux rester, reste;
Pars, s'il le faut. L'un court, et l'autre se tapit
Pour tromper l'ennemi vigilant et funeste,
Le Temps! Il est, hélas! des coureurs sans répit,

Comme le Juif errant et comme les apôtres,
A qui rien ne suffit, ni wagon ni vaisseau,
Pour fuir ce rétiaire infâme; il en est d'autres
Qui savent le tuer sans quitter leur berceau.

Lorsque enfin il mettra le pied sur notre échine,
Nous pourrons espérer et crier: En avant!
De même qu'autrefois nous partions pour la Chine,
Les yeux fixés au large et les cheveux au vent,

Nous nous embarquerons sur la mer des Ténèbres
Avec le cœur joyeux d'un jeune passager.
Entendez-vous ces voix, charmantes et funèbres,
Qui chantent: "Par ici! vous qui voulez manger

"Le Lotus parfumé! c'est ici qu'on vendange
Les fruits miraculeux dont votre cœur a faim;
Venez vous enivrer de la douceur étrange
De cette après-midi qui n'a jamais de fin?"

A l'accent familier nous devinons le spectre;
Nos Pylades là-bas tendent leurs bras vers nous.
"Pour rafraîchir ton cœur nage vers ton Électre!"
Dit celle dont jadis nous baisions les genoux.

VIII

O Mort, vieux capitaine, il est temps! levons l'ancre!
Ce pays nous ennuie, ô Mort! Appareillons!
Si le ciel et la mer sont noirs comme de l'encre,
Nos cœurs que tu connais sont remplis de rayons!

Verse-nous ton poison pour qu'il nous réconforte!
Nous voulons, tant ce feu nous brûle le cerveau,
Plonger au fond du gouffre, Enfer ou Ciel, qu'importe?
Au fond de l'Inconnu pour trouver du *nouveau!*

Charles Baudelaire

Notes

Introduction

1. Lowell writes: 'I have tried to write live English and to do what my authors might have done if they were writing their poems now and in America' (1962: xi).

Chapter 2

1. This proposal must raise some suspicions, that limits will soon be reached, or that extreme kinds of distortion are alienating and fruitless.
2. Venuti (1995: 24–5) suggests the cultural consequences that this procedural practice might have: 'Thus the translator consults many different target-language cultural materials, ranging from dictionaries and grammars to texts [...] Their sheer heterogeneity leads to discontinuities—between the source-language text and the translation and within the translation itself—that are symptomatic of its ethnocentric violence. A humanist method of reading translations elides these discontinuities by locating a semantic unity adequate to the foreign text, stressing intelligibility, transparent communication [...] A symptomatic reading, in contrast, locates discontinuities at the level of diction, syntax, or discourse that reveal the translation to be a violent re-writing of the foreign text [...].'
3. We might recall that Valéry identified rhythm as an agent of personal memory (of the involuntary kind), and insisted on its psychological or psychosomatic nature, on its being a certain state in the perceiver (see Ince 1982).
4. Bonnefoy's opinion has not held entirely firm. His translations of Shakespeare's 'Venus and Adonis' and 'Rape of Lucretia' are in prose (1993). Bonnefoy is somewhat embarrassed by his apparent change of heart, but argues that the poems have in them that painterly element which calls for the framing of prose paragraphs (separated by line-spaces), and that verse no longer has at its disposal that conventional, decorative phraseology that these poems, and particularly 'Venus and Adonis', draw upon so readily (pp. i–xv).
5. Elsewhere (Schulte and Biguenet 1992: 188), Bonnefoy suggests that translation is a dialogue between the source poet and the translator poet, in

which the latter intuits the motives of the former and plays out the drama of those motives on his own existential keyboard: 'We should in fact come to see what motivates the poem; to relive the act which both gave rise to it and remains enmeshed in it; and released from that fixed form, which is merely its trace, the first intention and intuition (let us say a yearning, an obsession, something universal) can be tried out anew in the other language'..

6.   Bonnefoy has published five *Hamlet* translations to date: 1957 (Club Français du Livre), 1959 (Club Français du Livre), 1962 (Mercure de France), 1978 (Gallimard), 1988 (Mercure de France).

Chapter 3

1.   Philip Berk (1974) also traces parallels between this opening of the Sixth Satire and the opening of Baudelaire's 'La Lune offensée', in which he uncovers other references to the Sixth Satire.

2.   For comment on Lowell's debt to Baudelaire (and Rimbaud), see Doreski 1986.

3.   Baudelaire expresses this idea in the article entitled 'Méthode de critique. De l'idée moderne du progrès appliquée aux Beaux-Arts. Déplacement de la vitalité', devoted to the Exposition universelle of 1855. In the same article is to be found his argument that *'le beau est toujours bizarre'* [*the beautiful is always bizarre*], that the bizarre is what makes the world 'multicolore et versicolore' [multicoloured and variegated], thanks to the relativities of climate, race, custom, religion (*OC*, II, 578–9). Self-replenishment as a function of translation is mentioned by Robert Lowell in the 'Introduction' to his *Imitations*: 'This book was written from time to time when I was unable to do anything of my own' (1962: xii).

Chapter 4

1.   If such an implication is upsetting to admirers of Rilke, then they can, of course, take consolation in Steiner's claim that, in Rilke's *Umdichtung* of Louise Labé, the translation is 'of a higher magnitude' than the original (1975: 298; see also 402–3). Steiner also prefers Celan's version of Supervielle's 'Chanson' to its source (1975: 404–5).

2.   Walters (1969: 51–2), amongst others, has remarked on the anthropomorphic possibilities of the physiological 'palpite'. In my version, the identification of poet and fire derives from 'can't make up its mind'; I have also tried to prefigure the second tercet by anthropomorphizing the recollections, 'coming up for air'.

3.   Walters (1969: 53–4) comments on the sexually generative implications of 'peupler': 'Hence, the verb "peupler" translates spiritual impotence into physical terms; it constitutes a response to the physical nature of the memories of the past ("Les souvenirs lointains lentement s'élever"), and suggests further that the poet longs for a return to physical vitality through musical expression' (p. 54). The connection between 'peupler' and 'souvenirs' is, of course, a feature of the opening stanza of 'La Chevelure':

> [...]
> Extase! Pour peupler ce soir l'alcôve obscure

Des souvenirs dormant dans cette chevelure,
Je la veux agiter comme un mouchoir!

Chapter 5

1. For a fuller and more careful categorization of compensation mechanisms, see Keith Harvey 1995.
2. In this respect, I could not agree with Jean Boase-Beier's view that 'it is often the repetition in itself, rather than the repetition of a particular element, which matters' (1994: 406).
3. Most editors, following the first edition of *Poèmes saturniens* (1866), plump for 'détone' rather than 'détonne', as the final word of the first stanza. Jacques Robichez (1969: 503), however, argues: 'Plutôt que d'admettre une "détonation" de la bise, je me range à l'avis de Bouillane de Lacoste (*Cours familier d'orthographe*, p. 16), qui voit dans *détone*, donné par les éditions que Verlaine a revues, une faute d'orthographe. [...] (Il y a donc lieu de corriger en "détonne" (solution adoptée par les *Oeuvres complètes*): la bise fait entendre une fausse note, de mauvais augure dans ce décor de torpeur' [Rather than accepting a 'detonation' of the North wind, I favour the view of Bouillane de Lacoste (*Cours familier d'orthographe*, p. 16), who sees in *détone*, given in editions revised by Verlaine, a spelling error. [...] (There are grounds, therefore, for correcting 'détone' to 'détonne' (the solution adopted by the *Œuvres complètes*): the North wind blows out of tune, which augurs ill in this torpid setting]. The case for 'détonne' is a persuasive one.
4. Benjamin notes 'the profound gulf between the quatrains which present the occurrence and the tercets which transfigure it' (1973: 46). Transfiguration is not something that I find here.
5. In his presentation of the villanelle (1909 [1872]: 213–15), Banville quotes a villanelle by Philoxène Boyer ('La Marquise Aurore') which has twenty-five lines, while 'L'Ornière', one of Maurice Rollinat's large output, has as many as eighty-five lines; Leconte de Lisle, on the other hand, uses only thirteen lines in his 'Villanelle', and eighteen in 'Dans l'air léger', which omits the final *A2* and takes other liberties with the final stanza's rhyme-scheme.
6. As we have already noted, Manet's 1862 portrait of Jeanne Duval depicts her as a mulatto woman, a native, 'amaigrie et phthisique' [wasted and tubercular], and yet as if awkwardly imprisoned in the billowing acres of a dress 'soulevée, balancée par la crinoline ou les jupons de mousseline empesée' [lifted, set swinging by crinoline or petticoats of starched muslin].
7. It is customary, of course, to demonstrate a virtuosity in refrain poems by subtly nuancing the meaning of the refrain at its each appearance. But here, as mentioned earlier, I am courting a parallel with minimalism. I have therefore attempted to restrict variation to features of pacing, intonation, syncopation, by controlling punctuation and clausal grouping.
8. In a recent treatment of Dylan Thomas's poem, Seamus Heaney describes the villanelle in the following terms: 'Yet that form is so much a matter of crossing and substitutions, of back-tracks and double-takes, turns and returns, that it is a vivid figure for the union of opposites [...]. The villanelle, in fact, both participates in the flux of natural existence and scans and abstracts existence in order to register its pattern. It is a living cross-section, a simultaneously open and closed form, one in which the cycles of youth and

age, of rise and fall, growth and decay find their analogues in the fixed rhyme cycle of rhymes and repetitions' (1995: 139). I would certainly want to agree with the majority of this eloquent case for the defence, but would still weight the villanelle towards flux; the refrains are, for me, as much to do with the function of repetition in Baudelaire's 'L'Horloge', unremittingly counting off the passing seconds, as with processes of abstraction:

> Trois mille six cents fois par heure, la Seconde
> Chuchote: *Souviens-toi!*—Rapide, avec sa voix
> D'insecte, Maintenant dit: Je suis Autrefois,
> Et j'ai pompé ta vie avec ma trompe immonde!

9.   Ernest Fouinet is usually credited with first introducing the pantoum into France. Hugo published a selection of Oriental poems translated by Fouinet in the notes of *Les Orientales* (1829), one of which was a pantoum ('Les papillons jouent à l'entour sur leurs ailes'). Fouinet went on to publish a *Choix de poésies orientales* in 1830.

10. In English practice particularly, the second line of the final stanza often repeats the third line of the first stanza.

11. Benoît de Cornulier seems to me mistaken when he claims that 'Harmonie du soir' 'en [of the pantoum] respecte l'apparence [...] mais en dénature ou transforme le système en supprimant la distinction entre deux thèmes entrelacés, ce qui prive la double structure parallèle d'enchaînement rétrograde de sa base sémantique' [respects the pantoum's look (...) but distorts or transforms its mechanism by suppressing the distinction between two interwoven themes, which deprives of its semantic foundation the double parallel structure of backward linkage] (1989: 69–70).

12. Other connections between the two threads are provided by religious lexical elements, and by the general synaesthetic experience (vibratory and localized in the first thread, swirling and spacious in the second).

Chapter 6

1.   Speaking of Edna St Vincent Millay, Clark and Sykes (1997, xli-xlii) remark: 'We must regret, too, that her example has not inspired many more women to translate Baudelaire: the ambiguous presentation of women in his poetry must act as a disincentive, but surely also offers possibilities for all manner of ironic and deconstructive approaches.'

2.   Pichois's argument in mitigation strikes me as ingenious but disingenuous: 'Ce passage n'est pas facile à interpréter. Voici comment nous le comprenons: Dieu étant un scandale [...], et donc un scandale, le Rédempteur incarné, il faut—soit dit ironiquement—exterminer les Juifs qui ont été les témoins de cette Rédemption. Tout anti-sémitisme est à écarter. On remarquera que c'est à peu près le seul passage de son œuvre où Baudelaire mentionne le Dieu rédempteur; partout ailleurs, Dieu est un tyran' [This passage is not easy to interpret. This is how we understand it: God being a scandal (...), and thus a scandal, too, the Redeemer incarnate, one must exterminate the Jews who were the witnesses of this Redemption (to be understood ironically). Any suggestion of anti-semitism is to be ruled out. Remarkably, this is almost the only passage in his work in which Baudelaire mentions God the

Redeemer; everywhere else, God is a tyrant] (*OC*, I, 1511). We might also do well to remember the lines from 'Les Sept Vieillards' which refer to 'la tournure et le pas maladroit/D'un quadrupède infirme ou d'un juif à trois pattes' (ll. 24–5).

3. 'Certainement, j'ai beaucoup à me plaindre de moi-même, et je suis tout étonné et alarmé de cet état. Ai-je besoin d'un déplacement, je n'en sais rien. Est-ce le physique malade qui diminue l'esprit et la volonté, ou est-ce la lâcheté spirituelle qui fatigue le corps, je n'en sais rien. Mais ce que je sens, c'est un immense découragement, une sensation d'isolement insupportable, une peur perpétuelle d'un malheur vague, une défiance complète de mes forces, une absence total de désirs, une impossibilité de trouver un amusement quelconque. [...] C'est là le véritable esprit de spleen' [Certainly, I have plenty to complain about on my own account, and I am surprised and alarmed by this condition. Do I need a change of scene, I could not say. Is it the ailing body which undermines the spirit and the will, or is it spiritual cowardice which exhausts the body, I have no idea. But what I do feel is an immense discouragement, an intolerable sense of isolation, a perpetual fear of some vague misfortune, a complete lack of trust in my powers, a total absence of desire, the impossibility of finding any amusement whatsoever. (...) That is the true spirit of spleen] (*Correspondance*, I, 437–8).

4. Eliot himself accounts for Baudelaire's failure to pass on the torch of modernism in these terms: 'For another thing, he had a great part in forming a generation of poets after him; and in England he had what is in a way the misfortune to be first and extravagantly advertised by Swinburne, and taken up by the followers of Swinburne. He was universal, and at the same time confined by a fashion which he himself did most to create' (1953: 174).

5. I have tried something similar, but without a framing 'other' voice, apart from that of the epigraph, in a rendering of 'Obsession':

>Grands bois, vous m'effrayez comme des cathédrales;
>Vous hurlez comme l'orgue; et dans nos cœurs maudits,
>Chambres d'éternel deuil où vibrent de vieux râles,
>Répondent les échos de vos *De profundis*.
>
>Je te hais, Océan! tes bonds et tes tumultes,
>Mon esprit les retrouve en lui; ce rire amer
>De l'homme vaincu, plein de sanglots et d'insultes,
>Je l'entends dans le rire énorme de la mer.
>
>Comme tu me plairais, ô nuit! sans ces étoiles
>Dont la lumière parle un langage connu!
>Car je cherche le vide, le noir, et le nu!
>
>Mais les ténèbres sont elles-mêmes des toiles
>Où vivent, jaillissant de mon œil par milliers,
>Des êtres disparus aux regards familiers.
>
>Obsession
>
>A culture is no better than its woods.
>   (W.H.Auden)

Petrifying
These great woods
Just like cathedrals
Winds in the trees
Organs bellowing
And our hearts
                        condemned and damned
Are rooms for dying in
                 filled with dying
Haunted by echoes
Of graveside prayers.

The ocean, hateful,
Rough tempestuous seas, heaving swell
These are what's inside my head;
And in the booming laugh
                 along the shore
Are notes of human laughter—
Convulsed, abusive, crushed.

The night would bring relief
If it were starless.
Give me the pitch-black, blank and bare.

But this is a well-mapped galaxy
                full of scores
                of shapes
Where I see,
                because I'm straining not to,
Ghosts from the past
Who look at me familiarly.

6.   The source usually quoted is Champfleury's *Hoffmann, Contes posthumes* (1856), in which *Moi* declares: 'C'est cependant une chose remarquable qu'on reconnaît immédiatement les aveugles à cette seule manière de tourner la tête en haut, qui est propre à tous les aveugles' [It is, however, a remarkable thing that we can recognize the blind immediately, merely from the way they have their heads turned upwards, which is a peculiarity of the blind everywhere] (quoted by Adam 1961: 386).

7.   Peter Nurse's excellent commentary on this poem (1969: 193–203) points out: 'In the 1860 version, line 12 read: "Cherchant la jouissance avec férocité." The superiority of the 1861 variant lies in the added symbolical significance of the noun: *atrocité*, by reason of its etymological origins: < *atrox* < *ater, atra* (black), recalling another aspect of *le noir illimité*.'

Chapter 7

1.   This translation also, of course, includes the second and third stanzas:

Il était tard; ainsi qu'une médaille neuve

> La pleine lune s'étalait,
> Et la solennité de la nuit, comme un fleuve,
> Sur Paris dormant ruisselait.
>
> Et le long des maisons, sous les portes cochères,
> Des chats passaient furtivement,
> L'oreille au guet, ou bien, comme des ombres chères,
> Nous accompagnaient lentement.

2. Let us remind ourselves again of the aims of the plain prose translation, this time in the words of Theodore Savory: 'Writers who have recommended the translation of poetry into prose have done so because they were thinking of one particular function of the translation, to show how the lines may be construed. When the student has learnt this he will be content with the original and will not need a translation in any form' (*The Art of Translation*, London, 1968, p. 82, quoted by Garfitt, 1998: 345).

3. I take these terms from Malcolm Bowie's delightful analysis of the rhythms of Mallarmé's late prose (1996: 175–86).

4. One may harbour some suspicion that Johnson over-interprets Baudelaire's distinction between stick and flowers, and attributes to him equivalences that he did not formulate.

5. One should also recall another of Barbey's references to *Niobé*, where he describes it as 'cette rêverie qu'on croirait traduite d'un poète anglais' [this revery that you might think translated from an English poet] (1966: 1612).

6. As Fumaroli puts it, in relation to Maurice de Guérin: 'Le propre du poème en prose, c'est de se donner pour le reflet imparfait, allusif, d'une œuvre idéale absente. Par là, du reste, il peut prétendre à un pouvoir de suggestion supérieur à l'œuvre close et parfaite à laquelle il donne l'impression de renvoyer. Il s'apparente à la traduction, elle aussi "énigme dans un miroir" d'une œuvre achevée, mais reposant ailleurs, dans une autre langue' [The peculiarity of the prose-poem is to present itself as the reflection, imperfect, allusive, of an ideal absent work. Besides, it can thereby pretend to a power of suggestion superior to the closed and polished work to which it seems to refer. It is related to translation, itself an 'enigma in a mirror' of a finished work, which, however, has its home elsewhere, in another language] (1984: 53).

Chapter 8

1. It should be said that Gaddis Rose's appraisal is somewhat marred by a highly misleading definition of the alexandrine—'A six-foot or 12-beat line of poetry. The foot is iambic (short/long). It is to French poetry what iambic pentameter is to English' (p. 85)—and by an inability to count syllables reliably, either in French or German.

2. Galand (1969: 455) asks: 'L'arche qui protège ce sommeil est-elle seulement l'arche d'un pont? Le mot n'évoque-t-il pas aussi la protection divine?' [Is the arch which protects this sleep only the arch of a bridge? Does not the word also evoke divine protection?].

3. For an account of the colon's fortunes in the early nineteenth century, and of its relation to comma and semi-colon as a syntactic stop, see Dürrenmatt

273

1998: 19–35. Jacques Drillon (1991) is another invaluable source of information, on all punctuation marks.

4. I use this term of approximation, even with an exact figure, simply because I am not entirely sure that all textual corruptions have been traced.
5. Is it possible that Leakey intends a reversed sonnet here?
6. There are nine colons in 'Le Voyage' as it appears in Pichois's (1861) edition (*OC*, I, 129–34).

Chapter 9

1. 'Quoi de plus absurde que le Progrès, puisque l'homme, comme cela est prouvé par le fait journalier, est toujours semblable et égal à l'homme, c'est-à-dire toujours à l'état sauvage' [What is more absurd than Progress, since man, as is proved every day, is still like, and equal to, man, that is to say, still in the primitive state] (*OC*, I, 663).
2. 'Perdu dans ce vilain monde, coudoyé par les foules, je suis comme un homme lassé dont l'œil ne voit en arrière, dans les années profondes, que désabusement et amertume, et devant lui qu'un orage où rien de neuf n'est contenu, ni enseignement, ni douleur' [Lost in this vile world, elbowed by the crowds, I am like an exhausted man who sees behind him, in the deep-reaching past, only disllusionment and bitterness, and in front of him only a storm which brings nothing new, neither instruction nor suffering] (*OC*, I, 667).
3. This poem is a close relative of Verlaine's 'Colloque sentimental'—Dowson's translation appeared in *Decorations*—but is addressed to Horace's Lalage and ends with a *carpe diem* exhortation, before recovering its Verlainian colouring:

> But pluck the pretty, fleeting flowers
> That deck our little path of light:
> For all too soon we twain shall tread
> The bitter pasture of the dead:
> Estranged, sad spectres of the night.

4. Another reason for opening the poem with this word is Baudelaire's own fondness for 'sondes':

> Bien loin des pioches et des sondes;
> ('Le Guignon')

> Homme, nul n'a sondé le fond de tes abîmes;
> ('L'Homme et la mer')

> Renaîtront-ils d'un gouffre interdit à nos sondes,
> ('Le Balcon')

5. About this collection, Pierre Albouy writes: 'Nul recueil, avant 1830, ne rompt, aussi radicalement que celui-ci, avec les formes post-classiques dont s'encombrent les *Odes* et, encore, la poésie d'un Lamartine ou d'un Vigny' [No collection, before 1830, breaks as radically as this one with the post-classical forms, with which the *Odes* and the poetry of Lamartine or Vigny

are still encumbered] (Hugo 1964: 1299).

6.   Hugo notes of one of Fouinet's renderings—'Les lances en se plongeant dans le sang rendaient un son humide comme celui de la pluie qui tombe dans la pluie' [As they plunged into the blood, the lances made a wet sound, like rain falling into rain]—'La langue française n'a pas de mot pour rendre ce bruit de l'eau qui tombe dans l'eau: les anglais [*sic*] ont une expression parfaite, *splash*. Le mot arabe est bien imitatif aussi, *ghachghachâ*' [The French language has no word for this noise of water falling into water: the English have a perfect expression, *splash*. The Arabic word is also highly imitative, *ghachghachâ*] (Hugo 1964: 697).

7.   But perhaps part VIII will bring to mind Eliot's 'Marina', Pericles recovering his daughter, thought to be lost at sea, and the poet able to think forward into a world he will no longer inhabit:

> This form, this face, this life
> Living to live in a world of time beyond me; let me
> Resign my life for this life, my speech for that unspoken,
> The awakened, lips parted, the hope, the new ships.

Bibliography

Adam, Antoine (ed.), 1961. *Charles Baudelaire: 'Les Fleurs du Mal'* (Paris: Garnier).

Adams, J.N., 1982. *The Latin Sexual Vocabulary* (London: Duckworth).

Adatte, Emmanuel, 1986. *'Les Fleurs du Mal' et 'Le Spleen de Paris': Essai sur le dépassement du réel* (Paris: Corti).

Alexander, Michael, 1997. 'Pound as Translator', *Translation and Literature*, 6/1, 23–30.

Arrojo, Rosemary, 1998. 'The Revision of the Traditional Gap between Theory and Practice and the Empowerment of Translation in Postmodern Times', *The Translator*, 4/1, 25–48.

Banville, Théodore de, 1909. *Petit Traité de poésie française* (Paris: Bibliothèque-Charpentier) (1st pub. 1872).

Barbey d'Aurevilly, Jules, 1966. *Œuvres romanesques complètes II* (ed. Jacques Petit) (Paris: Gallimard).

Barthes, Roland, 1970. *S/Z* (Paris: Éditions du Seuil).

Baudelaire, Charles, 1973. *Correspondance*, 2 vols. (ed. Claude Pichois and Jean Ziegler) (Paris: Gallimard).

—— 1975 and 1976. *Œuvres complètes*, 2 vols. (Paris: Gallimard).

Beare, W., 1957. *Latin Verse and European Song: A Study in Accent and Rhythm* (London: Methuen).

Beaugrande, Robert de, 1978. *Factors in a Theory of Poetic Translating* (Assen: Van Gorcum).

Benjamin, Walter, 1973. *Charles Baudelaire: A Lyric Poet in the Era of High Capitalism* (trans. Harry Zohn) (London: NLB).

Bergson, Henri, 1984. *Œuvres*, 4th edn. (ed. André Robinet and Henri Gouhier) (Paris: PUF).

Berk, Philip R., 1974. 'Echoes of Juvenal in Baudelaire's "La Lune offensée"', *Romance Notes*, 16/1, 73–82.

Berman, Antoine, 1984. *L'Épreuve de l'étranger: Culture et traduction dans l'Allemagne romantique* (Paris: Gallimard).

—— 1995. *Pour une critique des traductions: John Donne* (Paris: Gallimard).

Boase-Beier, Jean, 1994. 'Translating Repetition', *Journal of European Studies*, 24, 403–9.

Bonnefoy, Yves (trans. and ed.), 1978. *Shakespeare: 'Hamlet', 'Le Roi Lear'* (Paris: Gallimard).

—— 1979. 'On the Translation of Form in Poetry', *World Literature Today*, 53/3, 374–9.

—— (trans. and ed.), 1993. *William Shakespeare: Les Poèmes* (Paris: Mercure de France).

Bowie, Malcolm, 1996. 'Pierre Ménard, Author of "La Musique et les Lettres": Towards a Poetic of Mallarmé's Late Prose', in Christopher Smith (ed.), *Essays in Memory of Michael Parkinson and Janine Dakyns (Norwich Papers IV)*, 1996, 175–86.

Burton, Richard, 1988. *Baudelaire in 1859: A Study in the Sources of Poetic Creativity* (Cambridge: Cambridge University Press).

Campbell, Roy, 1960. *The Collected Poems of Roy Campbell III* (London: The Bodley Head).

Cargo, Robert T. (ed.), 1965. *A Concordance to Baudelaire's 'Les Fleurs du Mal'* (Chapel Hill: University of North Carolina Press).

Chamberlain, Lori, 1992. 'Gender and the Metaphorics of Translation', in Lawrence Venuti (ed.), *Rethinking Translation: Discourse, Subjectivity, Ideology* (London: Routledge).

Champigny, Robert, 1963. *Le Genre poétique* (Monte Carlo: Regain).

Chapelan, Maurice (ed.), 1946. *Anthologie du poème en prose* (Paris: René Julliard).

Chesters, Graham, 1988. *Baudelaire and the Poetics of Craft* (Cambridge: Cambridge University Press).

Clark, Carol (trans. and ed.), 1995. *Baudelaire: Selected Poems* (London: Penguin Books).

Clark, Carol, and Sykes, Robert, 1997. *Baudelaire in English* (Harmondsworth: Penguin Books).

Clements, Patricia, 1985. *Baudelaire and the English Tradition* (Princeton, NJ: Princeton University Press).

Cornulier, Benoît de, 1989. 'Métrique des *Fleurs du Mal*', in *Baudelaire 'Les Fleurs du Mal': L'Intériorité de la forme* (Paris: CDU/SEDES) (Actes du colloque du 7 janvier 1989) (Colloques de la Société des Études Romantiques), 55–76.

Creekmore, Hubert (trans. and ed.), 1963. *The Satires of Juvenal* (New York: New American Library).

Dale, Peter (trans. and ed.), 1986. *Poems of Jules Laforgue* (London: Anvil Press Poetry).

Derrida, Jacques, 1972. *La Dissémination* (Paris: Éditions du Seuil).

Diderot, Denis, 1959. *Œuvres esthétiques* (ed. Paul Vernière) (Paris: Garnier).

Dorchain, Auguste, 1933. *L'Art des vers* (Paris: Garnier) (1st pub. 1905).

Doreski, William, 1986. 'Borrowed Visions: Robert Lowell's Imitations of Baudelaire and Rimbaud in *History*', *CEA Critic*, 48/3, 38–49.

Drillon, Jacques, 1991. *Traité de la ponctuation française* (Paris: Gallimard).

Dürrenmatt, Jacques, 1998. *Bien coupé, mal cousu: De la ponctuation et de la division du texte romantique* (Saint-Denis: Presses Universitaires de Vincennes).

Eco, Umberto, 1995. *The Search for the Perfect Language* (trans. James Fentress) (Oxford: Blackwell).

Edwards, Michael, 1997. 'Translation and Repetition', *Translation and Literature*, 6/1, 48–65.

Eliot, T.S., 1953. *Selected Prose* (ed. John Hayward) (Harmondsworth: Penguin Books).

—— 1958. *Collected Poems 1909–1935* (London: Faber & Faber).

Elliot, Alistair, 1993. 'Translating Poetic Forms', *Translation and Literature*, 2, 67–83.

Evans, Margery A., 1993. *Baudelaire and Intertextuality: Poetry at the Crossroads* (Cambridge: Cambridge University Press).

Fairclough, Rushton (trans. and ed.), 1916. *Virgil I: 'Eclogues', 'Georgics', 'Aeneid I–VI'* (London: William Heinemann; New York: G.P. Putnam).

Fish, Stanley, 1980. *Is There a Text in This Class?* (Cambridge, Mass.: Harvard University Press).

Flotow, Luise von, 1997. *Translation and Gender: Translating in the 'Era of Feminism'* (Manchester: St Jerome Publishing; Ottawa: University of Ottawa Press).

Flower, Desmond (ed.), 1967. *The Poetical Works of Ernest Dowson* (London: Cassell).

Fongaro, Antoine, 1973. 'Aux sources de "Recueillement"', *Études baudelairiennes III* (Neuchâtel: A la Baconnière), 158–77.

Fox, John, 1969. *The Lyric Poetry of Charles d'Orléans* (Oxford: Clarendon Press).

Gaddis Rose, Marilyn, 1997. *Translation and Literary Criticism: Translation as Analysis* (Manchester: St Jerome Publishing).

Galand, René, 1969. *Baudelaire: Poétiques et poésie* (Paris: Nizet).

Garfitt, Toby, 1998. 'A Plural Approach to Translating Mallarmé', *Forum for Modern Language Studies*, 34/4, 345–52.

Gasparov, M.L., 1996. *A History of European Versification* (trans. G.S. Smith and Marina Tarlinskaja) (ed. G.S. Smith and Leofranc Holford-Strevens) (Oxford: Clarendon Press).

Genette, Gérard, 1982. *Palimpsestes: La Littérature au second degré* (Paris: Éditions du Seuil).

—— 1987. *Seuils* (Paris: Éditions du Seuil).

Geninasca, Jacques, 1980. 'Forme fixe et forme discursive dans quelques sonnets de Baudelaire', *Cahiers de l'Association internationale des études françaises*, 32, 123–39.

Gentzler, Edwin, 1993. *Contemporary Translation Theories* (London: Routledge).

Gracq, Julien, 1980. *En lisant, en écrivant* (Paris: Corti).

Green, Peter (trans. and ed.), 1974. *Juvenal: The Sixteen Satires* (Harmondsworth: Penguin Books).

Grimaud, Michel (ed.), 1992. *Pour une métrique hugolienne: Textes de Wilhem Ténint, Gustave Aae, Philippe Martinon* (Paris: Minard).

Guérin, Maurice de, 1984. *Poésie* (ed. Marc Fumaroli) (Paris: Gallimard).

Hargreaves-Heap, Shaun, Hollis, Martin, *et al.*, 1992. *The Theory of Choice: A Critical Guide* (Oxford: Blackwell).

Harvey, Keith, 1995. 'A Descriptive Framework for Compensation', *The Translator*, 1/1, 65–86.

Hatim, Basil, and Mason, Ian, 1997. *The Translator as Communicator* (London: Routledge).

Heaney, Seamus, 1995. *The Redress of Poetry: Oxford Lectures* (London: Faber & Faber).

Heylen, Romy, 1992. 'Translation as Allegory: Yves Bonnefoy's *La Tragédie d'Hamlet*', *Comparative Literature Studies*, 29/4, 339–56.

Hiddleston, J.A., 1987. *Baudelaire and 'Le Spleen de Paris'* (Oxford: Clarendon Press).

Howard, Richard (trans. and ed.), 1982. *Charles Baudelaire: 'Les Fleurs du Mal'* (London: Picador).

Howarth, W.D., and Walton, C.L., 1971. *Explications: The Technique of French Literary Appreciation* (London: Oxford University Press).

Hughes, Ted, 1995. 'Myths, Metres, Rhythms', in *Winter Pollen: Occasional Prose* (ed. William Scammell) (London: Faber & Faber).

Hugo, Victor, 1964. *Œuvres poétiques I: Avant l'exil 1802–1851* (ed. Pierre Albouy) (Paris: Gallimard).

Hutcheon, Linda, 1989. *The Politics of Postmodernism* (London: Routledge).

Ince, Walter, 1982. 'Some of Valéry's Reflections on Rhythm', in Malcolm Bowie, Alison Fairlie, Alison Finch (eds), *Baudelaire, Mallarmé, Valéry: New Essays in Honour of Lloyd Austin* (Cambridge: Cambridge University Press), 384–97.

Johnson, Barbara, 1979. *Défigurations du langage poétique: La Seconde Révolution baudelairienne* (Paris: Flammarion).

Jouve, Pierre Jean (trans.), 1969. *Shakespeare: Sonnets* (Paris: Gallimard).

Krauss, Rosalind, 1985. *The Originality of the Avant-Garde and Other Modernist Myths* (Cambridge, Mass.: MIT Press).

Kristeva, Julia, 1974. *La Révolution du langage poétique: L'Avant-garde à la fin du XIXe siècle–Lautréamont et Mallarmé* (Paris: Éditions du Seuil).

Ladmiral, Jean-René, 1979. *Traduire: Théorèmes pour la traduction* (Paris: Payot).

Lawrence, D.H., 1944. *Sea and Sardinia* (Harmondsworth: Penguin Books) (1st pub. 1923).

Leakey, F.W. (trans. and ed.), 1994. *Baudelaire: Selected Poems from 'Les Fleurs du Mal'* (London: Greenwich Exchange).

Lee, Guy (trans. and ed.), 1968. *Ovid's 'Amores'* (London: John Murray).

Lefebvre, Jean-Pierre (ed.), 1993. *Anthologie bilingue de la poésie allemande* (Paris: Gallimard).

Lewis, R.A., 1976. *'La Cloche fêlée': An Essay in Analysis of a Poem*, supplement to *Zambezia*, 4/2 (Salisbury: University of Rhodesia).

Leyris, Pierre (trans.), 1994. *William Shakespeare: 'La Nuit des rois'/'Twelfth Night: Or What You Will'* (Paris: Flammarion).

Linfield, Nicholas, 1995. 'Baudelaire's "Les Bijoux": A Case Study of Verse Translation', *Perspectives: Studies in Translatology*, 1, 35–54.

Longaker, Mark (ed.), 1962. *The Poems of Ernest Dowson* (Philadelphia: University of Pennsylvania Press).

Lowell, Robert (trans.), 1962. *Imitations* (London: Faber & Faber).

McFarland, Ronald, 1982a. 'The Contemporary Villanelle', *Modern Poetry Studies*, 11/1–2, 113–27.

—— 1982b. 'The Revival of the Villanelle', *Romanic Review*, 73, 167–83.

—— 1982c. 'Victorian Villanelle', *Victorian Poetry*, 20/2, 125–38.

McGowan, James (trans. and ed.), 1993. *Charles Baudelaire: 'Les Fleurs du Mal'* (Oxford: Oxford University Press).

Mallarmé, Stéphane, 1945. *Œuvres complètes* (ed. Henri Mondor and G. Jean-Aubry) (Paris: Gallimard).

Martin, Walter (trans. and ed.), 1997. *Charles Baudelaire: Complete Poems* (Manchester: Carcanet).

Maulnier, Thierry, 1939. *Introduction à la poésie française* (Paris: Gallimard).

Mazzaro, Jerome (trans.), 1965. *Juvenal: 'Satires'* (ed. Richard E. Braun) (Ann Arbor: University of Michigan Press).

Meschonnic, Henri, 1973. *Pour la poétique II: Épistémologie de l'écriture; Poétique de la traduction* (Paris: Gallimard).

—— 1982. *Critique du rythme: Anthropologie historique du langage* (Lagrasse: Verdier).

Miller, Christopher, 1985. *Blank Darkness: Africanist Discourse in French* (Chicago: University of Chicago Press).

Moore, Nicholas, 1990. *Spleen ('Le Roi Bonhomme'): Thirty-One Versions of Baudelaire's 'Je suis comme le roi...'* (ed. Anthony Rudolf) (London: The Menard Press).

Morier, Henri, 1975. *Dictionnaire de poétique et de rhétorique* (2nd ed.) (Paris: PUF).

Mounin, Georges, 1963. *Les Problèmes théoriques de la traduction* (Paris: Gallimard).

Nurse, Peter H., 1969. 'Baudelaire: "Les Aveugles"', in Peter H. Nurse (ed.), *The Art of Criticism: Essays in French Literary Analysis* (Edinburgh: Edinburgh University Press).

Nussbaum, G.B., 1986. *Vergil's Metre: A Practical Guide for Reading Latin Hexameter Poetry* (Bristol: Bristol Classical Press).

Oriol-Boyer, Claudette, 1992. 'Rythme et fonction poétique', *Champs du signe*, 2, 57–76.

Pearson, Roger, 1996. *Unfolding Mallarmé: The Development of a Poetic Art* (Oxford: Clarendon Press).

Pizzorusso, Arnaldo, 1973. 'Deux Commentaires', *Études baudelairiennes III* (Neuchâtel: A la Baconnière), 241–53.

Pound, Ezra, 1954. *Literary Essays of Ezra Pound* (ed. T.S. Eliot) (London: Faber & Faber).

Prévost, Jean, 1953. *Baudelaire: Essai sur l'inspiration et la création poétiques* (Paris: Mercure de France).

Ramsay, G.G. (trans.), 1961. *Juvenal and Persius* (London: William Heinemann; Cambridge, Mass.: Harvard University Press).

Richardson, Joanna (trans. and ed.), 1975. *Baudelaire: Selected Poems* (Harmondsworth: Penguin Books).

Riffaterre, Michael, 1971. *Essais de stylistique structurale* (Paris: Flammarion).

Ripoll, Frédéric, and Roux, Dominique, 1995. *La Photographie* (Toulouse: Éditions Milan).

Robb, Graham, 1996. *Unlocking Mallarmé* (New Haven: Yale University Press).

—— 1998. 'As Nygh as Possible', *The Times Literary Supplement*, 4964 (May 22), 30–1.

Robichez, Jacques (ed.), 1969. *Verlaine: Œuvres poétiques* (Paris: Garnier).

Robinson, Steven (trans.), 1983. *Juvenal: Sixteen Satires upon the Ancient Harlot* (Manchester: Carcanet New Press).

Ruthven, K.K., 1969. *A Guide to Ezra Pound's 'Personae' (1926)* (Berkeley, Cal.: University of California Press).

Saunders, David, 1970. 'Baudelaire's Personified Abstractions', *Modern Language Review*, 65, 768–77.

Scarfe, Francis (trans.), 1964. *Baudelaire* (Harmondsworth: Penguin Books).

Schulte, R., and Biguenet, J. (eds), 1992. *Theories of Translation: An Anthology of Essays from Dryden to Derrida* (Chicago: University of Chicago Press).

Scott, Clive, 1980. *French Verse-Art: A Study* (Cambridge: Cambridge University Press).

—— 1982. 'The Liberated Verse of the English Translators of French

Symbolism', in Anna Balakian (ed.), *The Symbolist Movement in the Literature of European Languages* (Budapest: Akadémiai Kiadó), 127–43.

—— 1990. *Vers Libre: The Emergence of Free Verse in France 1886–1914* (Oxford: Clarendon Press).

—— 1993. *Reading the Rhythm: The Poetics of French Free Verse 1910–1930* (Oxford: Clarendon Press).

—— 1998. *The Poetics of French Verse: Studies in Reading* (Oxford: Clarendon Press).

Scott, David and Wright, Barbara, 1984. *Baudelaire: 'La Fanfarlo' and 'Le Spleen de Paris'* (London: Grant and Cutler).

Séféris, Georges, 1989. *Poèmes 1933–1955 suivis de Trois poèmes secrets* (trans. Jacques Lacarrière, Egérie Mavraki, Lorand Gaspar, Yves Bonnefoy; pref. Yves Bonnefoy) (Paris: Gallimard).

Shapiro, Norman P. (trans. and ed.), 1998. *Charles Baudelaire: Selected Poems from 'Les Fleurs du Mal'* (ill. David Schorr) (Chicago: University of Chicago Press).

Siegel, Patricia J. (ed.), 1986. *Wilhelm Ténint et sa 'Prosodie de l'école moderne'* (Geneva: Éditions Slatkine).

Simon, Sherry, 1996. *Gender in Translation: Cultural Identity and the Politics of Transmission* (London: Routledge).

Sperber, Dan, and Wilson, Deirdre, 1986. *Relevance: Communication and Cognition* (Oxford: Blackwell).

Steiner, George, 1970. *Poem into Poem: World Poetry in Modern Verse Translation* (Harmondsworth: Penguin Books).

—— 1975. *After Babel: Aspects of Language and Translation* (London: Oxford University Press).

Stevenson, Robert Louis, 1996. *Treasure Island* (ill. François Place) (New York: Viking).

Symons, Arthur (trans. and ed.), 1925. *Charles Baudelaire: 'Les Fleurs du Mal', 'Petits Poèmes en prose', 'Les Paradis artificiels'* (London: The Casanova Society).

Thélot, Jérôme, 1983. *Poétique d'Yves Bonnefoy* (Geneva: Droz).

Valéry, Paul, 1957. *Œuvres I* (ed. Jean Hytier) (Paris: Gallimard).

Venuti, Lawrence, 1995. *The Translator's Invisibility: A History of Translation* (London: Routledge).

—— 1998. *The Scandals of Translation: Towards an Ethic of Difference* (London: Routledge).

Wagner, Geoffrey (trans.), 1971. *Selected Poems of Charles Baudelaire* (London: Panther).

Walters, Gordon B., 1969. 'A Reading of "La Cloche fêlée"', *Romance Notes*, 11/1, 51–6.

Widdowson, Henry G., 1991. 'Types of Equivalence', *Triangle*, 10, 153–65.

Will, Frederic, 1993. *Translation Theory and Practice: Reassembling the Tower* (Lewiston, NY: The Edwin Mellen Press).

Index

(This index does not, for obvious reasons, track all references to Baudelaire; but it does list all references to his poems)